ECONOMIC ACTIVITY IN IRELAND

Economic Activity in Ireland

A STUDY OF TWO OPEN ECONOMIES

Editors
NORMAN J. GIBSON
and
JOHN E. SPENCER

Contributors:
W. Black, J. A. Bristow, P. T. Geary,
N. J. Gibson, M. J. Harrison, D. McAleese,
J. W. O'Hagan, J. E. Spencer, B. M. Walsh

GILL AND MACMILLAN
MACMILLAN OF CANADA
MACLEAN—HUNTER PRESS

First published in 1977

Gill and Macmillan Ltd
15/17 Eden Quay
Dublin 1
and in America with
Macmillan of Canada/Maclean-Hunter Press
and elsewhere through
association with the
Macmillan Publishers Group

7171 0779 5

ISBN 0–7705–1478–2

Text set in 10/11pt IBM Press Roman, printed by photolithography,
and bound in Great Britain at The Pitman Press, Bath

Contents

Chapter 1
The Structure and Behaviour of the Irish Economies (with an Illustrative Model)
J. E. Spencer and M. J. Harrison   1

Chapter 2
Industrial Development and Regional Policy
W. Black   40

Contributors

Chapter 1
J. E. SPENCER
Professor of Economics, The New University of Ulster,
Coleraine

M. J. HARRISON
Lecturer in Economics, Trinity College,
Dublin

Chapter 2
W. BLACK
Professor of Applied Economics, The Queen's University
of Belfast

Chapter 3
B. M. WALSH
Research Professor, The Economic and Social Research Institute,
Dublin

Appendix
J. W. O'HAGAN
Lecturer in Economics, Trinity College,
Dublin

Chapter 4
D. McALEESE
Lecturer in Economics, Trinity College,
Dublin

Chapter 5
P. T. GEARY
Lecturer in Economics, University College,
Dublin

Chapter 6
J. A. BRISTOW
Associate Professor of Economics, Trinity College,
Dublin

Chapter 7
N. J. GIBSON
Professor of Economics, The New University of Ulster,
Coleraine

List of Tables

List of Figures

Preface

Historically the Irish economy has long been greatly influenced by the economy of her larger neighbour, Great Britain. This influence persists to the present day and in important respects makes the operation and the problems of the economies of the Irish Republic and Northern Ireland very similar, notwithstanding that one is an independent state and the other a region of the United Kingdom. Both economies have chronic and longstanding problems of unemployment, and both are small, highly open economies dominated by Britain. Furthermore, membership of the European Economic Community by both the United Kingdom and the Irish Republic is almost certain to increase the economic links and co-operation between both parts of Ireland, hopefully to the benefit of each. But fruitful co-operation demands at least some understanding of each other's economy and this book is directed to that purpose and, ideally, to a greater understanding generally amongst the people of this island.

Despite the contiguity of the Irish Republic and Northern Ireland, there are many important differences between the two economies. Northern Ireland, as a region of the United Kingdom, possesses very little autonomy in economic matters. Thus there is no ability to alter tariff levels or change tax rates. On the other hand, the Republic has all the autonomy of an independent democratic state, though that autonomy is necessarily constrained by arrangements and agreements with other states.

The book is built around Chapter 1 which describes in some detail the structures of the two economies. An algebraic model for each economy (eighteen equations for Northern Ireland, fifteen for the Republic) is provided and manipulated. This broad framework facilitates an understanding of the fundamental notion of economic interdependency both within Northern Ireland and the Republic and between them and with Great Britain. How, for example, does a change in fiscal policy, affect unemployment? Does a change in government spending in Northern Ireland have any impact on, say, the level of Gross Domestic Product in the Republic?

The remaining chapters of the book may be viewed as an elaboration of the skeletal construct of Chapter 1. This approach is, of course, more suited to some chapters than others. The editors were anxious that each contributor should have a free hand to develop his chapter in his own way. However, each author has attempted to develop it within the overall framework and to suggest where the analysis would require substantive development or modification of the structures of Chapter 1. Thus it is hoped that the reader will find it possible to move from chapter to chapter without losing sight of the overall structure, and in the process gain considerable knowledge about the operation of the Irish economies.

The main emphasis throughout the book is on the present and recent past, from about 1960 onwards. It is not one of the purposes of the book to forecast the economic future of the two economies; forecasting at best is a hazardous enterprise and is much more so in the present violent and uncertain atmosphere, especially in Northern Ireland.

Nor is it a purpose of the book to present policy conclusions. Nevertheless, it will be found that various themes and conclusions keep recurring throughout the various chapters. Perhaps the most central theme, to which reference has already been made, is the significance for the Irish economies of their openness to economic influences from the rest of the world. This is especially true as regards the British economy and the ease with which goods, people and finance have moved and are able to move between the two islands, even though the share of Britain in Irish foreign trade has shown some decline in the last ten years.

Given this ease of movement, it is to be expected that wages, prices, interest rates and economic conditions generally in Britain exercise a major determining influence on both Irish economies. In Northern Ireland these influences are reinforced by the importance to its economy of the large-scale financial transfers from the United Kingdom government. The Irish Republic also receives transfers, mostly from the EEC, and while these are of considerable importance, they are not on anything like the scale of those received by Northern Ireland.

If the Irish economies are greatly affected by economic conditions in the rest of the world and particularly in Britain, it should not come as a surprise that the ability of the two economies to influence their own overall economic conditions is correspondingly constrained. Furthermore, this applies to the Irish Republic as well as to Northern Ireland despite the political autonomy of the former.

This state of affairs has important implications. For instance, as long as there is a determined policy to maintain a fixed exchange rate between the Irish pound and the pound sterling, price levels in the Irish Republic are likely to diverge relatively little from those in Britain. In these circumstances neither fiscal nor monetary policy nor a prices and incomes policy can have significant effects on domestic prices. Indeed, monetary policy will have

very limited power as an instrument of economic policy generally. Thus
political autonomy does not necessarily confer economic autonomy, and
the question arises whether governments and perhaps trade unions in the
Irish Republic have tended to exaggerate the power they have in relation to
their own economy.

It should not be inferred from the foregoing that economic power would
automatically be achieved by abolishing the fixed exchange rate between
the Irish pound and sterling. While in principle to do so would give the
Irish Republic more control over its domestic economy and especially
domestic prices, it would still remain a very small economy in relation to
the rest of the world and Britain and to that extent would continue to be
subject to many economic constraints. The question of fixed versus flexible
exchange rates is a difficult one, and an adequate treatment of the Irish
case would involve considerable research effort which has not yet been
undertaken and which would go beyond the scope of the present book.
However, it can be said that flexible exchange rates for a small open economy would not by themselves confer economic autonomy.

If a small open economy is vulnerable to economic conditions in the
rest of the world and especially to those amongst its large and economically dominant neighbours, then there is a powerful case for the small
economy to try to influence the economic policies of such neighbours.
From this point of view, membership of the EEC is advantageous for the
Irish Republic, and its insistence on the development of Community social
and regional policies is not surprising. However, there has never, so far as is
known, been any similar attempts by the Irish Republic to influence economic and social policies in Britain. Something similar is, of course, true within the United Kingdom. Neither Northern Ireland nor other regions of the
United Kingdom have found it possible to exercise significant influence on
the economic and social policies of the central government, though they
may have had some influence on regional policy. It may be expected, however, that with devolution this position will change markedly and that
Scotland, Wales and perhaps Northern Ireland will between them ensure
that their influence is felt more strongly in the determination of central
government economic, social and regional policy.

This book is aimed at several different groups of people. First, it should
be relevant to students of the Irish economies at every level. Secondly, it is
hoped that it will prove helpful to civil servants, politicians, trade unionists
and others. Thirdly, it should be of value to economists interested in the
problems and activities of small open economies.

For readers unfamiliar with the usage of names in Ireland it should be
noted that the terms Irish Republic, Republic of Ireland, the South each
refer to the same physical and constitutional entity and are used inter-
changeably throughout the text. The same is true with regard to Northern
Ireland and the North.

The editors gratefully acknowledge the permission given by the Central Bank of Ireland to quote material from its *Annual Reports* and *Quarterly Bulletins.* Finally, we would like to thank on our own behalf and on behalf of the authors the individuals who have commented on the various chapters. At the risk of being invidious we would wish to mention in particular Brendan Dowling, John Martin and Rodney Thom. As usual, full responsibility for the contents rests with the editors and authors.

The Editors

Abbreviations

AnCO An Comhairle Oiliúna (Industrial Training Authority)
AIFTA Anglo-Irish Free Trade Area Agreement
BD   Bank Dispute 1970
BEQB *Bank of England Quarterly Bulletin*
CAP   Common Agricultural Policy in the European Economic
      Community
CBQB *Central Bank Quarterly Bulletin*
CBR   *Central Bank Annual Report*
CEEP European Centre for Public Enterprises
c.i.f. Cost Including Insurance and Freight
CIO   Committee on Industrial Organisation
CIP   Committee on Industrial Progress
CPI   Consumer Price Index
CPT   Corporation Profits Tax
CSO   Central Statistical Office
EEC   European Economic Community
EFTA European Free Trade Area
ESRI Economic and Social Research Institute
FES   Family Expenditure Surveys
FIS   Family Income Supplement
FR   Federal Republic
GATT General Agreement on Tariffs and Trade
GB   Great Britain
GDP   Gross Domestic Product
GNP   Gross National Product
GPCF Gross Physical Capital Formation
HBI   Household Budget Inquiries
HMSO Her Majesty's Stationery Office
IDA   Industrial Development Authority
IMF   International Monetary Fund
LEDU Local Enterprise Development Unit
n.a. not available
n.e.s. not elsewhere specified

NESC	National Economic and Social Council
NIEC	National Industrial Economic Council
NI	Northern Ireland
NIFC	Northern Ireland Finance Corporation
NIHE	Northern Ireland Housing Executive
OECD	Organisation for Economic Co-operation and Development
REP	Regional Employment Premium
RI	Republic of Ireland
RPI	Retail Price Index
SET	Selective Employment Tax
SITC	Standard Industrial Trade Classification
UK	United Kingdom
US, USA	United States of America
VAT	Value-Added Tax
WPI	Wholesale Price Index

CHAPTER 1

The Structure and Behaviour of the Irish Economies

WITH AN ILLUSTRATIVE MODEL

J. E. SPENCER AND M. J. HARRISON

1   INTRODUCTION

In discussing the economic activity of any country, the concept of 'economic structure' is fundamental. There are two ways in which the term may be used. One way is to describe such things as the country's resources, its industrial pattern, and the kinds and amounts of goods it trades internationally. Another way is to indicate how the economy of the country operates, how changes in one part of the system are transmitted to other parts of the system. Due to the interdependencies of economic behaviour within the system, this second type of description is facilitated by the specification of a mathematical model of the economy. Moreover, analysis of the model, such as the calculation of partial derivatives or elasticities, can add substantially to the description by indicating the rates at which certain independent or policy variables exert an influence on the other variables of the system.

In this chapter a blend of both of these interpretations is used. The specification of a simple macro-economic model of the salient behavioural characteristics of the economies of Northern Ireland and the Republic of Ireland forms the basis of the discussion. This is supplemented by a broad statistical description of the two economies using recent data on many of the variables appearing in the model. The description of structure and behaviour that emerges is further enriched by some analysis of the model focusing on selected aspects of the functioning of the systems. The intention is to provide a simple overall view of the Irish economies which highlights the nature of the interdependence of economic activity within and between the two areas. Such a view also serves to emphasise the essential interdependence of the chapters which follow. Each one in turn adds considerable detail and realism to the framework provided in this chapter; together they provide an insight into how the two economies operate and should be seen as constituting a unified whole.

2   THE STRUCTURE OF THE IRISH ECONOMIES

The model, which is presented in this section, is a short-run model based, like many macro-economic models, on standard Keynesian theory and its extensions. Keynesian theory is chiefly used for explaining those aspects of economic activity which are the concern of national economic policy. Therefore, while the objectives and strategies of policy are not discussed explicitly, the relationships of the model nevertheless describe the structure of the two economies in terms of the variables which economic policy seeks to influence, such as national income, employment, balance of payments, and the price level. The policy issues themselves are discussed in Section 3 below and in later chapters. In explaining how the key macro-variables are determined the Keynesian system attaches fundamental importance to the concept of aggregate expenditure. Consideration of aggregate expenditure therefore provides the starting-point for the discussion of the construction of the model.

Aggregate expenditure is made up of a number of important components. Consider, first, total domestic expenditure (E). This comprises private expenditures on consumption (C) and investment (I), and public or government expenditure (G_1) on goods and services. Thus, symbolically,

$$E = C + I + G_1 \tag{1.1}$$

For national accounting purposes, consumption is defined to include the personal expenditure of residents on all final goods and services except new houses, which are regarded as investment goods. Consumption, therefore, specifically excludes expenditure by tourists, which is regarded as part of exports, and expenditure by private firms on consumption goods, which is considered to be expenditure on intermediate goods. Investment, besides including expenditure on new houses, is also defined to include the value of physical changes in stocks of goods and in work in progress, so that if, for example, goods are produced but not sold, they serve to augment investment. The major constituent of investment, however, is the expenditure by firms in the private sector and by public authorities on fixed capital formation or the acquisition of physical assets such as plant and equipment and buildings. This expenditure is usually 'gross' expenditure in the sense that it includes both expenditure which is carried out in order to replace worn-out capital, and expenditure which adds to the existing capital stock of the country. Public expenditure includes the current spending of central and local government on goods such as health services, education and defence. It does not, however, include internal transfer payments (G_2) such as pensions and social security payments, since these are not payments made for goods and services. Transfer payments ultimately result in private expenditures, so they are in fact incorporated in consumption and investment.

The total spending measured by these three categories of domestic expenditure must, of course, be exhausted by that part of domestic output (Q) which is not exported and any foreign output which is imported. Thus

$$E = Q - X + M \qquad (1.2)$$

where X stands for exports, and M for imports, of goods and services, excluding factor income flows such as receipts of interest, profits and dividends by residents from activities carried out abroad; in the national accounts these factor income flows are reduced to a separate single item called net factor income from abroad. Equation (1.2) may also be interpreted as stating that total domestic expenditure equals domestic output plus the current trade deficit, that is, the difference between imports and exports. It then follows from equations (1.1) and (1.2) that

$$Q = C + I + G_1 + X - M \qquad (1.3)$$

or, verbally, that gross domestic output equals the sum of consumption, gross investment and government current expenditure, minus the trade deficit. This is precisely the relationship which underlies the so-called expenditure method of measuring the total annual output of goods and services produced in an economy by its residents. More specifically, if the expenditures on the right-hand side of equation (1.3) are valued using market prices for the year in question, then the equation defines Gross Domestic Product (GDP) at current market prices; if the expenditures are valued exclusively of the indirect taxation and subsidies which enter into market prices, the equation defines GDP at factor cost; and if the values, whether at current market prices or factor cost, are deflated by an appropriate price index, the equation defines GDP in constant prices, or real GDP, which is the most suitable concept to use when comparisons of the volume of domestic production in different years have to be made.

Consider now the expenditure in an economy which is made possible by spending-power originating overseas. It is because net factor income from abroad falls within this category that it is not included in GDP. In addition to net factor income, an economy may receive net gifts or transfers from abroad, and in some economies, Israel for example, such transfers of spending-power may be substantial. Added together, Gross Domestic Product (Q) and net factor income yield Gross National Product (GNP); adding net gifts or transfers (TN) to GNP yields gross national disposable income (Y). As net factor income from abroad has remained fairly constant and negligible in the Republic of Ireland (£30 million, or 1·1 per cent of Y, in 1973), and as its extent in Northern Ireland is not known, it is taken to be zero for present purposes. Symbolically, therefore, gross national disposable income

may be written as

$$Y = Q + TN \qquad (1.4)^1$$

The identity (1.3) is a fundamental relationship in the model for both the Irish economies. Identity (1.4) is particularly important in the model for the North. An indication of the actual magnitudes and relative importance of the components of these equations in the economies of the Republic of Ireland and the United Kingdom of Great Britain and Northern Ireland is given by the figures of Table 1.1(a). All the figures relate to the year 1973 and are given in terms of the prices which prevailed in 1973. In the case of both the economies the figures are derived directly from the respective national accounts. Separate figures for Northern Ireland are sparse; for example, no figures exist for consumption expenditure in the North. Furthermore, of those figures that are available, some are rather unreliable, in particular those for merchandise trade (see Chapter 4, p. 118). Nevertheless, such figures have been included in Table 1.1(a) in parentheses. Table 1.1(b) shows the 1973 indirect tax and subsidy content in GDP at market prices, and hence GDP at factor cost, a figure which is available for Northern Ireland.

Consumption expenditure is clearly the dominant element in gross national disposable income in the Republic of Ireland and in the United Kingdom, accounting for over 60 per cent of the value of gross national disposable income in both countries in 1973. For the Republic this figure marks a decrease in the share of consumption in gross national disposable income compared with previous years. In 1965, for example, the share stood at about 70 per cent. On the other hand, the Republic's shares of investment and government expenditure in gross national disposable income have both risen somewhat since 1965, from approximately 21 per cent and 12 per cent respectively to their 1973 values of about 24 per cent and 15 per cent respectively.

Exports and imports are also large components of gross national disposable income in the Republic and the United Kingdom. The fact that they are larger as a proportion of gross national disposable income in the Republic indicates the relatively greater openness of the Republic's economy. Indeed, the proportion of exports to gross national disposable income in the Republic, which has remained very stable since 1965, was almost 60 per cent greater than the corresponding proportion in the United Kingdom in 1973, while the proportion of imports to gross national disposable income, which has fallen slightly since 1965, was about 70 per cent greater than the corresponding United Kingdom figure in 1973.

1 Equation (1.4) is difficult to measure in real terms because the measurement of changes in real gross national disposable income should take account of changes in the terms of trade, since the latter affect the volume of domestic output which may be exchanged for imports. (See Hibbert (1975).)

Table 1.1(a): Gross National Disposable Income in 1973 at Current Market Prices, Republic of Ireland and United Kingdom

	Republic		United Kingdom	
	£m	% of Y at market prices	£m	% of Y at market prices
Consumption (C)	1,776	64·2	44,855	62·9
Investment (I)	665	24·0	14,445 (388)	20·2
Public current expenditure (G$_1$)	403	14·6	13,270 (184)[a]	18·6
Exports (X)	1,017	36·8	16,494 (1,175)	23·1
Less imports (M)	−1,208	43·7	−18,338 (−1,305)	25·7
G D P at market prices (Q)	2,653	95·9	70,726	99·1
Net factor income	30	1·1	1,095	1·5
G N P at market prices	2,683	97·0	71,821	100·6
Net transfers (T N)	83	3·0	−461 (313)	0·6
Gross national disposable income (Y)	2,766	100·0	71,360	100·0

[a] Estimate.

Note: Figures in brackets relate to Northern Ireland.

Sources: R I: *National Income and Expenditure 1973*, Stationery Office, Dublin, Tables A5 and A7; U K: *National Income and Expenditure 1963–1973*, H M S O, London, Tables 1, 7 and 12; N I: *Digest of Statistics*, No. 43 (Mar. 1975), H M S O, Belfast, Tables 111, 118 and 120.

Table 1.1(b): Gross Domestic Product at Factor Cost in 1973 at Current
Prices, Republic of Ireland and United Kingdom

	Republic (£m)	United Kingdom (£m)
G D P at market prices	2,653	70,726
less Indirect taxes	−512	−10,006
plus Subsidies	119	1,456
G D P at factor cost	2,260	63,271 (1,120)[a]

[a]1972 N I figure.
Sources: R I: *National Income and Expenditure 1973*, Stationery Office, Dublin,
Table A3; U K: *National Income and Expenditure 1963–1973*, H M S O, London,
Tables 1 and 12; N I: *Northern Ireland Economic Report on 1973*, H M S O, Belfast,
p.17.

The figures for Northern Ireland's trade, referring only to merchandise
exchanges, suggest, despite their shortcomings, that the economy of the
North is even more open than the economy of the Republic. Net factor income from abroad and net transfers are very minor elements in gross
national disposable income in the Republic and in the United Kingdom.
In the Republic as mentioned above, net factor income has remained
fairly constant, its average level between 1965 and 1973 having been about
£25 million in current prices. Thus, as gross national disposable income has
risen continuously, net factor income as a proportion of gross national disposable income has declined. In 1965 it was about 2·6 per cent of gross
national disposable income; by 1973, as Table 1.1(a) shows, it had fallen
by more than half to a negligible 1·1 per cent of gross national disposable
income. By contrast, net transfers to the Republic have more than doubled
during the same period, keeping approximately in step with the proportionate increases in gross national disposable income. As a percentage of the
latter they remained fairly stable at about 1·8 per cent until 1972. Since
1973, of course, the net transfer has included the net receipts from the
European Economic Community, and has increased in significance to 3 per
cent of gross national disposable income in 1973. The relative smallness of
net factor income and net transfers in the Republic and the United Kingdom
means, of course, that there is little difference in the values of G D P, G N P
and Y within the two countries. Given the relatively large net transfer to
Northern Ireland, however, the difference between the North's G N P and Y,
whose actual values are not precisely known, is clearly of considerable significance. Hence the importance of equation (1.4) in the model for the North.

Perhaps the most striking feature to emerge from Tables 1.1(a) and
1.1(b) is that the two Irish economies are so small compared with the

economy of the United Kingdom as a whole. As Table 1.1(b) shows, the levels of production in the Irish economies are many times smaller than the level of production in the United Kingdom. Specifically, G D P at factor cost is about two-thirds greater in the Republic than in Northern Ireland, but it is a mere 3·6 per cent of the level of G D P at factor cost in the United Kingdom. In order to make more meaningful comparisons of such things as the levels of production and national income, and the levels of prosperity, in the three economies, account needs to be taken of the differences in their populations. Accordingly, Table 1.2 gives the annual population figures for the North, the Republic and Great Britain for the decade 1963–73; corresponding figures for real G D P and the derived series of real G D P *per capita* are also given.

The populations of all three areas increased fairly steadily during the period, with those of the two parts of Ireland increasing at slightly higher average annual rates than that of Great Britain. For the Republic this steady upward trend in population was in sharp contrast to the experience of the 1950s, in which emigration was so high compared with the rate of natural increase in population that in every year from 1948 to 1961 population actually declined in the Republic of Ireland. At the beginning of the 1960s the population of the Republic was about twice that of Northern Ireland. Owing to the similarity in the rates of increase of the populations during the 1960s, the population of the Republic, at a little over 3 million, remains about twice the size of the population of the North. The total population of the island of Ireland, therefore, stands at something over 4½ million, only 8½ per cent of the population of neighbouring Great Britain.

The level of real G D P also rose fairly steadily in each of the countries during the period covered by the data, although the individual rates of increase varied. The average annual rate of increase in real GDP was highest in the Republic of Ireland, followed by Northern Ireland, with Great Britain having the lowest rate. The fact that real G D P grew at a faster rate than population in the three regions means, of course, that the standard of living of the regions, as measured by real G D P per head of the population, also rose during the decade. The level of real G D P *per capita* rose most rapidly in the Republic, at an average annual rate of about 3·8 per cent. The North's average annual rate of growth was about 3·0 per cent, while Britain's rate was lowest at about 2·3 per cent. This growth experience is shown in Figure 1.1 in which the real G D P *per capita* series for each country is expressed in index form.

Despite the higher growth rates in recent years, real G D P *per capita* in Northern Ireland and the Republic of Ireland is still considerably below that of Great Britain. As is shown in Figure 1.2, real G D P *per capita* in Northern Ireland in 1963 was about 65 per cent of real GDP *per capita* in Britain; and in 1972, at £613 million, it was still only about 73 per cent of the British level. In the Republic in 1963 real G D P *per capita* was only a

Table 1.2: GDP at Constant (1970) Factor Cost, Population, and Real GDP *per capita*, Northern Ireland, Republic and Great Britain, 1963–73

	Northern Ireland			Republic			Great Britain		
	GDP (£m)	Population (000s)	GDP per capita (£m)	GDP (£m)	Population (000s)	GDP per capita (£m)	GDP (£m)	Population (000s)	GDP per capita (£m)
1963	644	1,446	445	1,056	2,841	372	35,744	52,089	686
1964	689	1,458	473	1,114	2,849	391	37,561	52,391	716
1965	731	1,469	498	1,146	2,873	399	38,231	52,706	725
1966	749	1,478	507	1,163	2,884	403	39,055	52,972	737
1967	785	1,491	526	1,221	2,899	421	40,163	53,255	754
1968	814	1,502	542	1,303	2,910	448	41,078	53,543	767
1969	832	1,513	550	1,360	2,921	466	41,339	53,759	769
1970	863	1,524	566	1,394	2,944	474	42,149	53,887	782
1971	896	1,538	583	1,475	2,978	495	43,378	54,072	802
1972	947	1,545	613	1,540	3,014	511	45,452	54,248	838
1973	n.a.	1,547	n.a.	1,647	3,051	540	46,810	54,386	861
Average Annual Growth Rates 1963–73 (%)		0.72	3·0	4.6	0.7	3·8	2.6	0.45	2·3

Sources: NI: *Digest of Statistics*, HMSO, Belfast, various issues; RI: *National Income and Expenditure*, Stationery Office, Dublin, various issues, *Report on Vital Statistics 1971*, Stationery Office, Dublin, Table 1; UK: *National Income and Expenditure 1963–73*, HMSO, London, Tables 1 and 8, *Annual Abstract of Statistics 1973*, HMSO, London, Tables 6 and 403.

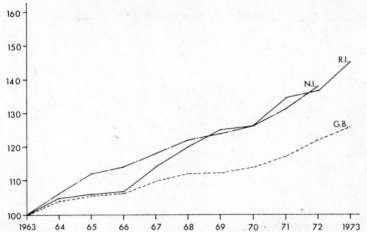

Figure 1.1: *Indices of Real GDP* per capita, *Northern Ireland, Republic and Great Britain, 1963–73 (1963 = 100)*

Source: Table 1.2.

little over a half, and in 1973, at £540 million, still only about 63 per cent of what it was in Britain in the corresponding years. Indeed, in 1972 neither the North nor the Republic had succeeded in reaching the level of real GDP *per capita* that Britain had had nine years earlier. Figure 1.3 shows this clearly; it depicts the real GDP *per capita* series for the three areas as

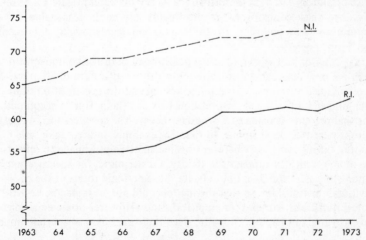

Figure 1.2: *Real GDP* per capita *in Northern Ireland and the Republic as a Percentage of Real GDP* per capita *in Great Britain, 1963–73*

Source: Table 1.2.

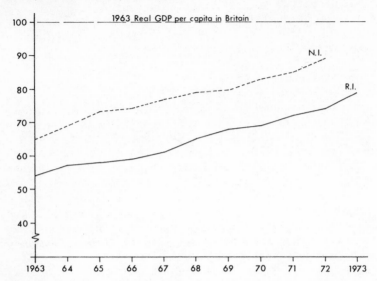

Figure 1.3: *Real GDP* per capita *in Northern Ireland and the Republic, 1963–73, relative to Great Britain's Real GDP* per capita *in 1963*

Source: Table 1.2.

series of indices based on the British real G D P *per capita* figure for 1963. Of course, these comparisons are meaningful only on the reasonable assumption that a pound[2] in the three areas commands roughly equivalent purchasing power.

Explanation of the simultaneous determination of the components of gross national disposable income requires the identification of all other relevant variables of the macro-economic system and the specification of behavioural and definitional relationships between them. It is to accomplish this that recourse is made to Keynesian theory. The specification of relationships is purposely kept simple, so that, for example, indirect taxes are ignored throughout; but wherever possible an attempt is made to reflect the more recent developments in theory. Furthermore, the specification is non-stochastic and does not indicate the functional forms of the behavioural relationships, so that the model could not, as it stands, be estimated statistically or used for empirical study. However, some equations are estimated in Chapter 5. Finally, since there are obviously certain import-

2 While the Republic of Ireland pound is generally accepted as a medium of exchange in Northern Ireland, it is not so accepted in Great Britain. However, there is effective one to one parity between the British and Irish pounds and the price levels in all three areas are rather similar. (See below and Chapter 5.)

ant structural differences between the economies of the North and the Republic, the basic model has been modified to yield two variants. Each of these is examined in turn in the following subsections.

2.1 Northern Ireland

Consumer expenditure (C) is one of the largest and one of the more stable elements in gross national expenditure in most economies. Although no data exist for consumer expenditure in Northern Ireland, the figures in Table 1.1(a) suggest that in the UK as a whole consumption accounts for about 63 per cent of GNP. Since Keynes's original work a good deal of theorising has been carried out concerning consumption, and for some economies there has been much statistical testing of this theory. The result is that the theoretical explanation of aggregate consumption is one of the more developed and satisfactory aspects of macro-economics. Of the several factors which appear to have a bearing on consumption expenditure, such as the availability of credit, accumulated wealth, and current and expected disposable income, there is little doubt that the income variables are by far the most important. For the Northern Ireland consumption function, therefore, current disposable income is chosen as the explanatory variable.

However, two types of disposable income may be distinguished, namely that which derives from domestically produced income and that which derives from the transfer payment from Great Britain. Domestic disposable income (Y_D) is simply gross domestic income (Q) less all income taxes and national insurance contributions (TX). The tax schedule is approximated by

$$TX = t_0 + t_1 Q \qquad (1.5)$$

where $t_0 < 0$ and t_1 is the rate of tax and insurance contributions levied by the British authorities. The assumed schedule, being of linear form, may not be a good approximation for taxes if Q were to vary much, but it should serve adequately in the neighbourhood of any particular level of Q. It implies progressive taxation, since the marginal rate of tax is greater than the average rate $\left(\dfrac{dTX}{dQ} > \dfrac{TX}{Q} \right)$ for $t_0 < 0$. Thus

$$Y_D = Q - TX = Q(1 - t_1) - t_0 \qquad (1.6)$$

The value of direct taxation in Northern Ireland amounted to about £138 million, or about 35·7 per cent of total taxation in 1971—72 (see Table 6.1). National insurance contributions in the same year totalled about £75·9 million. Detailed information on fiscal matters is contained in Chapter 6.

In addition to Q, national disposable income (Y) also includes the net transfer (TN) from Great Britain, an item which has been substantial in recent years. In current figures of the year concerned, the amount has risen from about £52 million in 1966—67 to £181 million in 1972—73 and an estimated £313 million in 1973–74. The latter figure is about 28 per cent of GDP at current factor cost. The gross transfer (T), which is equal to TN + TX, is made for a variety of reasons including the support of the health services, the provision of social security payments and regional employment premiums, and the financing of some of the security operations made necessary by political troubles.

Taxes levied in Northern Ireland are collected by the authorities in London. In return, a sum of money (the gross transfer) is made available by London for the use of the Northern Ireland authorities. The latter spend an amount $\dot{G}$, of which, as stated earlier, G_1 is on goods and services and G_2 is on transfers within Northern Ireland. The total spending (G) is financed by the gross transfer from London (T) and borrowing by the Northern Ireland authorities (B).

Thus, collecting these concepts,

$$TN = T - TX \tag{1.7}$$
$$G = G_1 + G_2 \tag{1.8}$$
$$G = T + B \tag{1.9}$$

As regards the extent of the gross transfer, it is clear that it is closely related to United Kingdom regional policy and, as such, may be expected to vary inversely with the level of activity in the Northern Ireland economy. Accordingly, it is plausible to write

$$T = \alpha + g(U) \tag{1.10}$$

where U is the level of unemployment in the province. It is assumed that $g(U)$ rises as unemployment rises, so that the transfer acts as a stabilising influence on the economy. The part of the transfer which is not dependent on the level of activity, for example, health service support, is represented by α (see Appendix to Chapter 3). This magnitude depends on external policy decisions in London which may, of course, be influenced by advice or requests from the authorities in Belfast. It is important to notice that, to the extent that T is greater than TX, the spending power in Northern Ireland is higher than that generated by domestic resources. As shown above, and as one would expect for a relatively poor region of the United Kingdom, the net transfer has indeed been positive in recent years. (See Northern Ireland Office (1974).)

Turning again to consumption, it is assumed that this consists of a part which depends on domestically produced disposable income $(Q - TX)$ and a part which is equal to a proportion, namely c_1, of G_2. For simplicity, it is assumed that the latter amount $(c_1 G_2)$ is not subject to taxation. In principle, of course, c_1 could be taken to be dependent on the rate of tax, although this is not done in the analysis of the equations below. Over a reasonably short period of time c_1 probably varies very little and can be taken to be constant. The complete Northern Ireland consumption relation is now written as

$$C = c(Y_D) + c_1 G_2 \qquad (1.11)$$

Investment may also be viewed as comprising two components, namely investment by domestic concerns ($\bar{I}$) and direct foreign investment (F). A satisfactory theoretical explanation of these components is not easy to achieve because each is such a heterogeneous aggregate. However, because investment is undertaken to produce goods in the future, expectations about future profits would seem to be the major consideration when investment decisions are being made. This implies that expected sales, the availability of funds within firms and the cost of borrowing funds will all have an important bearing on the decision. A variety of investment theories have been proposed in the literature. In specifying the present model's investment functions, the assumption is made that investment desires depend on the levels of gross national disposable income, which reflect aggregate demand and hence expected sales, and the real rate of interest (R) and various government-financed incentives, which reflect the costs of borrowing. These incentives depend on G_2 and are written as $\bar{d}(G_2)$ and $f(G_2)$. More specifically, domestic investment is assumed to depend on the level of British gross national disposable income (Y_{GB}) as well as on the domestic level. Thus $\bar{I} = i(Y, Y_{GB}, R, \bar{d}(G_2))$. Foreign investment is assumed to be similarly determined except that domestic income is deleted on the grounds that sales in Northern Ireland are not particularly important compared with expected sales in Great Britain, where most of the foreign investment originates. Indeed, it could be argued that foreign investment will rise in conditions of slack in Northern Ireland, given the conditions prevailing in Great Britain, since readily available cheap labour improves profit prospects. However, this possibility is ignored for simplicity, and total investment is written as

$$I = \bar{I} + F_z = i(Y, Y_{GB}, R, \bar{d}(G_2)) + f(Y_{GB}, R, \bar{f}(G_2)) \qquad (1.12)$$

The level of public current expenditure (G) is, of course, determined by the central authority (but see pp. 21–2 below). Again the single symbol conceals considerable heterogeneity, as is stressed in Chapter 6. It would be wrong to suppose that G is a particularly flexible instrument of policy, because most of public current expenditure is directed towards some major social need. For example, of the £121 million current expenditure by the Northern Ireland central authority on goods and services in 1972, £71·7 million, or 59 per cent, went towards health services alone.

As was mentioned above, the Northern Ireland economy is a very open economy. Merchandise exports and merchandise imports each amount in value to over 80 per cent of G D P at current prices. The majority of this trade is with Great Britain. At the beginning of the 1960s about 90 per cent of merchandise exports went to Britain and about 77 per cent of merchandise imports came from Britain. The proportions have fallen only slightly during the intervening years, standing in 1972, at 84 per cent and 74 per cent for exports to and imports from Great Britain, respectively. Detailed figures on the components of this trade are given in Table 4.4. Of the remaining trade, a relatively small amount, probably about 6 per cent of exports and about 10 per cent of imports, is with the Republic of Ireland.[3] The exports to the Republic consist mainly of cattle, textile yarn and non-electrical machinery, and the imports mainly of cattle, butter, beer, chemicals, and some textiles and paper products, details of which are contained in Table 4.2. In recent years the value of the imports from the Republic has been about twice the value of exports to the Republic, with the figures in 1973 being approximately £42 million for exports to the Republic and £82 million for imports from the Republic. Overall, too, Northern Ireland has sustained a visible trade deficit for many years. This reached a peak of about £83·6 million in 1970, but by 1972 had declined to about £20·4 million, both figures being in current prices.

Theoretically the volumes of exports and imports may be expected to depend essentially on two factors, namely income and relative prices, although more recently it has been argued that consumption, investment, government expenditure, and exports should also be considered as determinants of imports because of their different import components. Given the dominance of Great Britain in Northern Ireland's trade, export demand may therefore be assumed to depend on the level of income in Britain and the competitiveness of the North's products *vis-à-vis* Britain's as indicated by the Northern price level relative to that of Britain. The volume of exports to the Republic is small, and so for simplicity Republic of Ireland income and price variables are ignored. Thus the Northern Ireland export function is specified as

$$X = x(Y_{GB}, P_{GB}, P) \qquad (1.13)$$

where Y_{GB} is the British gross national disposable income, P_{GB} is the price level prevailing in Britain, and P is the Northern Ireland price level.

A similar argument applies to Northern Ireland's demand for imports, whereby it is assumed that imports depend on the North's spending (Z + G_1, where Z is C + I + X), the domestic price level (P), and the price level in Great Britain. Z and G_1 are incorporated separately into the import function in order to be able to capture potential differences in the marginal

3 As explained in Chapter 4, p. 118 (see also p. 126), there is probably an upward bias in both total exports from the North and exports from the North to the Republic of Ireland; there is probably a similar bias in imports. The North-Republic bias can be eliminated by using the Republic's trade figures, but the overall bias remains.

propensities to import with respect to the two components. 1
ignoring Republic of Ireland variables, the import function is

$$M = m(Z, G_1, P, P_{GB})$$

The model structure is now extended to incorporate equations ... _n_
explain how G D P (Q), unemployment (U), the price level (P) and the wage
level (W) are determined. These four variables will be considered in turn.

Like the other variables of the model, the level of G D P may be influenced
by many factors. However, by invoking the concept of the aggregate production function, it may be most simply regarded as being functionally related to the size of the employed labour force (N) and the stock of capital
(K) employed in the economy, viz

$$Q = \bar{h}(N, K) \tag{1.15}$$

Some figures for G D P have already been given in Tables 1.1 and 1.2.
More detailed information on the levels of production in individual sectors
of the Northern Ireland economy, and also on the sectoral levels of employment, is contained in Table 1.3. As can be seen, production in all sectors
has increased during recent years, with particularly large increases in the
government and other domestic service sectors. However, the sectoral shares
in total product have not changed markedly. The share of industry declined
slightly from 1967 to 1972, but industry, with a 42 per cent share in G D P
at factor cost, clearly dominates production in Northern Ireland. The share
of agriculture in total production also decreased slightly over the period to
8·4 per cent, while the share of the three service sectors together increased,
despite a small fall in the share of distribution, transport and communications.

Essentially the same trends are observable in the changes in sectoral
shares of total employment between 1967 and 1972, although total employment itself declined slightly. The main impact of this decline can be seen
to have fallen on the industrial sector, whose employment level fell by
about 15,000 or a little over 6 per cent. However, industry still provides
about 42 per cent of the North's employment, while agriculture only provides about 10 per cent and government administration and defence only
about 7 per cent. The government, transport, and other service sectors
combined provide about 48 per cent of employment.

The changes in sectoral shares in output and employment can be used
together to indicate the relative changes that have taken place in the productivity in the various sectors during the period covered. More specifically,
the ratio of a sector's percentage share in G D P at constant prices to its share
in employment may be used to ascertain whether or not that sector's productivity is greater than the productivity of the economy as a whole.[4] More-

---

4 Of course, this measure of productivity takes no account of the other productive
factors, in particular capital services, employed with labour.

Table 1.3: GDP at Factor Cost (1970 prices) and Employment by Sector, Northern Ireland, 1967 and 1972

| | 1967 | | | | 1972 | | | |
| | Output (Q) GDP at factor cost | | Employment (N) | | Output (Q) | | Employment (N) | |
Sector	Level (£m)	Share (%)	Level (000s)	Share (%)	Level (£m)	Share (%)	Level (000s)	Share (%)
Agriculture, Forestry and Fishing	68	8·8	61·1	11·0	75	8·4	55·3	10·2
Industry	344	44·9	242·2	43·5	376	41·8	227·0	41·8
Distribution, Transport, Communications	114	14·9	97·0	17·4	126	14·0	86·8	16·0
Public Administration and Defence	52	6·9	37·1	6·7	76	8·4	37·7	6·9
Other Domestic	188	24·5	119·1	21·4	247	27·4	136·0	25·1
Total economy	766	100	556·5	100·0	900	100·0	542·8	100·0

Source: *Digest of Statistics*, No. 42 (Sep. 1974), H M S O, Belfast, Tables 7 and 115.

over, upward changes in this ratio over time indicate that the relative change in productivity in the sector in question is greater, and downward changes that the relative change in productivity is smaller, than the corresponding change in nationwide productivity. Such ratios are given in Table 1.4 for Northern Ireland agriculture, industry and services for 1967 and 1972.

Table 1.4: Ratios of Percentage Share in G D P to Share in Employment, Northern Ireland, 1967 and 1972

Sector	1967	1972
Agriculture	0·800	0·824
Industry	1·032	1·000
Services	1·018	1·038

Source: Derived from data in Table 1.3.

The ratios indicate that while productivity in agriculture has remained lower than productivity for the entire economy, it has increased at a slightly faster rate than the latter. On the other hand, while productivity in the combined service sectors has also increased at a faster rate than overall productivity, it has remained slightly higher than it. Productivity in industry has declined slightly from a level just above the overall level of productivity to a level about equal to it. Greater detail on sectoral production, employment and productivity is given in Chapter 2.

There are no figures available for the capital stock (K) of Northern Ireland, although it has been suggested that it has been a rapidly increasing quantity (see Chapter 2, p. 54). Capital is a variable, newly introduced by the production function, which in principle could be explained by the model, since the capital stock is defined as the stock of capital inherited from the past ($\bar{K}$) plus new net investment. However, even a year's net investment is small relative to the capital stock, so it is a reasonable and simplifying approximation to regard capital as fixed in the short run and to write the production function as

$$Q = \bar{h}(\bar{K}, N) = h(N) \qquad (1.16)$$

The level of unemployment, which has been persistently high in Northern Ireland, is the difference between the total available labour force ($\bar{N}$) and the labour demanded and actually employed (N). It is further assumed that this difference is never negative (see Section 3 below). No attempt is made to explain employment, and hence unemployment, in terms of the marginal product of labour as is often done in macro-models. Symbolically, unemployment is defined simply as

$$U = \bar{N} - N, \quad (U > 0) \qquad (1.17)$$

The recent experience of unemployment in Northern Ireland is indicated by the figures in Table 1.5. Also included in Table 1.5 are figures for total civil employment and the total available labour force. For each year the un-employment figure gives the estimated number of registered wholly unem-ployed, and the employment figure gives the estimated number in employ-ment, including those temporarily stopped. The total available labour force estimate is the sum of the employment and unemployment figures. The unemployment percentage is simply the unemployment figure expressed as a percentage of the labour force figure. All the figures relate to June of the year in question, which, due to seasonal effects, means that the unemployment figure tends to be lower than the corresponding monthly average figure. The experience from 1960 to 1973, which is discussed more fully in Chapter 3, has been of a rate of unemployment that has varied fairly regularly around a mean of about 5·7 per cent. A low occurred in the mid-1960s following which the rate increased till the early 1970s, reaching a peak of 6·7 per cent in 1972; in 1973, it fell back to 5·2 per cent which is about the same as the average level was in the mid-1960s. In June 1974 the un-employment rate stood at about 5·4 per cent, and in December 1974 it was about 6·4 per cent. The unemployment situation in the province has always been more severe than elsewhere in the United Kingdom. In the mid-1960s the unemployment rate was over four times that of Britain, while the most recent figure is still more than twice that of Britain, whose rate in December 1974 was about 2·8 per cent. By contrast, unemployment is not quite as

Table 1.5: Employment and Unemployment in Northern Ireland, 1960–73

Year	Available labour (N) (000s)	Employment (N) (000s)	Unemployment (U) (000s)	% of $\overline{N}$
1960	574·0	545·0	29·0	5·0
1961	571·0	539·0	32·0	5·6
1962	574·0	540·0	34·0	5·9
1963	581·0	545·0	36·0	6·2
1964	581·0	549·0	32·0	5·5
1965	586·1	557·4	28·7	4·9
1966	591·4	563·2	28·2	4·8
1967	593·5	556·5	37·1	6·3
1968	592·0	556·5	35·5	6·0
1969	595·1	560·4	34·6	5·8
1970	592·9	561·2	31·7	5·3
1971	594·5	557·6	37·0	6·2
1972	581·6	542·8	38·8	6·7
1973	580·9	550·6	30·3	5·2

Source: *Digest of Statistics*, H M S O, Belfast, various issues.

severe in the North as it is in the Republic of Ireland. The Republic's unemployment rate for December 1974 was about 7·7 per cent. (See Chapter 3 for some discussion of the comparability of the statistics.)

Since the Northern price level is obviously very closely linked with the British price level (P_{GB}), it is assumed to be given by a function of the latter plus an element which is dependent on the rate of unemployment. Thus the price relationship is written as

$$P = \theta(P_{GB}) + \bar{\theta}(u^*) \qquad (1.18)$$

where $u^* = U/\bar{N}$ is the Northern Ireland unemployment rate. This equation is in line with, albeit a simplification of, certain recent economic theory which is outlined in the discussion of Chapter 5. Figure 1.4 is drawn to show the close similarity between the movements of the Northern Ireland price level and those of the United Kingdom price level. The index used for the North is the G D P deflator derived and discussed in Chapter 5. The United Kingdom index is the official annual (twelve-monthly average) index of retail prices for all consumption items. The U K price index is not markedly different from the UK GDP deflator, which suggests that the Northern

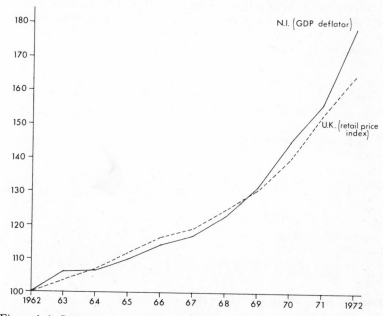

Figure 1.4: *Prices, Northern Ireland and United Kingdom, 1962–1972*

Source: N I: Chapter 5; U K; *Annual Abstract of Statistics 1973,* H M S O, London, Tables 6 and 403.

Ireland GDP deflator may also be a good proxy for the unavailable retail price index. The experience of the North, in common with most economies, has been of a steadily increasing price level during the 1960s, with a rise in the rate of increase occurring round about 1967.

Because of the close proximity of the large British labour market, the level of money wages in Northern Ireland is considerably influenced by the level of wages in Great Britain. It is assumed, therefore, that the wage level in Northern Ireland is described by the equation

$$W = \psi(W_{GB}) + \bar{\psi}(u^*) \qquad (1.19)$$

where W_{GB} is the wage level in Britain. This equation is similar in form to equation (1.18), and like equation (1.18) it accords well with modern theory. The equation can be viewed as a variant of the Phillips curve, according to which the growth rate of wages is dependent on excess demand for labour (proxied by a suitable function of the unemployment rate) and various cost-push forces (see Chapter 5). The term $\bar{\psi}(u^*)$ stands for the former demand-pull element in wage determination, while the term $\psi(W_{GB})$ denotes the cost-push element. However, the equation is written as determining the level of wages rather than the rate of growth of wages.

The recent course of average weekly earnings in Northern Ireland is indicated in Figure 1.5(a). Average weekly earnings, which reflect wage

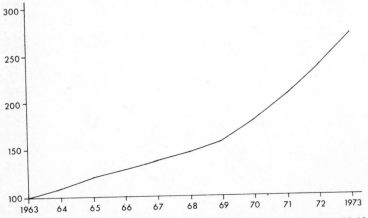

Figure 1.5(a): *Average Weekly Earnings of Males in Northern Ireland, 1963–73 (1963 = 100)*

Source: *Digest of Statistics*, H M S O, Belfast, various issues.

rates, but which are also influenced by the average length of the working week and hours of overtime, have been increasing quite rapidly. However, average earnings are somewhat lower in the North than they are in Great

Britain, although the gap has been narrowing. As Figure 1.5(b) shows, they have risen from about 80 per cent of the British level of average earnings in 1963 to close on 90 per cent in 1973.

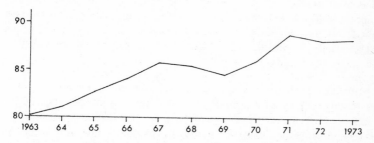

Figure 1.5(b): *Average Weekly Earnings of Males in Northern Ireland as a Percentage of Average Weekly Earnings of Males in Great Britain, 1963–73*

Source: *Northern Ireland Economic Report on 1973*, H M S O, Belfast, p. 23.

For convenience, the equations of the model are now rewritten and re-numbered. All the variables are considered to be in real terms.

$$Q = C + i(Y, Y_{GB}, R, \bar{d}(G_2)) + f(Y_{GB}, R, \bar{f}(G_2)) + G_1$$
$$+ x(Y_{GB}, P_{GB}, P) - m(Z, G_1, P, P_{GB}) \tag{1.20}$$
$$C = c(Y_D) + c_1 G_2 \tag{1.21}$$
$$Z = C + i(..) + f(..) + x(..) \tag{1.22}$$
$$Y_D = Q - TX \tag{1.23}$$
$$TX = t_0 + t_1 Q \tag{1.24}$$
$$TN = T - TX \tag{1.25}$$
$$T = \alpha + g(U) \tag{1.26}$$
$$Y = Q + TN \tag{1.27}$$
$$G = T + B \tag{1.28}$$
$$G = G_1 + G_2 \tag{1.29}$$
$$Q = h(N) \tag{1.30}$$
$$U = \bar{N} - N \tag{1.31}$$
$$u^* = U/\bar{N} \tag{1.32}$$
$$P = \theta(P_{GB}) + \bar{\theta}(u^*) \tag{1.33}$$
$$W = \psi(W_{GB}) + \bar{\psi}(u^*) \tag{1.34}$$

The variables I, M and X have been eliminated by replacing them with the functions determining them, i.e. $i(..) + f(..)$, $m(..)$ and $x(..)$ where the arguments (denoted by dots) are given in full in equation (1.20). These fifteen equations (1.20) to (1.34) serve to determine fifteen variables, i.e. the *endogenous* variables. Thirteen of these are Q, C, Y, P, Z, Y_D, TX, TN, T, N, U, u^*, W. Most of the other variables, for example P_{GB}, are clearly determined outside the system (i.e. are *exogenous*) since the Northern Ireland economy is too small to have a significant effect on them, but some discussion of the variables G_1, G_2, G and B is required. Various possible interpretations are permissible: for example, that B is determined exogenously. Since T is given from (1.26) for given α, it follows that G is determined endogenously, using (1.28). The division of G into G_1 and G_2 may be determined arbitrarily, i.e. exogenously by policy decision. This position is taken below, except that it is assumed that G_2 is determined exogenously by policy decision, subject to the constraint that $G_1 + G_2 = G$, $G_2 < G$. Thus G_1 is endogenous and positive. Although the model itself does not require it, it is assumed for economic realism that B cannot be varied limitlessly. While increasing B in the model implies increased government spending and is thus expansionary, it is important to remember that more borrowing involves more lending from somewhere, and increased interest costs or tougher terms may not be acceptable. This would be complicated to model explicitly and no attempt is made to do so here. If the authorities wish to increase G_2, it must be at the expense of G_1. If G is to be increased, then either B must be increased or the British authorities must increase T through α. Regarding G and G_1 as endogenous, the equations (1.20) to (1.33) constitute an integrated system of fourteen equations determining the endogenous variables listed above, except for W. The latter can be found by substituting the solved u^* value into equation (1.34). Since W does not appear in (1.20) to (1.33), these equations can be solved independently of it.

The treatment of British variables (Y_{GB}, P_{GB}, W_{GB}, etc.) as exogenous is justified by the argument that Northern Ireland is too small for changes in its variables to have noticeable impact on the British economy. Thus British variables are determined outside the system and these values feed into the Northern Ireland economy. A similar argument applies to the Republic of Ireland — Great Britain variables are exogenous to it. The interest rate is assumed exogenous to both Irish economies on similar grounds. Given free mobility of funds, the nominal interest rate in Ireland (R^N) cannot differ from that in London, and the latter is essentially determined outside Ireland. This point is elaborated below and in Chapter 7. The real rate (R) is the nominal rate less the expected rate of inflation, and for simplicity the latter is also taken as exogenous.

An important feature of the model is that the real variables — output (Q), employment (N), etc. — are not affected by monetary factors. This does not necessarily mean that the model precludes a monetary sector nor that there is no link between the real sector and the monetary sector.

In order to explain the nature of the assumed monetary mechanism, three further equations need to be considered.

First, the demand for money equation

$$\frac{M^D}{P} = l(Y, R^N) \tag{1.35}$$

where M^D is the demand for nominal money balances. This equation is fairly standard in the macro-economics literature, although some authors include the expected rate of price change as an argument in the function. It can be seen that M^D is determined once the values of the endogenous variables in equations (1.20) to (1.33) are known, although M^D does not itself serve in the determination of Q, Y, N, etc.

The demand for money is assumed to be equal to the supply of money, M^S (for which there are no official statistics in Northern Ireland). Thus

$$M^S = M^D \tag{1.36}$$

Justification of this equality requires consideration of the balance of payments. The change in foreign reserves (ΔV) is equal to the total currency flow and is defined as

$$\Delta V = Px(..) - P_{GB}\, m(..) + B_L + TN + H + P\epsilon_1 f(..) - A \tag{1.37}$$

where B_L is net long-term foreign borrowing, H is short-term capital inflows, $P\epsilon_1 f(..)$ is the component of direct foreign investment directly affecting the balance of payments, and A is the outward currency flow stemming from Northern Ireland investment abroad. Since the flows are in monetary terms, the real variables are multiplied by appropriate prices (imports being assumed to come only from Great Britain).

Of course, as Northern Ireland is a region of the United Kingdom, it does not have an officially recorded balance of payments. Indeed, no capital flows are recorded by the official statisticians. None the less, it does have a balance of payments in principle, even though it does not act as an obvious constraint on its economic behaviour. As with the monetary variables M^D and M^S, it is clear from equations (1.20) to (1.33) that there is no feedback from the balance of payments situation to the real sector. This is further discussed below.

Equation (1.37) is based on the principles of accounting which are the basis of international accounts in the United Kingdom. For further detail, the reader is referred to Chapter 4 on the foreign sector. As regards the interaction of equations (1.35) to (1.37), suppose that $\Delta V > 0$ so that there is an inflow of funds into the economy. Since in the model the demand for money is not affected, this inflow will give rise (eventually if $M^D > M^S$, immediately if $M^D = M^S$) to the supply of money exceeding the demand. This, in turn, will lead to a tendency for the nominal interest rate to fall, as the banking sector attempts to expand credit. The domestic decline in the interest rate, however, will lead to an outflow of funds from the economy seeking the higher interest rate in Great Britain. The only way in which these funds can be stabilised is for ΔV to be zero and M^S to equal M^D. The interest rate is thus treated as exogenous since it cannot be different in Ireland and Great Britain, except instantaneously, and the latter economy is so much larger that the Irish influence on the actual magnitude of R^N is negligible.

It is not true to say that Irish conditions have absolutely no effect, however. For suppose an initial position of equilibrium, with $M^S = M^D$ and $\Delta V = 0$. Let this position be disturbed by an exogenous shift which increases income and hence the demand for money. This gives rise to immediate upward pressures on the interest rate inducing inflows of funds. ΔV becomes positive and M^S rises. In the new position of equilibrium, with $\Delta V = 0$ and $M^S = M^D$ as argued above, there may well be a slightly higher rate of interest than previously obtained, since, given Q etc. as determined independently of monetary factors, there is a lasting increase in the demand for money in Northern Ireland. Assuming the same demand for money in Britain as previously obtained and an unchanged supply of money in all the economies combined, the rate of interest must be slightly higher than before in order for monetary equilibrium to obtain everywhere.

It is important to treat these arguments as applying to a relatively short time period. The assumption that monetary and balance of payments considerations do not have repercussions on the real variables of the system is untenable as a general principle. The equality of ΔV to zero and M^S to M^D as outlined above may well involve the various components of the balance of payments being at undesirable levels. Borrowing may be at an unhealthy level, for example, and the authorities might wish to use policies aimed at increasing exports relative to imports. In the medium to long run, these policies would probably be induced *because of* balance of payments problems of the kind alluded to, so that there would indeed be feedbacks to the real sector. Formalisation of points of this kind, which would be realistic for the Irish cases, is worthy of considerable research effort.

Even the relatively simple arguments outlining reasons why it is permissible to equate ΔV to zero and M^S to M^D are quite difficult to model formally, involving, as they do, dynamic considerations. Since they act without feedback on the rest of the model, there is no attempt here to write down differential or difference equations pertaining to the postulated dynamics.

2.2   Republic of Ireland

The model of the Republic of Ireland economy is purposely kept as similar as possible to that of Northern Ireland. It is unnecessary, therefore, to specify the entire structure of the Republic of Ireland model separately. Rather, it is sufficient simply to draw attention to the modifications of the structure as set out in equations (1.20) to (1.37) which the differences in the two economies suggest might usefully be made. Without implying any change in the basic theory underlying the model, three such modifications are introduced; they concern the Republic's net transfers, its export function, and its balance of payments function.

As is shown in Table 1.1(a), the transfers to the Republic amounted to £83 million, or only 3 per cent of gross national disposable income, in 1972. Despite the payments from the European Economic Community, which commenced in 1973, transfers as a proportion of gross national disposable income are still only very small in the Republic compared with their significance in Northern Ireland. In view of this, and in the interest of simplicity, it seems reasonable to omit the transfers variable (TN) from the Republic of Ireland model, just as net factor income is omitted. This means that there are no counterparts to equations (1.25), (1.26) and (1.27) in the model of the Republic; that T is replaced by TX in equation (1.28); and that wherever the variable Y appears in the model it is replaced by Q, for with TN omitted there is no difference between G D P (Q) and gross national disposable income (Y) in the model.

It was pointed out in the previous subsection that the proportion of Northern Ireland's total merchandise exports which goes to the Republic is small. By contrast, merchandise exports from the Republic to Northern Ireland, which in 1973 accounted for nearly 10 per cent of the Republic's total merchandise exports, are considered to be a significant proportion of the Republic's export trade (see Chapter 4, p. 120). This suggests that a change in the specification of the Republic's export function would be appropriate. In fact, in the Republic of Ireland variant of the model the export equation is written as

$$X = x (Y_{GB}, P_{GB}, Y_{NI}, P_{NI}, P) \qquad (1.38)$$

implying that the level of the Republic's exports is dependent on the income (Y_{NI}) and the price level (P_{NI}) in Northern Ireland as well as on the income and price levels in Britain. Thus in the Republic of Ireland model a link exists not only with Great Britain but also with the Northern Ireland economy, although this latter link is a rather tenuous one in comparison with the former. Like Northern Ireland, the Republic's major trading partner is still Great Britain. In 1973, for example, £393·1 million worth, or 45 per cent, of the Republic's total merchandise exports went to Britain, and £534·8 million worth, or 47 per cent, of its total merchandise imports came from Britain. However, during the 1960s, and particularly the early 1970s, there has been a clear lessening of the dependency of the economy of the Republic on that of Great Britain, and a corresponding increase in trade with the countries of the E E C and the rest of the world. In 1960, for example, the proportion of total merchandise exports going to Britain was about 60 per cent; in 1968 it was about 57 per cent. Accompanying this trend there has been a continuing change in the composition of the Republic's merchandise trade, particularly its merchandise exports, with the proportion of exports accounted for by live animals declining markedly from about 26 per cent in 1965 to a little under 10 per cent in 1973, and the proportion of exports accounted for by raw materials and manufactured goods increasing from about 35 per cent to about 50 per cent over the same period. Details of these changes in trading pattern and composition of trade are given in Chapter 4.

The Republic has a well-defined balance of payments which, no doubt, has significant economic effects. However, to preserve the basic similarity of the two models, the balance of payments equation does not, in the model of the Republic, serve to influence any of the other structural variables. As was mentioned above (p. 24), this course may be justified, at least partially, by appealing to the essential short-run nature of the model. Hence the Republic's balance of payments equation could be written as

$$\Delta V = Px(Y_{GB}, P_{GB}, Y_{NI}, P_{NI}, P) - P_{GB}m(Z, G_1, P, P_{GB}) + B_L + H + P_{e}f(..) - A \tag{1.39}$$

Given the movements in the exogenous variables, output, unemployment and all other endogenous variables are determined, and ΔV is accordingly affected. If ΔV were significantly negative, which would be equivalent to there being a substantial fall in the level of the official external reserves, then offsetting flows would occur as described above.

In fact, during the period 1960–73 the changes in the Republic's official external reserves have invariably been positive (see Table 4.5), a fact which would be expected under the above analysis if the demand for money has been rising. The repeated and increasing annual deficits on the current account of the balance of payments, which in the 1960s averaged about £20 million and in the period 1969–73 averaged about £70 million, have been financed not by depletion of the external reserves but by expansion of the net capital inflow. The major part of this inflow of funds is accounted for by overseas borrowing on the part of the government and the semi-state bodies within the public sector. For example, during the five years up to 1973 this kind of borrowing accounted, on average, for 41 per cent of the total net capital inflow annually; inflows of funds through the commercial banks accounted for an annual average of about 36 per cent, and direct foreign investment and other inflows only for an annual average of about 23 per cent. The expansion of the net capital inflow during this period has been such as to increase reserves by over £150 million, with most of this increase having taken place in 1971 and 1972. It is interesting to note, however, that since 1972, reserves as a percentage of imports have fallen from about 50 per cent to little more than 30 per cent at the beginning of 1974, despite a further increase in reserves of about £89 million during 1973.

It remains to complete the statistical sketch of the economy of the Republic of Ireland. In doing this, data are given which, as far as is possible, permit some kind of comparison with those already given for Northern Ireland. It has to be stressed however, that owing to differences in the definition or in the methods of measurement of the variables, such comparisons can, generally, be only crude comparisons at best.

Table 1.6 gives the level of the Republic's G D P at constant factor cost and the level of employment in certain sectors of the economy in the years 1962, 1967 and 1973; like Table 1.3, it also gives the percentage shares in total production and total employment accounted for by each of the sectors. The figures in the table indicate clearly that a marked structural change has taken place within the economy during the period covered by the data. Although output has increased in absolute terms in all sectors during the period, with particularly large increases of over 100 per cent occurring in industry and the government sector, there has, in common with many developing countries, been a substantial decline in the share of agriculture in total output and a corresponding increase in the share of industry. The shares of the three service sectors have altered only marginally. These changes are paralleled by the sectoral employment experience. Employment in agriculture has fallen continuously during the decade, with a loss of about 109,000 reducing the agricultural share in total employment from about 35 per cent in 1962 to about 25 per cent in 1973. During the same period employment in industry increased by about 50,000, and the industrial share in total employment increased from about 25 per cent to about 30 per cent. Employment in the combined service sectors also increased, taking the share of all services together to about 45 per cent of total employment in 1973, slightly less than the corresponding figure for Northern Ireland. The trend towards increasing industrialisation has probably been considerably aided by the activities of the Industrial Development Authority in attracting foreign capital and by the various programmes for economic expansion. As can be seen by comparing the figures of Table 1.6 with those of Table 1.3, however, the Republic is still relatively highly dependent on its agricultural sector; in 1972 the Republic's agricultural shares in total output and total employment were more than twice the corresponding shares for Northern Ireland, while its industrial shares in total output and employment were about 71 per cent and 83 per cent, respectively, of the Northern Ireland equivalents.

Structural changes have also taken place *within* sectors of the economy of the Republic during the period 1962–73. For instance, in agriculture there has been increasing specialisation in the production of livestock; and in industry, production and employment in the traditional manufacturing areas of drink, tobacco, clothing, and footwear have become less significant as production and employment in such industries as cement, chemicals, metals and engineering have increased rapidly. Production of cement and chemicals, for example, increased over the period by about 200 per cent and 140 per cent respectively. These issues of industrial growth and changing production patterns are discussed in Chapter 2, while Chapter 3 examines the employment issues more closely.

Using the shares for production and employment given in Table 1.6, sectoral productivity ratios for the Republic are given in Table 1.7 for com-

Table 1.6: GDP at Factor Cost (1968 prices) and Employment by Sector, Republic of Ireland, 1962, 1967 and 1973

Sector	1962 Output (Q) Level (£m)	1962 Output (Q) Share (%)	1962 Employment (N) Level (000s)	1962 Employment (N) Share (%)	1967 Output (Q) Level (£m)	1967 Output (Q) Share (%)	1967 Employment (N) Level (000s)	1967 Employment (N) Share (%)	1973 Output (Q) Level (£m)	1973 Output (Q) Share (%)	1973 Employment (N) Level (000s)	1973 Employment (N) Share (%)
Agriculture, Forestry and Fishing	188	25·3	370	34·9	196	19·2	320	30·2	286	19·4	261	24·8
Industry	240	32·3	270	25·5	342	33·5	297	28·0	487	33·1	320	30·4
Distribution, Transport, Communications	122	16·4	215	20·2	174	17·1	226	21·3	245	16·6	235	22·4
Public Administration and Defence	38	5·1	41	3·9	61	6·0	44	4·2	92	6·2	55	5·2
Other Domestic	155	20·9	164	15·5	247	24·2	173	16·3	365	24·7	181	17·2
Total economy	743	100·0	1,060	100·0	1,020	100·0	1,060	100·0	1,475	100·0	1,052	100·0

Sources: *National Income and Expenditure 1967 and 1973*, Stationery Office, Dublin, Table A4; *Trend of Employment and Unemployment 1966 and 1972*, Stationery Office, Dublin, Table 1; *CBR* (1975), Table 55.

parison with those given in Table 1.4 for Northern Ireland. As in Table 1.4, the three service sectors have been combined for this exercise.[5] Comparing the ratios for 1967 and 1973, the picture that emerges for the Republic is very similar to that which emerged from Table 1.4 for Northern Ireland. Productivity in the Republic has been higher in the industrial and services sectors, and lower in the agricultural sector, than productivity in the economy as a whole, although in industry and services there is evidence of a slight fall in productivity from 1967 to 1973, and in agriculture a slight rise, relative to overall productivity.

Table 1.7: Ratios of Percentage Share in GDP to Share in Employment, Republic of Ireland, 1962, 1967 and 1973

Sector	1962	1967	1973
Agriculture	0·725	0·636	0·782
Industry	1·267	1·196	1·089
Services	1·070	1·132	1·060

Source: Derived from data in Table 1.6.

Table 1.8 contains figures for the total available labour force and the levels of employment and unemployment in the Republic for the years 1960–74. The figures in the first three columns of the table are based on the Censuses of Population taken in 1961, 1966 and 1971. For non-censal years the census information is supplemented by various indicators obtained from the annual censuses of production and distribution. The rate of unemployment in column 4 of the table is obtained by expressing the unemployment figure for each year as a percentage of the labour force figure, which is in line with the definition of the unemployment rate in the model. However, this is not a very reliable estimate of the year-to-year unemployment rate. A better estimate is that given by the ratio of currently insured persons on the Live Register of the Department of Social Welfare to the total currently insured population; such figures are given in the final column of Table 1.8. Although the latter series suggests a higher rate of unemployment than the former, there is a correspondence in the direction of the year-to-year changes in the unemployment rate between the two series.

The total labour force of the Republic remained fairly stable around an average of about 1,118,000 persons from 1960 to 1973. This average level is nearly double that of the Northern Ireland labour force for the same period. The level of the Republic's total employment has not been quite so

5 Kennedy (1971) (p. 11) has calculated similar ratios for the Republic of Ireland for selected years up to 1967. His ratios for 1967 are only very slightly different from those in Table 1.4; they yield precisely the same conclusions.

Table 1.8: Employment and Unemployment in the Republic of Ireland,
1960–74

Year	Available labour ($\overline{N}$) (000s)	Employment (000s)	Unemployment		
			U(000s)	u* (%)	%
1960	1,118	1,055	63	5·6	6·7
1961	1,108	1,052	56	5·1	5·7
1962	1,114	1,060	54	4·8	5·7
1963	1,122	1,066	56	5·0	6·1
1964	1,124	1,071	53	4·7	5·7
1965	1,120	1,069	51	4·5	5·6
1966	1,118	1,066	52	4·7	6·1
1967	1,116	1,060	56	5·0	6·7
1968	1,123	1,063	60	5·3	6·7
1969	1,122	1,066	56	5·0	6·4
1970	1,118	1,053	65	5·8	7·2
1971	1,120	1,055	65	5·8	7·2
1972	1,117	1,046	71	6·4	8·1
1973	1,118	1,051	67	6·0	7·2
1974[a]	1,122	1,058	64	5·7	7·9

[a]1974 figures supplied by the C S O, Dublin.
Source: *Trend of Employment and Unemployment,* Stationery Office, Dublin,
various issues.

stable. Its general trend was upward till the mid-1960s, reaching a peak of
1,071,000 persons in 1964, then downward till 1972. In 1973, at about
1,051,000 persons, it was about the same as it had been in 1961. Unemployment in the Republic, as in Northern Ireland, tended to fluctuate during
the 1960s, but it moved about a somewhat higher average annual rate than
in Northern Ireland, as indicated in Figure 1.6. Moreover, the recent unemployment experience has been rather more severe than earlier in the
1960s, with the average rate for the first four years of the 1970s being 7·4
per cent as compared with an average rate of 6·1 per cent for the first four
years of the 1960s. The lowest annual rate of unemployment experienced
during the 1960s was 5·7 per cent.

Finally, Figure 1.7 is drawn to illustrate the Republic's recent experience
with regard to consumer prices, average weekly earnings in transportable
goods industries, the money supply, and, for comparison, the level of real
GDP. The money supply used is the so-called narrow money supply measured
by the sum of currency outstanding and the Associated Banks' current
accounts. Owing to the bank dispute in 1970, no money supply figure is
available for that year.

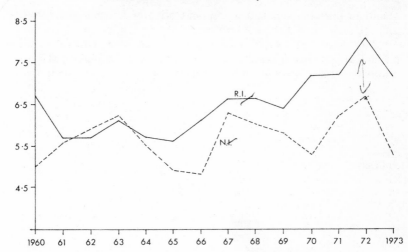

Figure 1.6: *Rates of Unemployment in Northern Ireland and the Republic, 1960–73*

Source: R I: Table 1.8; NI: Table 1.5.

The Republic's level of prices has grown at a very similar rate to that of Northern Ireland during the period 1963–72, with both rates appearing to accelerate round about 1967–68. The steep trend has continued, with the Republic having the highest increase in consumer prices of the nine EEC countries in 1973. The inflation experience of the Republic is discussed and analysed in Chapter 5.

Average earnings, too, have paralleled quite closely the experience of Northern Ireland, growing even more rapidly than consumer prices in both areas. Like prices, earnings also appear to have increased at a higher annual rate since about 1967. Comparing the growth of earnings with the growth of GDP provides an insight into how the share of labour in gross domestic income has been changing. As can be seen from Figure 1.7, earnings increased considerably more rapidly than GDP from 1963 to 1973, implying that during this period labour's share in income has been increasing. Indeed, calculating the ratio of agricultural and non-agricultural wages and salaries to national income indicates that in the Republic, labour's share has risen from about 52 per cent in 1959 to about 56 per cent in 1963 and about 62 per cent in 1973.

Substantial growth also took place in the Republic's money supply from 1963 to 1973. In 1973 the narrow money supply stood at about £506 million, which is about twice the nominal value of the money supply in 1963. However, the money supply as a percentage of GNP has declined by about one-third to around 20 per cent of GNP over the same period. Notes and coins constituted about 42 per cent of the narrow money supply in 1973, or about 8 per cent of GNP. Again, this percentage marks a fall during the period. The money supply measured on the broad definition, which includes the deposit accounts of the commercial banks, has been about twice

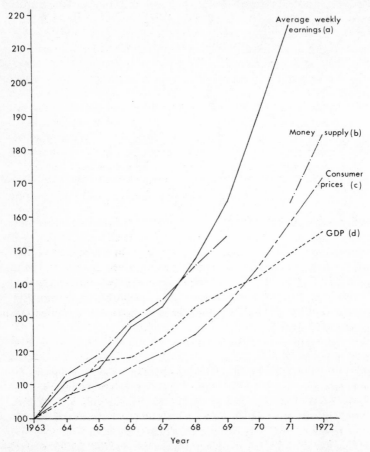

Figure 1.7: *Consumer Prices, Average Weekly Earnings, Real GDP and the Money Supply in the Republic of Ireland, 1963–72*

Sources: (*a*) *Statistical Abstract of Ireland,* Stationery Office, Dublin 1970–71, Table 114.
   (*b*) *CBR,* various issues.
   (*c*) *Irish Statistical Bulletin,* Stationery Office, Dublin, various issues.
   (*d*) *National Income and Expenditure,* Stationery Office, Dublin, various issues.

as large as the narrow money supply, and has grown approximately in step
with it. These various money magnitudes and their economic significance
are discussed more fully in Chapter 7.

In concluding this brief statistical description of the economy of the
Republic of Ireland it is worthwhile to point out the stark contrast between
the growth experience and structural changes that have been described and
the economic experience of the previous decades. In the mid-1950s, for
example, there was chronic stagnation of the agriculture-dominated
economy, with a high rate of unemployment and negligible economic
growth. Indeed, during the mid-1950s, growth was virtually nil for three
years and in one year actually declined, and emigration reached its highest
level since the late nineteenth century. The growth experience from 1960
to 1974 has been about twice as fast as that during the previous thirty years,
there has been a continuing shift from agriculture to industry, and net
emigration has given way to a modest net immigration. The impact of becoming a member of the EEC in 1973 could be such as to reinforce these
trends and raise still further the prosperity of the Republic of Ireland.

3   ASPECTS OF THE MODELS

A great advantage of specifying a structural model, as is done in the preceding section, is that the interdependencies of the different sectors and
variables of an economic system are thereby brought out explicitly. Furthermore, the approach favours the explicit making of assumptions and helps
in understanding the behaviour of particular economies. Mathematical
analysis of the structure is usually the most efficient way of deriving the
implications of the assumptions made, but before turning to the analysis,
further comment on the models developed above is required.

It is of the utmost importance to understand that the models are static
and are intended to replicate reality in the *short run* only. To ease exposition of this point, consider the Northern Ireland model, equations (1.20) –
(1.34). If all the exogenous variables were constant, and implied that net
investment were positive, it is true that the capital stock, and hence productive capacity, would be growing through time. This would clearly be
important and could not be ignored in the long run. Since the model is not
intended to be used in this way and is regarded as an approximation to reality in the short run only, this inherently dynamic problem is henceforth
ignored.

Neither of the models implies balance of payments equilibrium. It is
assumed, for simplicity, that a surplus or deficit does not have repercussions
which feed back into the model in the short run. This is not to say, of
course, that disequilibrium could obtain in the medium and long term.
Either self-correcting forces would be at work, which are not contained in
the model as presently developed, such as the monetary mechanism dis-

cussed above (see also Chapter 4, Section 3.4, and Chapter 7, pp. 249–50, or else the authorities would take action in order to affect some or all of the variables involved.

An important logical necessity for the models to be sensible is that the equations generate positive unemployment. If the demand for labour exceeded the supply in either economy, the equations cannot make sense as they stand, even in the short run. As has already been mentioned, both economies, in fact, suffer from long-standing problems of unemployment, so it is natural to assume that the equations of the structure do imply positive unemployment.

As a final general comment on the models, consider the so-called 'adding-up' problem. This problem concerns the logical question of whether the implied payment to factors precisely exhausts the implied output. Again illustrating with the model for Northern Ireland, and temporarily ignoring the transfer problem, it is assumed that the capital payments or rentals, which do not explicitly appear in the equations, are such that factor income is equal to the value of output. The model does not logically imply that the 'adding-up' problem is solved, but the assumption that the model approximates reality, together with the degree of freedom concerning the payments to capital, allows the problem to be ignored. What if the wage rate in Great Britain rises, however? Then, given unemployment, the wage rate in Northern Ireland changes according to equation (1.34). In fact, W will rise, on the understanding that $\dfrac{\partial \psi}{\partial W_{GB}} > 0$, and since this equation does not feed back into the system, employment is unchanged, so that wage income rises. Logically, this implies a squeeze on capital payments, at least in the short run, which is permitted by the model. However, another possibility is open here, subject to a mathematical refinement, namely that prices in Great Britain are not independent of wages in Great Britain. Hence, with the change in W_{GB} is associated a change in P_{GB} which affects P through θ (P_{GB}) in equation (1.33) and hence employment, output, etc. The conclusion is that the 'adding-up' problem need not be of concern in the analysis below.

3.1   Analysis of the Models

The method of analysis adopted is to consider the effects of exogenous variable changes on the endogenous variables of the system. The tool of analysis is the implicit function theorem of differential calculus, an exposition of which appears in any advanced calculus text. Certain mathematical requirements, such as differentiability, are assumed for all the functions appearing in the models. Given these assumptions, we can evaluate precisely and uniquely the effect of a change in any exogenous variable on any endogenous variable. For example, consider the effect of a change in the tax rate (t_1) on the endogenous variable unemployment (U); this would be given by $\frac{\partial U}{\partial t_1}$, and routine calculations give (for Northern Ireland)[6]:

$$\frac{\partial U}{\partial t_1} = -Q\left(1 - \frac{\partial m}{\partial Z}\right)\left(\frac{\partial c}{\partial Y_D} + \frac{\partial i}{\partial Y}\right)/D \qquad (1.40)$$

where $D = -\frac{\partial h}{\partial N}\left[1 - \left(1 - t_1\right)\left(1 - \frac{\partial m}{\partial Z}\right)\left(\frac{\partial c}{\partial Y_D} + \frac{\partial i}{\partial Y}\right)\right]$

$$-\frac{\partial g}{\partial U}\left[1 - \frac{\partial m}{\partial G_1} + \left(1 - \frac{\partial m}{\partial Z}\right)\frac{\partial i}{\partial Y}\right] - \frac{1}{N}\frac{\partial \bar{\theta}}{\partial u^*}\left[\left(1 - \frac{\partial m}{\partial Z}\right)\frac{\partial x}{\partial P} - \frac{\partial m}{\partial P}\right]$$

The expression for the denominator D occurs throughout the analysis of derivatives and its sign is considered first.

(a) $0 < \frac{\partial h}{\partial N}, 0 < \frac{\partial m}{\partial Z} < 1, 0 < \frac{\partial c}{\partial Y_D} < 1, 0 < \frac{\partial i}{\partial Y} < 1, 0 < t_1 < 1$

$\frac{\partial m}{\partial Z}$ is, like $\frac{\partial m}{\partial G_1}$ and $\frac{\partial c}{\partial Y_D}$, quite high in both parts of Ireland, possibly around 0·8. The aggregate marginal tax rate is probably less than 0·5, and the marginal propensity to invest with respect to income is probably close to zero.

(b) $0 < \frac{\partial g}{\partial U}$

(c) $\frac{\partial \bar{\theta}}{\partial u^*} < 0, \frac{\partial x}{\partial P} < 0, \frac{\partial m}{\partial P} > 0$

Thus $D < 0$. Since the numerator is also negative, $\frac{\partial U}{\partial t_1} > 0$. That is, an increase of the tax rate increases unemployment.

The effect on output follows at once since $\frac{\partial Q}{\partial t_1} = \frac{\partial h}{\partial N}\frac{\partial N}{\partial t_1} = -\frac{\partial h}{\partial N}\frac{\partial U}{\partial t_1}$, using equations (1.30) and (1.31). Thus $\frac{\partial Q}{\partial t_1} < 0$, so that increasing the tax rate reduces domestic output.

---

6 Of course such a tax change would be carried out in London, since Northern Ireland does not have fiscal autonomy. Furthermore, the change would influence British variables which would have further effects on Northern Ireland. These are ignored partly since a Great Britain model has not been specified and partly in order to highlight the pure tax effects. $\partial U/\partial Y_{GB}$ is discussed below.

Next, consider as alternative fiscal policy, an increase in government borrowing (B) (holding other exogenous variables including government transfer spending (G_2) constant).

$$\frac{\partial U}{\partial B} = \left(1 - \frac{\partial m}{\partial G_1}\right)/D < 0$$

That is, increased borrowing reduces unemployment, the beneficial effects being mitigated (given D) by increased imports arising from the increased government spending on goods and services (G_1). Imports, of course, constitute a leakage from the system.

The effect of increased borrowing on the net transfer (TN) results from two considerations. Since unemployment falls, there is a fall in the gross transfer (given α) and a rise in taxes resulting from increased output. Formally,

$$\frac{\partial TN}{\partial B} = \frac{\partial T}{\partial B} - \frac{\partial TX}{\partial B} \qquad\qquad \text{from (1.25)}$$

$$= \frac{\partial g}{\partial U}\frac{\partial U}{\partial B} - t_1\frac{\partial Q}{\partial B} \qquad\qquad \text{from (1.24) and (1.26)}$$

$$= \frac{\partial g}{\partial U}\frac{\partial U}{\partial B} - t_1\frac{\partial h}{\partial N}\frac{\partial N}{\partial B} \qquad\qquad \text{from (1.30)}$$

$$= \frac{\partial U}{\partial B}\left(\frac{\partial g}{\partial U} + t_1\frac{\partial h}{\partial N}\right) \qquad\qquad \text{from (1.31)}$$

$$< 0$$

Thus Northern Ireland could reduce the net transfer from London by increased borrowing.

It is of interest to compare borrowing with gifts from London. To do so, consider an exogenous increase in α.

$$\frac{\partial U}{\partial \alpha} = \left[1 - \frac{\partial m}{\partial G_1} + \frac{\partial i}{\partial Y}\left(1 - \frac{\partial m}{\partial Z}\right)\right]/D < 0$$

Clearly $\left|\frac{\partial U}{\partial \alpha}\right| > \left|\frac{\partial U}{\partial B}\right|$

so that an extra pound in α reduces unemployment by more than an extra pound borrowed. The reason is the increased investment caused by the increase in gross national disposable income (Y), the latter increase being occasioned by the increase in gifts (α). More important, of course, are the interest costs and repayments associated with borrowing but not with gifts.

This is not picked up by the model. (See also note 1 of this chapter, p. 4.)

It should be pointed out that the net transfer will not rise by as much as $d\alpha$, since the fall in unemployment and rise in taxes will lessen the increase in the net transfer. Specifically,

$$\frac{\partial TN}{\partial \alpha} = \frac{\partial T}{\partial \alpha} - \frac{\partial TX}{\partial \alpha} \qquad \text{from (1.25)}$$

$$= 1 + \frac{\partial U}{\partial \alpha}\left(\frac{\partial g}{\partial U} + t_1\frac{\partial h}{\partial N}\right) \qquad \text{using (1.24), (1.30--31)}$$

$$< 1$$

It is of interest to consider some direct consequences of the openness of the Northern Ireland economy. Some of these are listed at the beginning of Chapter 4. For example, it is stated there that cyclical swings in the economies of major trading partners tend to be transmitted rapidly to the open economy. This fact can be exemplified by considering the effects of an increase in British income (Y_{GB}) on Northern Ireland unemployment, i.e.

$$\frac{\partial U}{\partial Y_{GB}} = \left[\left(1 - \frac{\partial m}{\partial Z}\right)\left(\frac{\partial x}{\partial Y_{GB}} + \frac{\partial i}{\partial Y_{GB}} + \frac{\partial f}{\partial Y_{GB}}\right)\right]/D$$

Since $\frac{\partial x}{\partial Y_{GB}} > 0$, the numerator is certainly positive. Since $D < 0$, an increase in Y_{GB} decreases unemployment in Northern Ireland. The effect arises through stimuli to exports and direct and foreign investment.

Next, consider a change in the British price level (P_{GB}). What, for example, is the effect on the Northern Ireland price level (P) of an increase in P_{GB}?

$$\frac{\partial P}{\partial P_{GB}} = \left\{ \frac{\partial \theta}{\partial P_{GB}} \left[-\frac{\partial h}{\partial N}\left(1 - \left(1 - t_1\right)\left(1 - \frac{\partial m}{\partial Z}\right)\left(\frac{\partial c}{\partial Y_D} + \frac{\partial i}{\partial Y}\right)\right)\right.\right.$$

$$\left.-\frac{\partial g}{\partial U}\left(1 - \frac{\partial m}{\partial G_1} + \left(1 - \frac{\partial m}{\partial Z}\right)\frac{\partial i}{\partial Y}\right)\right] + \frac{\partial \bar{\theta}}{\partial u^*}\left(\frac{1}{\bar{N}}\right)\left[\left(1 - \frac{\partial m}{\partial Z}\right)\frac{\partial x}{\partial P_{GB}} - \frac{\partial m}{\partial P_{GB}}\right]\right\}/D$$

Since $\frac{\partial \theta}{\partial P_{GB}} > 0$, $\frac{\partial m}{\partial P_{GB}} < 0$, $\frac{\partial x}{\partial P_{GB}} > 0$,

the numerator is negative and so the expression is positive. On the additional assumption that $\frac{\partial \theta}{\partial P_{GB}} \leqslant 1$, manipulation shows that

$$\frac{\partial P}{\partial P_{GB}} < 1 \text{ if } \left(1 - \frac{\partial m}{\partial Z}\right)\left(\frac{\partial x}{\partial P_{GB}} + \frac{\partial x}{\partial P}\right) < \frac{\partial m}{\partial P_{GB}} + \frac{\partial m}{\partial P}$$

The above analysis has concentrated on calculating the effects of changes in exogenous variables on Northern Ireland. The results are similar for the Republic. They are simpler in that a transfer is not involved; they are more complex in that they are affected by changes in Northern Ireland. For example, a change in P_{GB} affects variables in Northern Ireland as well as directly affecting the economy of the Republic, and the changes in Northern Ireland variables also have consequent effects in the Republic through the trade relationship.

This may be illustrated by two examples:

$$\frac{\partial U}{\partial t_1} = -Q\left[\left(1 - \frac{\partial m}{\partial Z}\right)\frac{\partial c}{\partial Y_D} - \left(1 - \frac{\partial m}{\partial G_1}\right)\right]/D_R$$

where $D_R = -\frac{\partial h}{\partial N}\left\{1 - \left(1 - \frac{\partial m}{\partial Z}\right)\left[\frac{\partial c}{\partial Y_D}\left(1 - t_1\right) + \frac{\partial i}{\partial Q}\right] - t_1\left(1 - \frac{\partial m}{\partial G_1}\right)\right\}$

$$- \frac{\partial \theta}{\partial u^*}\frac{1}{N}\left[\left(1 - \frac{\partial m}{\partial Z}\right)\frac{\partial x}{\partial P} - \frac{\partial m}{\partial P}\right]$$

and

$$\frac{\partial U}{\partial Y_{GB}} = \left(1 - \frac{\partial m}{\partial Z}\right)\left(\frac{\partial i}{\partial Y_{GB}} + \frac{\partial f}{\partial Y_{GB}} + \frac{\partial x}{\partial Y_{GB}} + \frac{\partial x}{\partial Y_{NI}}\frac{\partial Y_{NI}}{\partial Y_{GB}} + \frac{\partial x}{\partial P_{NI}}\frac{\partial P_{NI}}{\partial Y_{GB}}\right)/D_R$$

D_R is negative, but the sign of $\frac{\partial U}{\partial t_1}$ is uncertain. With fixed borrowing, the change in taxes is transmitted wholly to government spending on goods and services (G_1). $\frac{\partial U}{\partial Y_{GB}}$ involves Northern Ireland effects since a change in Y_{GB} affects Northern Ireland endogenous variables, including Y_{NI} and P_{NI}. These two variables affect the Republic's exports as shown by the equation. $\frac{\partial Y_{NI}}{\partial Y_{GB}}$ and $\frac{\partial P_{NI}}{\partial Y_{GB}}$ can be readily evaluated. Using (1.27), (1.25) and (1.24)

$$\frac{\partial Y_{NI}}{\partial Y_{GB}} = \frac{\partial Q_{NI}}{\partial Y_{GB}} + \frac{\partial T_{NI}}{\partial Y_{GB}} - t_1 \frac{\partial Q_{NI}}{\partial Y_{GB}}$$

$$= (1 - t_1)\frac{\partial Q_{NI}}{\partial Y_{GB}} + \frac{\partial g}{\partial U}\frac{\partial U_{NI}}{\partial Y_{GB}} \qquad \text{using (1.26)}$$

$$= \left[\frac{\partial g}{\partial U} - \left(1 - t_1\right)\frac{\partial h}{\partial N}\right]\frac{\partial U_{NI}}{\partial Y_{GB}} \qquad \text{using (1.30)}$$

$\frac{\partial U_{NI}}{\partial Y_{GB}}$ has been shown negative, and it appears reasonable to treat the expression in brackets as negative so that the whole expression is positive.

$$\frac{\partial P_{NI}}{\partial Y_{GB}} = \frac{1}{N}\frac{\partial \theta}{\partial u^*}\frac{\partial U}{\partial Y_{GB}} \qquad \text{using (1.32) and (1.33)}$$

and is positive.

Since $\frac{\partial x}{\partial Y_{NI}}$ and $\frac{\partial x}{\partial P_{NI}}$ are both positive (higher Northern Ireland income and prices boost the Republic's exports), it follows that $\frac{\partial U}{\partial Y_{GB}}$ is negative, just as it was for the North.

These results illustrate the richness of comparative static results of even a fairly simple model. More than two hundred derivatives can be calculated for the two models combined. Of course, they merely indicate at best the direction of change resulting from exogenous variable or parameter shifts, but they do allow for the complexities of a highly interdependent system which is necessarily a feature of the Irish and other economies.

It has not been considered to be part of the scope of this book to obtain quantitative results from the models or some variant of them, as this would require a major departure into econometric work. However, it is hoped that such a task will be undertaken by economists in Ireland before too long.

REFERENCES

Hibbert, J. (1975): 'Measuring Changes in the Nation's Real Income', *Economic Trends*, No. 255 (Jan.), H M S O, London.

Kennedy, K. (1971): *Productivity and Industrial Growth: The Irish Experience*, Clarendon Press, Oxford.

Northern Ireland Office (1974): *Northern Ireland: Discussion Paper: Finance and the Economy*, H M S O, London.

CHAPTER 2

Industrial Development and Regional Policy

W. BLACK

1 INTRODUCTION

Two small economies, situated on an island on the periphery of Europe, subject to similar broad influences of distance, meagre raw material resources, demonstration effects from contiguous economies, etc., might be expected to exhibit similar economic structures and problems. To some extent they do. Both have been seriously affected by the long-term decline in agricultural employment that has been a feature of Western Europe generally; both suffer from heavy unemployment; and both are struggling to provide jobs and incomes to meet the needs created by high birth rates (see Chapter 3).

Yet in terms of industrial structure the differences are more striking than the similarities. As can be seen from Table 2.1, the Republic of Ireland is much more heavily dependent on agriculture than Northern Ireland. Indeed, in its reliance on agriculture the Republic is more akin to Italy or Portugal than to Northern Ireland; and by the same measure Northern Ireland is more akin to Britain than to the Republic. As in many developing economies, the size of the agricultural sector in Ireland should be regarded, to some extent, as a residual: it reflects the lack of industrial development rather than the profitability of agriculture at the margin. This is true of both areas but it is particularly important for an understanding of the economy of the Republic.

Employment in manufacturing industry is relatively more important in Northern Ireland than in the Republic. In terms of industrial structure the Northern economy has had a developed industrial base for more than half a century; over a long period of time the proportion of employment in manufacturing was relatively stable, with counterbalancing changes taking place in the proportions in agriculture and services. But this apparent stability concealed dramatic changes within the structure of manufacturing industry, with the older traditional sectors declining and new activities develop-

Table 2.1: Structure of Employment in Northern Ireland and the Republic, 1960 and 1973

| | Northern Ireland | | | | Republic | | | |
	1960 (000s)	1973 (000s)	1973 (%)		1960 (000s)	1973 (000s)	1973 (%)
Agriculture, Forestry and Fishing	79	50·6	9·0		390·0	261·0	24·8
Construction	40	52·1	9·3		57·0	79·0	7·5
Mining and Quarrying	3	2·9	0·5		9·0	10·0	1·0
Manufacturing	190	174·4	31·1		172·0	217·0	20·6
Services	233	279·9	50·0		427·0	485·0	46·1
Total numbers at work	545	559·9	100·0		1055·0	1052·0	100·0

Sources: NI: Civil employment 1960: *Digest of Statistics*, H M S O, Belfast, various issues. Figures have been adjusted to the basis of the standard industrial classification, 1968. Civil employment 1973 on comparable basis: Department of Manpower Services, Belfast; RI: *Trend of Employment and Unemployment 1965 and 1973*, Stationery Office, Dublin.

ing to fill the gap. In recent years the declines have outweighed the new growth with the consequence that manufacturing employment has fallen. In the Republic, on the other hand, manufacturing employment has grown rapidly in recent years. Over the period between 1960 and 1973 the proportion of the labour force engaged in the sector increased from 16 per cent to 20·6 per cent. This growth reflects a process of industrial development that has had far-reaching effects on the economic life of the country during the past fifteen years.

Services, too, are relatively more important in Northern Ireland than in the Republic. It will be argued below that the main reasons for this difference stem from the fact that Northern Ireland is part of the United Kingdom. In the Republic the level to which public services have developed is partly determined by the capacity of the economy to meet the costs of providing them. In Northern Ireland this structural constraint does not apply: public services may be partly financed by transfers from the rest of the United Kingdom. This is only one example of the ways in which the interrelationships with the rest of the United Kingdom affect economic activity in the North. There are many others. Indeed, in what follows it should be borne in mind that although the discussion is couched in terms of the Northern Ireland economy, in a highly significant sense Northern Ireland is simply a region of the British economy.

The broad structural patterns in the two economies and the changes in those patterns since 1960 define the context within which the analysis of this chapter will be developed. Both economies have problems that can be solved only by the development of manufacturing industry. But the problems have distinctively different roots. In the Republic the main need is to offset the decline in agricultural employment by developing manufacturing industry, if not from scratch, at least from the very low levels that existed until quite recently. In this the problem in the Republic is similar to the problem in the southern part of Italy. Northern Ireland, too, has to cope with surplus agricultural employment, but in addition it must replace declining traditional manufacturing industry by new and vigorous manufacturing industry; Northern Ireland's difficulties are very similar to those of the problem regions in the rest of the United Kingdom.

While the provision of employment is a first policy objective in both economies, the need to increase incomes is a very close second. Income per head is higher in the North than in the South, but the differences between the two economies are small compared to the differences between both and, for example, the rest of the European Economic Community. To raise incomes to Western European standards within an acceptable period of time would be a formidable task. What are the possible sources of this growth?

Attention has been drawn in Chapter 1 to a major determinant of income that has important implications for the pattern of industrial development — the size of the capital stock. Obviously there are great gains to be reaped from improvements in organisational efficiency and from increases in the capital stock embodied in human beings as a result of education and training. But in both economies a considerable part of the required increase in income can only be achieved by making available to each employee an increased amount of non-human capital. In agriculture it is probable that increased amounts of capital per head will continue to be associated with declining employment. But the evidence of the past decade is that opportunities for concurrent growth in employment and capital per employee exist in manufacturing and services. To benefit from these opportunities both economies must sustain the high rates of industrial investment that have been achieved in recent years.

The main aim of this chapter is to disentangle from the flux of short-term changes the broad patterns of development in the two economies. It will be readily apparent that one major factor has affected the patterns during the last five years — the existence of civil unrest in Northern Ireland. No attempt can be made here to assess in detail the effects of that unrest on the Northern economy, not only on the performance of existing industry but on inward investment and on industrial development generally. But the bombing campaign has not had any dramatic direct impact on industry — apart from retail distribution; and the economy has proved extremely resilient in the face of widespread unrest and security problems. The eventual consequences of unchecked violence could be catastrophic, not only for the economy but for Irish life in general; but those consequences are not yet apparent in the Northern economy.

2   AGRICULTURE, INDUSTRY AND SERVICES

2.1   Agriculture

The relative importance of agriculture in the economies of Northern Ireland and the Republic can be assessed from the figures presented in Table 2.2. By all of the measures the sector is much more important in the Republic than in Northern Ireland; but it is in the contribution to total exports that the dependence of the Republic on agriculture is most striking. This dependence is, however, diminishing: as recently as 1960 agricultural products accounted for 58 per cent of total exports. Against this background it is somewhat paradoxical that agriculture is more export-orientated in Northern Ireland than in the Republic: in 1972 exports of agricultural produce — some of which was, of course, further processed in manufacturing industry — represented about three-quarters of the gross output of the agricultural sector in Northern Ireland compared with about half in the Republic.

The relationship between the contributions of the sector to employment and GDP in both areas is also striking. In Northern Ireland the percentage contribution to GDP is slightly lower than the percentage of total employment represented by the sector: the inference is that GDP per head is slightly lower in agriculture than the average for all other activities. In the Republic, on the other hand, 26 per cent of those in employment produced only 18 per cent of GDP; output per head in agriculture was only 64 per cent of the average for all other activities.

Table 2.2: Percentage of Employment, Gross Domestic Product and Exports in Agriculture for Northern Ireland and the Republic, 1972

	Northern Ireland	Republic
Employment[a]	9·0	26·0
Gross Domestic Product[a]	8·4	18·0
Exports	20·0	43·0

[a]Includes Forestry and Fishing.

Sources: NI: *Digest of Statistics.* No. 41 (Mar. 1974), HMSO, Belfast; R I: *Trend of Employment and Unemployment 1973, National Income and Expenditure 1972, Trade Statistics of Ireland* (Dec. 1972), all Stationery Office, Dublin.

As can be seen from Table 2.1, the rates of decline in agricultural employment have been very similar for the two areas over the period 1960—73: 36 per cent for Northern Ireland and 34 per cent for the Republic. But because of the greater importance of the sector in the economy the absolute size of the problem created by this outflow is much greater in the Republic. This can be readily established by considering the numbers involved: over the period the average annual outflow of people from agricultural employment in Northern Ireland was about 1,400; the corresponding figure for the Republic was close to 10,000. Alongside these declines in employment there were rapid increases in productivity and Gross Domestic Product from agriculture continued to increase in both areas. Agricultural GDP per head at constant prices increased by 154 per cent between 1961 and 1972 in Northern Ireland and by 172 per cent in the Republic.

The differences in the nature of farming in the two parts of Ireland can be seen from Table 2.3 which sets out the broad patterns of output in 1972. The Republic relies heavily on cattle and milk products — 57 per cent of gross output compared with 47 per cent in Northern Ireland — and on crops etc. — 14 per cent compared with 7 per cent in the North. In Northern Ireland, farmyard enterprises, pigs, eggs and poultry accounted for 34 per cent of gross output compared with 14 per cent in the South. Traditionally farmers in the Republic have concentrated on enterprises which make maximum use of their main natural asset, grass. Farmers in the North have found that their holdings are not large enough to provide satisfactory incomes from extensive operations dependent mainly on grass and, aided by the levels of support which were available to British agriculture generally, have turned instead to enterprises which make greater use of other factors — high-yield dairying, pigs and poultry. Thus in 1972, when the gross output of the Republic's agriculture was more than two and a half times that of the North, the total cost of inputs other than wages, rent and interest was slightly lower than in the North. Farms in Northern Ireland are more highly capitalised than those in the Republic and have greater access to machinery and equipment of all types; but the major part of the higher level of inputs in the North represents inputs of feeding-stuffs. Northern Ireland agriculture is feeding-stuff-intensive.

Although the differences in structure are still substantial, the agricultural industries in both areas are undergoing changes which are tending to reduce

Table 2.3:   Production Patterns in Agriculture, Northern Ireland, 1971—72, and the Republic, 1972

	Northern Ireland		Republic	
Livestock and livestock products	£m	%	£m	%
Cattle	53	29·0	156	33·0
Milk	34	18·6	114	24·2
Pigs	36	19·7	49	10·4
Eggs	22	12·0	10	2·1
Poultry	5	2·7	10	2·1
Other	5	2·7	28	5·9
Total livestock	155	84·7	367	77·7
Crops and Horticulture				
Barley	2	1·1	21	4·4
Wheat	0	0·0	8	1·8
Potatoes	5	2·7	12	2·5
Other	6	3·3	26	5·5
Total crops	13	7·1	67	14·2
Other[a]	15	8·2	38	8·1
Gross Output	183	100·0	472	100·0

[a]Including changes in stocks but excluding turf production.

Sources: NI: *Digest of Statistics,* No. 41 (Mar. 1974), HMSO, Belfast; RI: *Review of 1973 and Outlook for 1974* (Prl 3774), Stationery Office, Dublin.

the differences between them. From the earliest stages of the negotiations on entry to the E E C it was apparent that the pattern of enterprises in Northern Ireland would be vulnerable in the face of the high grain prices which have been a feature of the Common Agricultural Policy in the Community. It was also apparent that there were large potential gains available for the Republic from access to the continental beef market at Community prices. Anticipation of these pressures encouraged a shift in the pattern of output away from the traditional feeding-stuff-intensive farmyard enterprises in Northern Ireland: pigs, poultry and eggs accounted for 46 per cent of gross output in 1964–65 compared with the figure of 34 per cent in 1971–72 shown in Table 2.3. In the Republic, on the other hand, the attempts to expand cattle numbers rapidly have necessitated increased reliance on imported feeding-stuffs.

In the event the hopes and fears of the late 1960s were realised, although their realisation owed less to the effects of the E E C Common Agricultural Policy than to the dramatic increase in world agricultural prices in the early 1970s. Agriculture in both parts of Ireland benefited: farmers in the Republic were particularly affected by the high level of beef prices in 1972 and 1973. By the end of 1973, however, livestock prices were beginning to sag and farmers in both areas were caught in the squeeze between low output prices and persistently high input prices, particularly for feeding-stuffs. After increasing by around 30 per cent in each of the previous two years, agricultural incomes (in money terms) in the Republic are expected (at the time of writing) to fall by about $12\frac{1}{2}$ per cent between 1973 and 1974 (Durkan and Kelleher (1974)).

Although there have been structural changes resulting from amalgamations in both areas over the last decade, the average size of agricultural holdings is still small, 42 acres in Northern Ireland and 56 acres in the Republic. Moreover, many of the holdings are very small: in 1970 36 per cent of holdings in the North and 24 per cent of those in the South were under 15 acres.

In a sense there are two types of agriculture existing side by side in both areas, one full-time, viable, providing incomes comparable with those obtained in other forms of economic activity, the other either part-time or sub-marginal, a residual which persists, at least in part, because of the absence of other employment opportunities. In 1973, for example, there were 35,000 farms in Northern Ireland, only 18,500 of which could be regarded as full-time businesses. Although the remaining 16,500 were too small ever to be viable, Department of Agriculture surveys suggest that about half of them provided the only source of income for their occupiers. Comparable figures are not available for the Republic for the same year, but earlier investigations suggested the existence of a non-viable sector proportionately larger than that in Northern Ireland. These are structural problems which Northern Ireland and the Republic share with many other European countries. Experience suggests that their resolution will not come quickly; what does seem certain is that the decline in agricultural employment, so distinctive a feature of both economies for so many years, will continue.

2.2 Manufacturing Industry

The main constituent elements in manufacturing employment are set out in Table 2.4. In terms of employment the sector is slightly larger in the Republic than in Northern Ireland, although it still represents a much smaller proportion of total employment. While there are many differences of detail, the main configurations of the structures have been growing more alike in recent years. These similarities reflect common locational forces in the two areas: both economies are small, and have very small domestic markets; both are situated on the periphery of Europe; neither has — at least at the time of writing — large supplies of domestic industrial materials or fuel. Much of the raw material for industry must be imported, and, if economies of scale are to be realised, much of what is produced must be sold abroad. This limits the range of potentially viable industry. There has, for example, been no large-scale development of the iron and steel and heavier metal-working trades. On the other hand, both economies are heavily dependent on the more locationally footloose textile and clothing industries and on light engineering: these groups accounted for 66 per cent of manufacturing employment in Northern Ireland in 1973 and for 44 per cent of employment in the Republic. The food, drink and tobacco group is also

Table 2.4: Manufacturing Employment in Northern Ireland and the Republic, 1960 and 1973

	Northern Ireland			Republic		
	1960 (000s)	1973 (000s)	1973 (%)	1960 (000s)	1973 (000s)	1973 (%)
Food, Drink and Tobacco	27·2	27·9	16·2	44·7	52·9	26·1
Textiles	60·9	43·2	25·0	20·5	23·1	11·4
Clothing and Footwear	26·4	25·5	14·8	21·4	22·1	10·9
Shipbuilding	25·5	10·0	5·8	0·9	1·8	0·9
Engineering and Metal Goods	21·5	30·9	18·0	14·4	30·3	15·0
Vehicles	8·0	8·0	4·7	8·7	11·8	5·8
Chemicals	1·7	2·3	1·3	5·4	9·0	4·5
Other Manufacturing	17·4	24·3	14·1	34·6	51·5	25·4
Total Manufacturing	188·6	172·1	100·0	150·7	202·4	100·0

Sources: NI: Department of Manpower Services, *Employees in Employment,* Belfast; RI: Census of Industrial Production report, 1973 (employment in firms employing more than three persons).

important in both areas, but, as might be expected from its heavy reliance on agriculture, relatively more important in the Republic.

A more detailed examination of the structures, however, reveals very significant differences. The textile sector in the Republic, for example, is still heavily engaged in the processing of natural fibres. At one time textiles and linen were synonymous in Northern Ireland; by 1973, however, the sector had become much more diversified. Only about half of textile employment was in firms engaged in the processing of flax. Moreover, even this overestimates the importance of linen in the North, for in many of these firms flax had given way to cotton and man-made fibres as the basic material input. Man-made fibres accounted for about one-quarter of textile employment in Northern Ireland and for a much larger proportion of textile net output. The synthetics industry is represented by six large plants, owned by major multi-national companies, producing a wide range of viscose and synthetic yarns and fibres. Other sectors of the industry which have shown rapid development in recent years are those engaged in the production of hosiery, knitted goods, and carpets.

In engineering, too, there are significant differences of detail. Shipbuilding, which accounted for 5·8 per cent of employment in 1973, no longer occupies the dominant position that it once held in Northern Ireland, and there has been some decline in the more traditional mechanical engineering sectors engaged in the production of textile machinery. These have been more than offset by growth in other sectors of the industry, in electrical and instrument engineering as well as in the production of a wide range of other metal goods. One particularly interesting development has been in the production of components and accessories for motor-cars. In the Republic the major part of the employment in the vehicle sector is in the heavily protected motor-car assembly industry; in Northern Ireland there is some employment in the production of trailers and bodies for trucks etc., but the main employment in the sector is in the aircraft industry.

The main engineering growth in the Republic has been in the fields of electrical engineering and electronics. These groups employed almost 12,000 people in 1973, and the potential for growth in new firms already in production is substantial. A number of the older-established firms are involved in the production of domestic appliances, radio and television sets for the home market, but the main growth in recent years has been in the telecommunications field, in computers and in the production of components. One of the first of the overseas electronics companies to invest in Ireland, General Electrics Inc. (USA), set up a plant in the Shannon Industrial Estate in 1963. Since then there have been developments in a number of centres, including Dundalk and Galway as well as the Dublin area.

Another major success story in the Republic in recent years has been the development of the chemical industry. In 1973 the industry provided jobs for 9,000 people in the Republic, compared with 2,300 in Northern

Ireland. It thus accounted for over 4·5 per cent of manufacturing employment in the former compared with about 1·3 per cent in the latter. The main developments have been in the production of fine chemicals rather than basic materials. These, which are generally high in value in relation to bulk, include enzymes, hormones, vitamins, pharmaceutical products, insecticides, steroids, adhesives, etc. As in the electronics field, the expansion of the industry has reflected the inward movement of the large multinationals, particularly in the pharmaceuticals field, and this has been a consequence of a deliberate and highly selective policy by the I D A.

The 'other manufacturing' sector is considerably larger, both in absolute terms and as a proportion of all manufacturing employment, in the Republic than in Northern Ireland. Moreover, this relationship is true not only of the group as a whole but also of major sub-sectors within the group. Bricks, pottery and glass, timber and furniture, paper, printing and publishing, leather goods, etc. are all relatively more important in the industrial structure of the South than in the North. Although there are exceptions, it is characteristic of many of the firms in these groups that they have found their main outlets in the protected domestic markets in the Republic. To a more limited extent the same is true of Northern Ireland; but the absence of barriers to imports of manufactured goods, particularly from the rest of the United Kingdom, left fewer opportunities for survival in the North.

What general observations can be made about the industrial structures of the two areas? First, that the Northern Ireland structure is more specialised than that of the Republic. No attempt is made here to produce precise measures of specialisation relative to, for example, the U K or the E E C. But attention has already been drawn to the very heavy dependence on textiles, clothing and engineering in Northern Ireland and to the proportionately greater importance of the varied group 'other manufacturing' in the Republic.

Secondly, and this is obviously related to the first point, manufacturing industry is much more export-orientated in Northern Ireland than in the Republic. In 1970, the last year for which Census of Production data are available, about 70 per cent of the gross output of manufacturing industry in the North was exported; the corresponding figure for the South was 27 per cent (*Review of 1973 and Outlook for 1974*). This, of course, reflects a basic characteristic of a considerable part of Irish industry, developing as it has to serve the needs of a heavily protected domestic market.

The third general observation is that both structures are changing rapidly: the Irish economies are economies in transition. In a general way, too, these changes are tending to make the characteristics which have already been observed less true: the Northern economy is becoming less specialised; the Southern economy is becoming more export-orientated.

To highlight the main changes in structure, figures for 1960 have been included in Table 2.4. The most striking difference in performance is that

Review

between 1960 and 1973 manufacturing employment grew by more than one-third in the Republic but declined by 9 per cent in Northern Ireland. In the Republic the growth of employment affected both males and females, although the growth in male employment was faster. In Northern Ireland, on the other hand, female employment fell by 11 per cent and male employment showed a slight increase. These changes in the balance of employment in the North reflect the changes in industrial structure over the period. The traditional textile sector lost about 27,000 jobs, over 20,000 of them for females. This was partially offset by the growth in synthetic textiles, hosiery and knitwear, but most of the 10,000 new jobs in these sectors were for men. The 15,000 male jobs lost in shipbuilding were more than balanced by the growth in employment in engineering and metal goods and in 'other manufacturing', where again most of the new jobs were for men.

In the Republic the growth of manufacturing employment was apparent in most sectors but, as in Northern Ireland, the star performers were engineering, metal goods and 'other manufacturing'. As has already been noted, employment in chemicals also showed rapid expansion. Although at the level of disaggregation in the table no substantial sector showed an absolute decline, the slow growth of textiles and clothing reduced their relative importance in the total.

In both economies a major part of the growth of employment resulted from an influx of new industry. In Northern Ireland government-assisted projects employed over 75,000 people in 1973, about 43 per cent of all manufacturing employment. The corresponding figure for the Republic was probably between 25 and 30 per cent. In Northern Ireland the growth in new projects has been more than offset by the decline in the older-established industries; the evidence of decline in employment to some extent conceals a dramatic transformation in industrial structure. In the Republic too there have been redundancies in the older industries, but these have been small in relation to total employment: much of the new industry represents a net addition to manufacturing employment and capacity.

In both areas the newer sectors of industry are heavily export-orientated. This has had little effect on the balance between domestic and external markets in Northern Ireland, where the proportion of manufacturing gross output which is exported — about 70 per cent in 1970 — has shown little change since the early 1960s. The newer sectors in the industrial structure are no more heavily export-orientated than were the old sectors which are in decline. In the Republic, on the other hand, the influx of new projects has brought about a dramatic increase in the relative importance of export markets: the proportion of gross output which is exported increased from 18 per cent in 1960 to 33 per cent in 1973. To a considerable extent industrial growth in the Republic in recent years has been export-led.

In this, of course, the Republic is now moving along the path of industrialisation which had been taken by the North almost a century before. But the end result of the process may be very different from that experienced by Northern Ireland. The developments which shaped the Northern economy were characterised by the locational forces of the day: an area had to succeed in one line or a small number of lines, usually materials-orientated, in which the existence of economies of scale provided the basis for regional expansion. Other industries and service activities grew around the export base and in turn generated further growth. Changes in technology and improvements in transportation have widened the range of potentially viable industry. Today there is a wide and probably increasing range of activities which are mobile in the sense that neither the attraction of the market nor the anchor of material supplies constitutes an overwhelming reason for a particular location. Thus the new export-orientated structure need not be as specialised as the old. To the extent that this is true the process of industrial development is likely to reduce the amount of specialisation in the economy of Northern Ireland, and it need not lead to any dramatic increase in specialisation in the Republic.

These potential patterns of development have important implications for trade between the two economies. Because Northern Ireland's past structure was highly specialised, so that it was selling a narrow range of products to a wide range of customers on the world market, there were few opportunities for sales to the Republic. To put the same matter differently, there were only limited markets in the Republic for Northern producers of ships, linen and textile machinery. At the same time producers in the Republic had little incentive to forgo their concentration on the protected domestic market in order to compete with British producers in Northern markets. The consequence was the emergence of a pattern of commodity flows in which both parts of the island traded heavily with Great Britain and with the rest of the world but only to a very limited extent with each other.

The process of development is tending to change this situation. The potential market in Northern Ireland is small; but Southern industry, eager to increase exports, cannot afford to ignore it. In Northern Ireland, on the other hand, the increasing diversification of industry is likely to increase the potential for sales to the Republic. The markets in the South may have been small in relation to the North's massive output of ships, linen and textile machinery; they may appear much more significant in relation to the much more varied output of, among other things, carpets, engineering components and packaging materials.

2.3   Comparative Performance in Northern Ireland and the Republic

General assessments of the efficiency of industry within an economy are fraught with problems of measurement and interpretation; judgments about relative efficiency in two economies are even more difficult to make. Yet the differences in the market environments in which industry has developed in Northern Ireland and the Republic are so fundamental and so obvious that some comments on comparative performance are essential. Industry in Northern Ireland has had to operate in the context of competitive world markets, and in the last analysis its efficiency must be judged in terms of its ability to survive in those markets. Industry in the Republic has for many years operated in a domestic market which has been heavily protected; survival in these conditions is not *prima facie* evidence of efficiency. But the changing trade relations between the Republic and the outside world are altering the competitive climate; and the ability of industry in the Republic to compete in world markets is critical to the success of the development strategy which has been pursued since 1958.

Judged in terms of their ability to continue to provide employment, the major traditional staple industries in Northern Ireland, linen and shipbuilding, are weak elements in the industrial structure. As has already been noted, employment in the two groups fell by 42,000 between 1960 and 1973. The reasons for the decline in linen employment are fairly obvious. Coupled with the increases in productivity in the world textile industry there has been a general tendency for the balance of production of yarns and fabrics to shift in favour of the developing countries, particularly in the East. Employment in textiles in the E E C, for example, fell by about half a million in the ten years up to 1972. Against the background of intense competition engendered by the growth of world textile capacity, linen has had to struggle for markets, not only against its old rival cotton but also against an increasing range of cheap, purpose-designed synthetic fabrics. In the course of the struggle a number of firms have gone to the wall; most of the survivors are now organised into a small number of substantial groups. Whether this more compact structure can arrest the decline of the industry remains to be seen.

Almost all of the shipbuilding activity in the North is carried on in one Belfast firm, Harland and Wolff Ltd. Here again the problem has been one of responding to a major shift in demand. Harland and Wolff developed as a major supplier of passenger ships, particularly for the Atlantic route. With the decline in sea passenger transport it has attempted to redirect its activities towards the building of very large bulk carriers, both for oil and for dry cargo. To achieve the increases in labour productivity necessary to survive in this highly competitive market the company recently undertook, with government assistance, a massive programme of investment in new equipment. Assistance from public funds in the form of both grants and loans amounted to £68 million between 1966 and 1974. Unfortunately the hoped-for increases in productivity have been slow to materialise, and at the time of writing the company is experiencing severe financial difficulties. Against this background, future levels of shipbuilding employment must be regarded as uncertain.

The main sources of general information about the efficiency of industry in the Republic are the reports of the Committee on Industrial Organisation (C I O) in the early 1960s and the reports of the Committee on Industrial Progress (C I P) about a decade later. The C I O carried out a number of surveys aimed at identifying the major weaknesses in industry in the Republic and proposing remedies designed to prepare industry for increased competition. The C I P was appointed in 1968 to examine the action that had been taken and to assess the capacity of industry to compete in a free trading environment.

The C I O reports had revealed widespread weakness in industry in the Republic, particularly in those sectors catering mainly for the domestic market which would come under pressure from imports in free trade conditions. There was evidence of the existence of weak firms in all the sectors investigated, but textiles, clothing, footwear and furniture were among those that gave special cause for concern. Some indication of the seriousness with which the Committee viewed the situation is indicated by the fact that in 1963 it reported that over 25 per cent of the employment in the twenty-two trades examined was at risk in free trade conditions. The symptoms of weakness were widespread — old buildings, machinery unsuited to mass-production techniques, short production runs, highly diversified production, and relatively high costs of production.

Action taken on the basis of the C I O reports and government aids towards expenditure on adaptation and re-equipment — over £40 million up to 1973 — contributed towards a substantial improvement in the competitive strength of the more traditional sectors of Irish industry. But the C I P report (C I P (1973)) revealed that in many firms the fundamental defects persist, and that there is still serious doubt about the ability of some sectors of industry to survive in free trade conditions. The problems are still serious for small and medium-sized firms in footwear, furniture, printing and in some sectors of the textile and clothing trades, and particularly serious amongst those older-established firms which are largely dependent on the home market. Again and again the reports return to two main critical themes: management which is production- rather than marketing-orientated, and management which in a number of trades is unwilling to face up to the problems of rationalisation and reorganisation on which increased efficiency depends.

The evidence thus suggests that there are weak elements in the structure of industry in both Northern Ireland and the Republic, and it is hardly surprising that those firms that give main cause for concern are in the older-established sectors of industry. But in both economies there are vigorous and growing new fields of industrial activity. It is these that have contributed most to the rapid growth of industrial exports from the Republic during the last decade and that have offset much of the decline in employment in the traditional sectors in Northern Ireland over the same period.

Moreover, the process of industrial change is increasing the weight of the newer sectors in manufacturing employment in both economies.

2.4　Output and Output per Head

Indices of production for manufacturing industry in Northern Ireland and the Republic are shown in Table 2.5. For comparative purposes the corresponding figures for the U K and the E E C are also presented. Since 1960 both of the Irish economies have enjoyed growth rates for manufacturing output which far exceed the rate for Great Britain. In view of Britain's abysmal performance since the war, this represents no great feat. Perhaps more surprising, the rate of growth of output in the Republic compares favourably with that achieved by the E E C (six) since 1960. The increase in output over the period can be disaggregated into two main elements: changes in employment, and changes in output per head. The more rapid growth of output in the Republic than in Northern Ireland can be attributed wholly to increased employment; as can be seen from the table, output per head grew more rapidly in the latter than in the former.

Table 2.5: Output and Output per Head in Manufacturing Industry, 1965 and 1970–73 (1960 = 100)

| Year | Output | | | | Output per head | |
	Northern Ireland	Republic	U K	E E C	Northern Ireland	Republic
1965	122	137	118	130	126	119
1970	156	188	133	179	159	144
1971	165	195	133	183	172	150
1972	164	204	147	194	178	157
1973	178	222	148	n.a.	193	167

Sources: NI: *Digest of Statistics,* H M S O, Belfast, various issues: R I: *Review of 1973 and Outlook for 1974* (Prl 3774), Stationery Office, Dublin; U K: *Monthly Digest of Statistics,* H M S O, London, various issues; E E C: Commission of the European Communities, *Basic Statistics of the Community,* Eurostat, Brussels 1972.

What were the underlying reasons for this rapid growth? Because increases in output per head are sometimes described as increases in 'labour productivity' there is some temptation to attribute the changes to harder working, improved training and increased efficiency. This, however, is only part of the story. As well as improved inputs of labour and management over the period there were substantial increases in inputs of capital: a significant part of the increase in output must be attributed to an increase in the stock of capital in manufacturing. Slattery (1973) suggests that in the Republic the gross stock of capital embodied in machinery and equipment (excluding agricultural machinery and transport equipment) increased by over 250 per cent between 1960 and 1972. Jefferson (1968) reported a similarly rapid rate of growth for Northern Ireland in the early 1960s. The general picture that emerges is not only that the stock of capital was increasing in both economies but that it was increasing much faster than employment; the increase in output per head was to a large extent due to increases in the amount of capital per head in manufacturing industry.

Part of the increase in the capital stock per head resulted from the application of more capital-intensive methods in existing industries in the course of the drive to make them more efficient: for example, considerable sums were spent in both areas on the modernisation of plant in the traditional textile industries. But a major part was due to the growth of new industry which appears to have been on average more capital-intensive than existing industry in the Republic and was certainly more capital-intensive than the industry which it replaced in Northern Ireland. The most obvious example of this process is in the textile sector in Northern Ireland, where the growth of more capital-intensive synthetic textiles has partially offset the decline in less capital-intensive traditional textiles: between 1960 and 1973 employment in the sector fell by 29 per cent and output increased by 175 per cent; output per head increased by a massive 287 per cent.

Thus while output per head in individual firms in both economies may have risen because of improvements in the quality of labour and of management and because of increased amounts of capital available to each worker in existing industry, a considerable part of the recorded increase has been due to the growth of new industry, to a change in industrial structure.

From the censuses of production in Northern Ireland and the Republic it is possible to calculate comparative figures of net output per head in the two economies. The results for 1970 — the latest year available — are set out in Table 2.6. Although average net output per head for manufacturing industry as a whole was very similar for the two areas, there were considerable variations between sectors. Northern Ireland led in food, drink and tobacco, textiles, timber and furniture and 'other manufacturing'; the Republic led in clothing, mineral products, paper and printing and in the engineering and metals group.

In some ways these results are surprising. Such fragmentary evidence as exists (Slattery (1973), Jefferson (1968)) suggests that the amount of capital per person employed in manufacturing industry is higher in Northern Ireland than in the Republic. Certainly the official statistics show that gross investment in fixed assets per person employed has been running at a slightly higher level in recent years: the figure for the Republic varied between 81 per cent and 98 per cent of that for Northern Ireland between 1966 and 1969. If, in manufacturing industry, capital per head is greater in Northern Ireland than in the Republic, then there is at least a presumption that output per head should be higher also.

Part of the explanation of the paradox may lie in differences in output price levels in the two areas. Since the major part of output in Northern Ireland is sold in Great Britain or in world markets, it is sold either at world prices or at the prices ruling in the relatively free British market. By contrast, some 73 per cent of the manufacturing output of the Republic was sold in the home market in 1970; and much of this output enjoyed substantial tariff protection. McAleese (1971a) estimated the average tariff protection for manufacturing industry in the Republic at about 20 per cent in 1966; it was not very different in 1970. To the extent that it raised the prices of the Republic's manufacturing output in 1970 this protection inflated the figures of net output per head. Valued at world prices or at UK prices, net output per head in the Republic was probably significantly lower than in Northern Ireland.

Table 2.6: Net Output per Head in Manufacturing Industry, Northern Ireland and the Republic, 1970 (£)

	Northern Ireland	Republic
Food, Drink and Tobacco	3,034	2,309
Engineering, Metal Goods and Vehicles[a]	1,514	1,935
Textiles	1,966	1,737
Clothing	890	1,136
Mineral Products	2,308	2,339
Timber and Furniture	1,688	1,486
Paper, Printing and Publishing	1,846	2,099
Other Manufacturing	4,784	3,071
All Manufacturing	2,029	2,052

[a]Including shipbuilding.

Sources: NI: Census of Production report, 1970, HMSO, Belfast; RI: Census of Industrial Production report, 1970, Stationery Office, Dublin.

2.5 Services

Attention has already been directed to the much greater development of service employment in Northern Ireland than in the Republic. In 1973 the sector accounted for 50·0 per cent of total employment in the former compared with 46·1 per cent in the latter. This is a long-standing divergence which shows little sign of diminishing. Between 1960 and 1973 service employment grew by over 20 per cent in Northern Ireland compared with under 14 per cent in the Republic.

The differences may, in part, reflect disparities in average income levels between the two parts of Ireland. (There is a strong tendency observed in many advanced countries, though with some notable exceptions, for the proportion of the working population engaged in services to be correlated with *per capita* income) Demand for many service activities – education, health services, catering, etc. – appears to be income-elastic, and this, combined with the fact that labour productivity is still growing more rapidly in manufacturing industry than in services, will probably tend to continue to shift the balance of employment in favour of services for some time to come.

It seems unlikely, however, that this explanation accounts for all the differences between the two economies. As can be seen from Table 2.7, there have been substantial differences in the experience of the various service groups, not only between the two economies but within each of them. Employment in distribution in Northern Ireland, for example, ran counter to the trend of the sector as a whole by declining by almost 12 per cent between 1960 and 1973. It is not possible to separate the figures for distribution from those for commerce in general in the Republic, but the group in total showed an *increase* of almost 11 per cent.

The distribution figures for Northern Ireland may, to some extent, reflect the difficulties encountered by traders as a consequence of the civil unrest of the last five years: there can be little doubt that retail trade must have suffered severe interruptions as a result of the bombing campaign.

Table 2.7: Employment in Services in Northern Ireland and the Republic, 1960 and 1973 (000s)

	Northern Ireland		Republic	
	1960	1973	1960	1973
Gas, Electricity and Water	7·0	8·5	10·0	14·0
Transport and Communications	29·9	22·7	54·0	61·0
Distribution	69·9	61·8	157·0	174·0
Insurance, Banking and Finance	6·9	14·4		
Public Administration	33·9	48·4	41·0	55·0
Professional and Scientific Services	46·2	83·1	165·0	181·0
Miscellaneous Services	39·1	40·0		
Total Services	217·0	278·9	427·0	485·0

Sources: NI: Department of Manpower Services, *Employees in Employment,* Belfast; RI: *Trend of Employment and Unemployment 1965* and *1973,* Stationery Office, Dublin.

But this can be only part of the explanation, for the major part of the decline took place between 1963 and 1970 before the worst of the 'troubles' occurred. To a much greater extent the fall reflects a process of rationalisation in which supermarkets, self-service stores and cash-and-carry methods have made significant inroads into traditional methods in retail and whole-sale trade. This process was hastened in the late 1960s by the effects of Selective Employment Tax. There have been increases in productivity in the Republic also; but, as the National Industrial Economic Council predicted in 1967 (N I E C (1967)), the growth in sales has more than offset the increase in productivity with the consequence that employment has continued to increase.

The transport and communications group also moved in opposite directions in the two economies: in the Republic employment increased by 13 per cent; in Northern Ireland it fell by 25 per cent. In Northern Ireland the reduction in rail services contributed to the fall in employment, but, unlike the experience in the Republic (and in the United Kingdom), there was no offsetting increase in employment in road transport services.

In terms of employment, the main contributors to the more rapid growth of services in Northern Ireland than in the Republic were public administration and professional and scientific services. Between 1960 and 1973 these two groups grew by 43 per cent and 80 per cent respectively. In the Republic employment in public administration grew by 34 per cent over the period. The figures for professional and scientific services in the South are combined with those for miscellaneous services for the years concerned: the total increased by just under 10 per cent. Evidence from the Census of Population suggests that between 1961 and 1971 the numbers engaged in miscellaneous services showed a decline of about 8,000, mainly because of the reduction in the numbers engaged in domestic service. The actual increase in the numbers engaged in professional and scientific services between 1960 and 1973 might have been of the order of 25,000–30,000. Even at the outside, however, this would have represented a percentage increase less than half that experienced by Northern Ireland.

What are the roots of these differences in growth rates? In the export-led growth of the economy of the Republic it is reasonable to regard the growth of the services sector as in some sense dependent upon the growth of income arising in agriculture and manufacturing industry. Of course, this is an approximation: employment in manufacturing industry catering for the home market is as much induced as employment in services; and employment in services may be as potent as employment in other sectors in inducing further growth in other sectors. But it is an illuminating approximation in the sense that it is unlikely that the growth of services would have taken place if the growth in other sectors had not. Moreover, it is likely to be true of public sector services as well as private sector services. The provision of the former grows with the expansion of the community's capacity to finance them either by taxation or by borrowing; the provision of the latter grows with the community's willingness to purchase them.

In Northern Ireland, however, the situation is different in one major respect. Services provided by the public sector may, in part, be financed by subventions from the rest of the United Kingdom: they are not wholly dependent on the growth of income produced in other sectors of the economy. And in terms of employment the public sector services — public administration, education and medical services — are an important group: in 1973 they accounted for 44 per cent of all service employment.

Employment in these sectors depends upon the emphasis put upon the provision of education, health and related services in the United Kingdom as a whole. But the expansion of the sectors in Northern Ireland has been faster than in the rest of the United Kingdom, for in addition to the increased employment required to keep pace with those services in which parity of standards has been achieved, there has been the increased employment arising from the drive to achieve parity where gaps in standards still existed. To the extent that they are financed by subventions from the rest of the United Kingdom these services play a similar role in the economy of Northern Ireland to that played by exports in the Republic. The growth of exports has been a critical factor in the growth of income and employment in the Republic since 1960; the growth of public sector services made a major contribution to the growth of incomes and to the maintenance of employment in Northern Ireland.

Moreover, there is considerable potential for further growth in services generally. The implementation of accepted objectives in education and health services in the United Kingdom will necessitate further expansion of employment in Northern Ireland, and after the rationalisation of recent years some growth might reasonably be expected in distribution and transport and communications. A few years ago Cuthbert (1970) forecast an increase in service employment of 78,000 between 1968 and 1990, most of it in public sector services. The direct impact of the 'troubles' and the probable consequential reduction in the rate of growth of population will necessitate some downward revision of this estimate. And the growth is, of course, dependent upon the willingness of the United Kingdom in general to finance national standards of public services in Northern Ireland. Subject to these qualifications, however, it seems likely that services will continue to play an active and important role in the development of the North for some time to come.

3 INDUSTRIAL DEVELOPMENT POLICY

The governments on both sides of the Irish border, faced as they are by serious economic difficulties, have not been content to leave the resolution of their problems to the unfettered working of the market mechanism.

Both have been markedly interventionist in their postures, particularly in their approach to industrial development policy.

The roots of that policy in Northern Ireland go back to the inter-war years. The depression of those years had highlighted the weaknesses of the staple textile and engineering industries and the need to provide alternative employment to offset their decline. The New Industries (Development) Acts of 1932 and 1937 set the mould for later developments by providing for grants, interest-free loans and rates exemptions designed to stimulate an inflow of new industry. Subsequent developments of policy were very much in the context of U K regional policy, and a pattern has emerged in which Northern Ireland can offer grants and other subventions similar in general type to those offered in other British regions but, recognising the exceptional severity of Northern Ireland's problem, at a somewhat higher rate. Some of the measures from which Northern Ireland benefits, for example the Regional Employment Premium, are operated from Whitehall for all regions of the U K.

In the Republic the impetus towards development based on new industry came much later. Indeed, the aims of policy until the mid-1950s had been based on the contrary objectives, to foster production for the home market by tariff protection and to ensure, through the Control of Manufactures Act of the early 1930s, that the control of industry in the Republic remained within the state. The main shift of direction in policy came after the publication of the First Programme for Economic Expansion in 1958 with the recognition that, against the background of continuing decline in agricultural employment, the industrial structure based on the domestic market could provide neither the jobs nor the incomes necessary to meet the aspirations of the population. The central aim of industrial policy since that time has been to develop an export-based industrial structure capable of generating, by competitive sales on the world market, incomes and job opportunities comparable with those available in Western Europe generally.

In the march of events during the last fifteen years this policy objective has been crystallised in relation to two major changes in the external commercial position of the Republic. First, it was presented as the need to make industry in the Republic competitive in face of the erosion of protection resulting from the Anglo-Irish Free Trade Area Agreement of 1961; secondly, it was given dramatic impetus by the need to face up to the increased competition from European suppliers resulting from accession to the E E C. Against this background it is not surprising that in the earlier years of the new economic policy major emphasis was placed on the need to adapt and strengthen industry to enable it to meet the strains of competition. There was early recognition, however, that domestic industry could not, by itself, provide the basis for the required expansion: a substantial development of new industry, much of which would have to come from outside, was a prerequisite for success.

From these diverse roots in the two parts of Ireland there emerged similar policy objectives: to promote jobs in manufacturing industry either by encouraging the expansion of the activities of domestic firms or by attracting inward direct investment. Clearly the development agencies, the Department of Commerce in Northern Ireland and the Industrial Development Authority in the Republic, are competitors in the search for new industry; moreover, they are both, in turn, in competition with a wide range of development agencies in other countries, ranging from the UK Department of Industry, attempting to pursue the interests of lagging regions in Britain, to the Casa per Il Mezzogiorno, attempting to bring jobs to Southern Italy. This competition is sharpened by the fact that both parts of Ireland are seeking similar types of jobs. In both areas the emphasis is on jobs in fast-growing, high value-added industry, on jobs in firms which will concentrate on export markets, and, perhaps most important, on jobs for males.

Before proceeding to a discussion of the details of the inducements which are offered to developing firms in each area, it is worth considering in a little more detail the economic justification for the policies in the two economies. As matters of political judgment they may seem obvious: they are simply the expressions in Ireland, North and South, of the view that it is the responsibility of the state to ensure full employment for its citizens. But the amounts which are spent on inducements to manufacturing industry could be spent on other things — on social security, on aid to agriculture, on education — and it is necessary to consider whether the benefits which are expected to accrue to the community in the form of increased income and employment outweigh the costs in terms of alternatives forgone.

For Northern Ireland the justification must be argued in terms which recognise that in constitutional as well as in economic terms the North is a region of the United Kingdom: the justification must be in terms of British regional economic policy as a whole. In this context two major lines of argument have been important, one of which emphasises the costs of regional policy, the other emphasising the benefits. It can be argued, for example, that if entrepreneurs require inducements to move, within the UK, to what might prove to be permanently high-cost locations, the effect may be to increase costs and reduce potential real output in the economy as a whole; there may, in other words, be a conflict between economic efficiency and what is socially desirable. On the other hand, if entrepreneurs are unwilling to move to peripheral areas, potential output can be realised only if the unemployed labour will migrate to the central areas where jobs are available; and there is clear evidence that, if income support is available at the levels currently offered by social security schemes, labour will not move in large enough numbers to eliminate regional unemployment. To an increasing extent therefore, the justification of regional policy has been couched in terms of the potential gains to UK national output from resources which would otherwise remain idle. These gains may accrue not only because resources in the problem regions are brought into operation but also because the pressures of congestion in other, more favoured regions are reduced. The important point in this way of looking at the matter is that part, at least, of the justification for regional policy in Northern Ireland is a benefit which accrues not only to the local economy but to the United Kingdom as a whole.

In the Republic, on the other hand, the justification for development policy must be argued in terms of the contribution of that policy to economic welfare in the Republic itself. Some elements of this contribution — the impact of immigrant managers on the level of management skill available from domestic sources, the increases in productivity forced on domestic firms by having to compete with new firms for scarce resources — are extremely difficult to quantify. But, as McAleese (1971b) argues, these are not likely to be of critical importance in the context of the Republic's economy. In the last analysis the justification of the policy must rest on the extent to which increases in income resulting from sponsored industrial development in the Republic outweigh the costs of inducements.

3.1   The Industrial Development Agencies

In Northern Ireland the organisation of industrial development machinery has followed the British pattern by locating the main grant-paying and promotional agency firmly within the government machine, in the Department of Commerce. The Republic has followed continental practice by creating a public body outside the administrative departments, the Industrial Development Authority (I D A). There are advantages and disadvantages in both procedures. Since these bodies are involved in large disbursements of public funds, it can be argued that it is desirable that they should be subject to close financial scrutiny and to direct ministerial control. In Northern Ireland particular value is set upon the close relationships which exist between the Department of Commerce and other government departments which may also be involved in negotiations on a development project, the Departments of Manpower Services, Environment, etc.; such negotiations are frequently a team effort. Against these advantages, it is argued in the Republic, must be set the fact that civil service attitudes are not particularly suited to industrial promotion procedures, that experience in industry and an ability to talk the language of industry are essential ingredients for success. This divorce between the mental attitudes of administrators and industrialists is, of course, frequently alleged, and it is difficult to make any objective assessment of its validity. It is worth noting, however, that in recent years the Department of Commerce in Northern Ireland has attempted to obtain the benefits of both worlds by taking into its Industrial Development Organisation a number of negotiators with industrial experience who work in harness with other civil servant members of the team.

The main concentration of development activities into the hands of the Industrial Development Authority came as a consequence of the Industrial Development Act (1969) with the increased emphasis in the Third Programme for Economic and Social Development on the need to attract foreign capital into Ireland as a means of achieving export-orientated growth. An Foras Tionscal, which had been engaged in the promotion of industry in the underdeveloped areas of the country since 1952, was amalgamated with the I D A, thus locating within one organisation the grant-giving and promotional aspects of industrial development policy for virtually the whole country. This organisational change marked an important stage in the evolution of policy, a shift from concern with the industrial development of particular problem areas in the country to concern with the industrial development of the country as a whole. Nevertheless, the special problems of the poorer areas continue to be recognised by the provision of assistance at higher rates in those areas than in the rest of the country. Two smaller organisations, the Shannon Free Airport Development Company and Gaeltarra Éireann, continue to cater for the needs of the Shannon Industrial Estate and the Gaeltacht regions respectively.

In contrast to the process of amalgamation which created the I D A in the Republic, the last few years in the North have seen the development of two new organisations working in parallel with the Department of Commerce in the field of industrial development. These organisations are concerned with special problems rather than particular geographical areas. The Local Enterprise Development Unit (L E D U) was established in 1971 to promote and expand small local industries — employing not more than fifty persons — in Northern Ireland. It thus fulfils a function similar to that undertaken by the Small Industries Programme within the I D A in the Republic. The Northern Ireland Finance Corporation (N I F C) was set up in 1972 with funds of £50 million and with the primary aim of assisting companies whose business had been affected by civil disorder; it was, to some extent, a response to what was seen at the time as a 'doomsday' situation. In the event doom did not materialise, and while it is still involved in the provision of rescue finance, the Corporation is to an increasing extent operating as a commercially orientated development bank, attempting to improve corporate structure and management, taking equity where necessary and even promoting new enterprise from scratch. While the N I F C can provide assistance in the form of loans and loan guarantees, the provision of grants is retained within the Department of Commerce.

3.2   Industrial Development Incentives

Details of the main incentives available in Northern Ireland and the Republic are set out in Table 2.8. The common element in the schemes, North and South, is the availability of grants towards the costs of purchase of fixed assets, buildings, plant, machinery and equipment. In the Republic the

Table 2.8: Industrial Incentives in Northern Ireland and the Republic, 1974

Northern Ireland	Republic
Grants towards costs of plant, equipment and buildings in new industry and major expansions (including small firms) 30%–40%	Grants towards costs of plant, equipment and buildings in new industry and major expansions 25%–50%
	Grants for small firms 40%–60%
Employment grants as an aid towards starting-up costs Negotiable	Tax exemption on export-generated profits Complete exemption for 15 years. Partial exemption thereafter
Regional Employment Premium:	
Males £3 weekly	
Females £1·50 weekly	
Grants towards re-equipment costs:	*Grants towards re-equipment costs*
(Automatic on capital expenditure in manufacturing and construction)	(Available on a selective basis) 25%–35%
Buildings 30%	
Plant, machinery and equipment 30%	
Industrial de-rating 75%	Industrial de-rating 66⅔%

(handwritten annotation: Now 10% 10–50)

Sources: NI: information supplied by the Department of Commerce, Belfast; RI: IDA, *Annual Report, 1972–73*

grants are available to medium- and large-scale enterprises at three basic rates, 50 per cent in the Designated Areas — broadly the Western and North-Western counties — 25 per cent in Co. Dublin, and 35 per cent elsewhere. In Northern Ireland the Industries Development Acts (1966 and 1971) do not set precise limits to the amounts that may be paid, but as a general administrative rule grants vary between 30 and 40 per cent, depending on the needs of the area where the project is to be located. Northern Ireland's 'edge' over the rest of the United Kingdom can be gauged from the fact that the corresponding rate of grant available in U K Special Development Areas is 22 per cent.

The main back-up to these common capital grant elements differ in the two economies. In Northern Ireland considerable emphasis is placed on the availability of grants towards starting-up costs, paid as revenue and negotiated on the basis of a *per capita* grant on employment during the build-up of the project. In the Republic there is the extremely attractive exemption from income tax on profits generated from export sales. Complete exemption is available for a fifteen-year period, and partial exemption thereafter.

No details are available on the rates of employment grant payable in Northern Ireland, but it is clear that, although they are not a major element in total grants paid — about 5 per cent in 1972–73 — they provide a useful opportunity for flexibility and for the exercise of selectivity in the industrial development programme. Whether or not they get employment grants, however, new manufacturing firms — and indeed all manufacturing firms — automatically qualify for the U K Regional Employment Premium. Current rates of R E P are £3 per week for each male employee and £1·50 for each female; the male rate is equivalent to about 7 per cent of mid-1974 average earnings for male manual workers in manufacturing industry.

Similarly, the precise value of tax exemption to a firm in the Republic is not easy to calculate in advance, depending as it does on the proportion of output exported and on the timing and expected rate of profit. It is clear from figures quoted by McAleese (1971b), however, that this is an extremely important element in the pattern of inducements: in the years 1967–71 the total value of tax relief (£33·2m) exceeded the total value of New Industry Grant Payments (£30·7m).

In addition to these main elements of grant and tax exemption, both areas offer a wide range of ancillary inducements: loans, interest relief grants, factories at subsidised rents, industrial de-rating, training grants, removal grants, etc. Both place great emphasis on the ability to negotiate a package deal, tailored to the needs of each particular client, and each is prepared to experiment in the development of new inducements to strengthen its competitive position in the struggle to increase its share of the total amount of mobile industry that is available for relocation in each year. Quite clearly they are competitors in an extremely competitive market.

Apart from the grants and tax reliefs available to new industry, both governments make substantial subventions to existing industry, mainly in the form of capital grants. In the Republic these subventions are offered for the re-equipment and modernisation of industrial premises as part of the programme of adaptation designed to prepare the country's industry for the rigours of free trade. They are administered selectively to meet the differing needs of different sectors of industry. By contrast, the capital grants available in Northern Ireland under the terms of the Industrial Investment Acts (1966–71) are completely non-selective, payable at a rate of 30 per cent on buildings, plant and equipment in respect of all expenditure on fixed capital in manufacturing industry. The relative scale of the two programmes can be gauged from the fact that in the year 1971–72 total grant payments for re-equipment were £6·4 million in the Republic and £13·9 million in Northern Ireland.

Because they are payable in respect of all expenditure on fixed assets, capital grants in Northern Ireland have important implications for the attraction of new industry. The immigrant industrialist is offered not only grants on his initial investment under the Industries Development Acts but also, as long as there is no amendment to the legislation, subsequent grants on replacement or expansion of fixed assets; this has obvious implications for profitability.

What are the relative attractions of the two sets of incentives to the potential industrialist? Obviously the answer to this question depends on the nature of the project under consideration. A firm that expects to make quick profits from export sales will probably pay close attention to the tax exemptions available in the Republic, although problems may arise for foreign firms that want to repatriate their earnings (McAleese (1971b)). A firm involved in a labour-intensive process may be attracted by the availability of employment grants and R E P in Northern Ireland. At first sight, the high rates of capital grants available particularly in the Designated Areas might be expected to give the Republic an advantage in the attraction of capital-intensive projects. But the cost per job restrictions limit the amount that can be paid on fixed assets, and the availability of automatic grants towards costs of re-equipment provide a powerful counter attraction in the North, particularly for those firms in which the potential life of equipment is short.

In general the arithmetic of the grants suggests that there is no decisive advantage on one side or the other. The Northern Ireland package is successful with some industrialists, the Republic package with others, and the detailed way in which the packages are arranged is probably at least as important as the total grant payments involved. Moreover, while financial inducements may play an important role in industrial development, other factors, such as the availability of labour and sites, easy access to markets and raw materials, etc., may in many instances be the critical considerations.

Whatever their relative effectiveness, it is clear that the financial inducements in both Northern Ireland and the Republic can involve a very significant subvention to industrialists. Over a large part of both areas firms may
qualify for assistance with a capitalised value representing as much as two-
thirds of the initial costs of fixed capital; in the Designated Areas in the
Republic the ratio of assistance to cost can be even higher. Many firms are
prepared to settle for less; but it seems probable that few new projects are
getting much less than one-third of their fixed capital costs and the bulk
are probably qualifying for something between one-third and one-half.

3.3   The Effects of Policy

Some indications of the effectiveness of the two industrial development
programmes in promoting new jobs can be obtained from Table 2.9. The
figures presented there represent the job targets negotiated with the firms
which concluded agreements in the periods concerned. The low level of
annual promotions recorded for the Republic during the 1960s reflects the
fact that the concentration on the development of new industry, particularly
foreign industry, and the reorganisation and enlargement of the I D A, did
not occur until 1968. The figures for 1969 indicate the speed at which the
new programme began to pay off, and the excellent results for recent years
indicate the way in which membership of the E E C has enhanced the attractions of location in the Republic for overseas investors. In its essential outlines the operation in Northern Ireland was well established by 1960, and
there was a steady inflow of new industry during the following decade.

The figures in the table refer to job promotions of all types, whether as
a result of the inflow of new firms, the creation of new firms from domestic

Table 2.9: Jobs Promoted in Northern Ireland and the Republic, 1960—73

Year	Northern Ireland[a]	Republic[b]
1960—68		
(annual average)	6,150	2,880
1969	5,943	11,100
1970	6,484	10,906
1971	7,665	6,400
1972	7,964	10,303
1973	9,482	20,151

[a]Calendar years.

[b]Financial year beginning 1 April.

Sources: N I: information supplied by the Department of Commerce, Belfast;
R I: I D A, *Annual Reports*.

sources or the expansion of existing firms. In Northern Ireland the importance of expansions in the total of new jobs promoted has shown a strong
upward trend through time. Jobs in major expansions represented 38 per
cent of all job promotions in the years 1960—64, 55 per cent in 1965—69,
and almost 70 per cent in 1970—73. In the years since 1970 the relative
importance of expansions in the total reflects, to some extent, the reduction in the inflow of new industry resulting from civil unrest. But expansions
have increased in absolute as well as in relative terms, and there is increasing
evidence that the new industrial structure is generating growing employment
opportunities from internal sources.

The companies coming to the two parts of Ireland have one thing in
common: they are heavily export-orientated. According to McAleese
(1971b), grant-aided establishments in the Republic export, on average,
75 per cent of their gross output compared with 25 per cent for all other
establishments. No detailed figures are available for Northern Ireland, but
general impressions suggest that almost all of the output of new firms is
exported. Access to export markets has, of course, been a major incentive
to firms to move into both areas. After the signing of the Anglo-Irish Free
Trade Area Agreement in 1961 a Republic location gave access to the UK market; up until 1972 firms coming to Northern Ireland had access to E F T A
markets, and since the beginning of 1973 there have been the added attractions in both areas of access to the E E C. Apart from these attractions there
is the fact that both the Department of Commerce and the I D A have concentrated their efforts on the development of export-orientated firms. In
the Republic this has been central to the strategy of economic development
since 1958; in Northern Ireland it reflects an understandable reluctance to
offer incentives to industrialists who will be competing with the small sector
of industry in the province that caters for the local market.

In both parts of Ireland, too, most of the jobs in new industry are for
men. Some 64 per cent of the jobs created in Northern Ireland until 1973
are for males, as are about 66 per cent of the new jobs in the Republic. This,
of course, reflects a major policy aim in both economies. There are areas
where female jobs are welcome, for female participation rates are still low
by comparison with the United Kingdom. But against the background of
decline in agriculture in the South and in the staple industries in the North,
the main preoccupation is with jobs for men.

The average size of immigrant firms appears to be significantly larger in
Northern Ireland than in the Republic. In mid-1973 in Northern Ireland
there were 72,376 people employed in 271 assisted projects (excluding
L E D U), giving an average project size of 267. Eighteen of the grant-aided
projects employed more than 1,000 persons. The employment figures of
44,800 in new industry projects (excluding the Small Industries Programme)
in the Republic in 1972 covered about 900 projects giving average project
employment of about 50. The Northern Ireland figures to some extent re-

flect the type of industry that has been attracted. The synthetic textile producers who came to the North in the early 1960s are typically large-scale plants in large-scale multi-national companies. The same is true of the electronic equipment and tyre producers who are now in operation. In the South, on the other hand, many of the early projects negotiated from domestic sources were very small in scale, and this tends to pull the average for all projects down. The average size of project appears to have increased substantially in recent years, and by 1973 there were at least a dozen projects involving total approved assistance exceeding £1 million.

The types of industry that have been attracted to both parts of Ireland, and the sources from which they have been attracted, show broad similarities but interesting differences of detail. Engineering and metal goods have been the most important sectors, accounting for about a third of the jobs created in Northern Ireland (Department of Commerce (1974)) and of the projects approved in the Republic (Buckley (1974)). Much of the new employment has been in light engineering, and firms engaged in the production of electronic components have made a substantial contribution in recent years. Textiles have been an important element in the success of the programme in Northern Ireland which now accounts for about one-third of the UK output of synthetics. But textiles and clothing together have also accounted for nearly a quarter of the projects approved in the Republic. Two sectors which have contributed more in the Republic than in Northern Ireland are chemicals and food, drink and tobacco. At one level these developments might be interpreted as an extension of the broad structure — textiles, clothing, engineering, food, drink and tobacco, etc. — which had already proved locationally viable in Northern Ireland. But this would underestimate the variety and potential of the new activities in both economies and particularly the amount of diversification that has been achieved in the economy of Northern Ireland.

The sources of new employment are shown in Table 2.10. The predominance of Britain, the United States and Western Germany is clearly apparent in both areas. Britain, as might be expected, has been a particularly important source for Northern Ireland. These sources illustrate the importance of a number of factors in the inward flow of new firms. First, contiguity: other things being equal, firms are more likely to consider nearby locations than those which are distant; hence the flow from Britain. Secondly, pressure on factor supplies in the home country: it is no accident that West Germany, which has sustained a high level of economic activity for a long period of time, has been seeking locations in Ireland. Thirdly, access to markets: a major factor affecting the inflow of American firms is access to the European market.

Although the industrial development strategies in the two economies have made a significant contribution to the maintenance of manufacturing employment in Northern Ireland and to the growth of employment in the

Linkages,

criticism
①

Republic, they have from time to time been subject to similar criticisms in both areas. It has been argued (for example by O'Farrell (1971)) that reliance on capital grants produces a bias in favour of the attraction of capital-intensive projects which is inappropriate to economies which suffer from heavy unemployment. Attention has also been drawn to the limited extent to which new firms either purchase inputs from or sell outputs to established firms, i.e. to the limited amount of inter-industry linkage that has followed from new industrial development (McAleese (1971b)). Finally, concern has been expressed about the divergence between the contribution which incoming firms make to Gross Domestic Product and the contribution that they make to national (or regional) income, i.e. concern about outward transfers of returns to capital.

Table 2.10: New Industry and Major Expansions by Country of Origin, 1973

	Northern Ireland Jobs created since 1945. Percentage of total	Republic Percentage of employment in approved projects
Domestic	13·6	23·9
Great Britain	47·2	19·9
USA	24·9	25·0
West Germany	4·2	12·4
Other Europe	9·3	18·8
Other	0·8	
Total	100·0	100·0

Sources: N I: Department of Commerce, *Facts and Figures,* Belfast 1974; R I: I D A, *Annual Report 1972–73.*

No detailed assessment of these criticisms can be offered here, but it is interesting to note that, if they have substance, they suggest, not that policy should be radically altered, but that it should be implemented more selectively. This is happening to some extent already in both parts of Ireland, not only because the industrial development agencies are acquiring the expertise and capacity necessary for a systematic and selective approach, but also because the nature of the economic problems is changing in such a way as to make such an approach essential. In Northern Ireland, for example, the fall in unemployment in the second half of 1973 produced problems of severe shortages of labour, particularly skilled labour, in some of the more developed centres. There is still a need for new industry in many areas in the province, but in view of the shortages it would have been extremely difficult to fit a large new employer into some centres in, for example, the Belfast area. A large area around Dublin faces exactly the same difficulty. Against this background it is necessary to develop an increasingly selective policy in both economies, not only in terms of particular geographical locations, but also in terms of the industries that will meet the — often highly specific — requirements of those locations.

4   REGIONAL PROBLEMS AND POLICY

While concern with the particularly severe economic problems of the remoter areas in Northern Ireland and the Republic has been a feature of public policy for many years, it is only in the last decade that the interrelations between industrial development policy as a whole and the regional implications of that policy have become a matter of major interest in both areas. These interrelations are exceedingly complex. The regional distribution of economic activity is partly dependent upon the relative costs of siting plants in particular locations. But the costs in those locations are affected by public policy on transport, housing and other infrastructure, and decisions on these matters must reflect social as well as economic aims.

Obvious similarities of pattern are apparent in the geographical location of economic activity in the two areas, in the dominance of the Belfast region in Northern Ireland and the dominance of the Dublin region in the Republic. In 1971 the Dublin region (East Planning Region), representing about 10 per cent of the area of the country, contained 36 per cent of the population, 37 per cent of total employment, 46 per cent of employment in industry (including construction), and 47 per cent of employment in services. In the same year the Greater Belfast Area (including Craigavon and Antrim), accounting for about one-fifth of the area of Northern Ireland, contained 55 per cent of the population, 60 per cent of total employment, and 66 per cent of employment in services. In the Republic, apart from Limerick, the major industrial centres are located along the coast between Dundalk and Cork. In 1971 two-thirds of all non-agricultural employment was located in the coastal counties between Louth and Cork plus Kildare. In Northern Ireland the only major industrial centre outside the Greater Belfast Area is Londonderry. Elsewhere towns are small: with the exception of Cork in the Republic, there are no settlements outside Belfast and Dublin with populations approaching 100,000.

Moreover, the imbalance which is apparent between Dublin and the rest of the Republic and Belfast and the rest of Northern Ireland is increasing. The share of the population in the East Planning Region in the Republic increased from 30 per cent in 1951 to 36 per cent in 1971. Similar trends are apparent for the Greater Belfast Area in the North. These trends are not too difficult to explain. Outward transport routes for industrial production are focused eastward, towards Great Britain and Europe, and locations convenient to the major ports are favoured by potential industrialists; the decline of agriculture produces a continuous movement of people from the land and some, at least, of these see their best opportunities in the larger centres; and the natural growth of population in the developed areas themselves provides a further source of expansion. It is this heavy concentration of economic activity in the eastern parts of both parts of the island that has given rise to the view that although the political division of Ireland is between North and South the fundamental economic dichotomy is between East and West.[1]

In the absence of intervention from government, the capital centres in both North and South would continue to grow, at least very much faster, and probably at the expense of the remaining areas. Even in the face of past attempts to produce a more balanced pattern, they have both continued to expand their proportions of the total populations in Northern Ireland and the Republic. Very rapid growth might in the end produce its own restraints. Pressures on the availability of industrial sites have been apparent for some time, particularly in Belfast; and pressures on existing infrastructure have also given cause for concern, particularly in Dublin. Moreover, both areas have now reached the point at which they are running into labour shortages. Unemployment rates in the Greater Belfast Area in June 1973 — Belfast 4·6 per cent, Lisburn 2·0 per cent, Antrim 2·9 per cent, Bangor 3·5 per cent — do not suggest that there is a readily available pool of labour for further expansion, particularly when it is borne in mind that the Belfast rate is inflated by heavy unemployment in West Belfast, largely a consequence of the civil unrest. But although the pressures of congestion might make further expansion in Belfast and Dublin more difficult, experience elsewhere suggests that, in the absence of control, rapid expansion would continue.

Against these similar backgrounds the broad objectives of regional policy have also been similar in both parts of Ireland. First, it has been accepted that it is necessary to limit the expansion of Belfast and Dublin and to foster viable economic development elsewhere in order to counteract the magnetic influence of the capital cities. This proposition is not self-evident. As Buchanan (1968) pointed out for the Republic, the concentration of expansion in the Dublin area might well be the best strategy to maximise economic growth. The main reasons for rejecting this concentration strategy are social rather than economic. Secondly, it follows that the regional structures which are fostered outside the ambits of the capital cities should be conducive to industrial development. While this has been accepted as a general aim in both areas, there has been considerable disagreement, particularly in the Republic, as to how it can be achieved. The

1 The imbalance is apparent not only in the location of employment but also in the location of unemployment (see Chapter 3, pp. 95–6, and particularly Table 3.9).

discussion has become polarised around the views of those who favour concentration on a limited number of growth centres and those who would disperse industrial development more widely. Thirdly — and the order of discussion here is not intended to reflect any judgment about the order of importance of the broad objectives — there is recognition that policy should reflect the balance between the aims of the community on the regional distribution of population and the costs of achieving those aims. There is, for example, in both areas, but particularly in the Republic, a strong lobby in favour of the preservation of rural communities. These views should be given due weight, but they should be assessed against the consequential costs, possibly in terms of economic development forgone and certainly in terms of the resources required to provide modern standards of infrastructure for dispersed communities.

4.1 Policy in the Republic

As the survey *Regional Policy in Ireland* (N E S C (1975)) points out, the roots of regional policy in the Republic lie in the successive attempts that were made over a long period of time to promote development in the poorer areas in the West and North-West of the country — the Congested Districts, subsequently the Undeveloped Areas and today the Designated Areas. The Undeveloped Areas Act of 1952 established An Foras Tionscal to provide grants to stimulate industrial development in the problem areas. Until the emergence of the new economic policy after the publication of *Economic Development* in 1958, however, no attempt was made to weld these efforts into a regional development strategy for the country as a whole.

In the early days of the new economic policy emphasis shifted away from the problems of the poorer areas to the more urgent task of achieving the take-off necessary for the economic development of the country as a whole. As expansion got under way in the early 1960s, however, the emerging strains on the capacity of the existing infrastructure in many areas made it clear that long-term plans for the physical development of the country were an essential part of the programme for economic development. In 1963 the government provided a regulative basis for new planning machinery in the Local Government (Planning and Development) Act, and gave a regional dimension to the planning process by defining nine planning regions. Consultants were commissioned in 1964 to prepare reports for the Dublin and Limerick regions, and in 1966 the government requested the United Nations to commission a consultant to undertake regional studies in the remaining seven regions and to report on regional development strategies for the country as a whole. This latter report (Buchanan (1968)) was a major landmark in the development of thinking about regional problems in the Republic. The methodology of the study was to consider the possible effects of a number of alternative development strategies: unrestricted expansion of Dublin, concentration on a number of growth centres, and widespread dispersal of economic development. Although, as has been noted above, the Buchanan Report concluded that the rate of economic growth might be maximised by concentrating on Dublin, it recommended the growth centre strategy as providing the best compromise between the need for growth and the desire for balanced development. The recommended strategy involved (a) the development of two major centres of industrial growth at Cork and Limerick/Shannon, and (b) expansion based on industrial development at Waterford, Dundalk, Drogheda, Sligo, Galway, Tralee, Letterkenny, Castlebar and Cavan.

The publication of the Buchanan Report focused attention on a debate about general policy on regional development that had been continuing since the publication of *Economic Development* in 1958: should development be polarised in the larger centres of population or should it be spread widely over the country as a whole? In its simplest form the contest was between centralisation and dispersion.

During the 1960s the use of growth centre policy as an instrument for regional development had received favourable attention in a number of Western European countries (Allen and Hermansen (1968)). Emphasis had been directed towards the external economies available from proximity to suppliers and markets, from larger and more diversified labour markets and from the availability of services for people and industry. At the same time research in the Republic of Ireland was producing evidence supporting the view that large towns provided a better environment than small towns for industrial survival and growth (O'Neill (1971)). This evidence, though persuasive, could hardly be said to be conclusive: it is doubtful if it is strong enough to bear the weight of the very strong version of growth centre policy that it has been used to justify (O'Farrell (1974)). The present state of the debate seems to be that although there is general agreement that some concentration of development effort is essential, there is little agreement about how much concentration there should be. Much detailed work remains to be done on the relationships between town size and the external economies and agglomeration economies that can accrue to industry.

Against this background, and bearing in mind the painful political decisions involved in the situation, it is hardly surprising that the government 'sat on the fence between the rival factions of the Centralists and the Dispersionists for a long time' (O'Neill (1973)). In May 1972, however, it issued a statement setting out overall regional strategy for a twenty-year period. The statement endorsed the plans for regional industrial development which had been published by the I D A in the same year and which, with job targets for 177 towns and villages, were clearly dispersionist in character. The main planks in the strategy are (a) restriction of the growth of Dublin to the natural increase of the present population, (b) expansion of the main

Buchanan growth centres, (*c*) development of other county towns and
rapid expansion of towns in areas remote from other existing towns, and
(*d*) continuation of the special measures for the development of the Gaeltacht. In this strategy the government appears to have attempted to get the
best of all possible worlds. The tone of the statement is dispersionist; but
as has been pointed out the population targets which accompanied the
statement — involving doubling of the population of the Cork area and
more than doubling the population of Limerick/Shannon by 1991 — are
those implied by the Buchanan growth centre strategy (O'Neill (1973)).
As was concluded in N E S C (1975), 'There is need for much greater clarity
in the specification of regional policy objectives.'

4.2 Policy in Northern Ireland

The first attempt at a comprehensive economic development strategy for
Northern Ireland was made in the programme for 1965–70, *Economic
Development in Northern Ireland* (1965), prepared by an interdepartmental
committee of civil servants advised by an economic consultant, Professor
Thomas Wilson. The physical strategy proposed in the programme, however,
was to a large extent an elaboration of proposals made in an earlier report,
the *Belfast Regional Survey and Plan* prepared by Sir Robert Matthew and
published in 1963. In the Republic physical planning followed economic
planning, growing out of the pressures created by expanding economic
activity; in Northern Ireland economic planning came after a number of
critical elements in the physical development strategy had been decided.

The Matthew Report was mainly concerned with the environmental problems arising out of the rapid growth of urban Belfast and with the prospect
that by the early 1980s unrestricted growth would produce a situation in
which nearly three-quarters of a million people, not far short of half the
population of Northern Ireland, would be living in a single conurbation.
The proposals designed to avoid this outcome were (*a*) to limit the expansion of Belfast by setting a stopline beyond which expansion would not
be permitted, (*b*) to expand a number of towns in the Belfast Region to
cater for overspill of population, and (*c*) to create a new city — subsequently
named Craigavon — based on the existing towns Lurgan and Portadown,
partly to cater for overspill from Belfast and partly to provide an alternative
magnet to Belfast for population moving from the rest of the province.
Although it was mainly concerned with the problems of the Belfast Region,
the report also suggested the designation of six key centres in the rest of
the province to provide suitable locations for industry and for the accommo-
dation of people moving from surrounding rural areas.

The Wilson team, coming to the problem somewhat later, found a regional
development strategy ready made. It was, moreover, a strategy which had
attractive features in the light of their view of the economic problems in
Northern Ireland. In addition to meeting the problems associated with

limiting the growth of Belfast, it appeared that the concentration of development in a small number of centres offered the best hope of achieving the industrial expansion that was a key element in economic policy. This was not simply a matter of accepting the growth centre philosophy that had become influential elsewhere. It also reflected the hard practical experience of the Ministry of Commerce that there were serious problems in attracting industry to small towns in which specialised skills were in short supply, services were poorly developed, and infrastructure was frequently unsuited to industrial needs.

The regional strategy outlined in the Wilson Report and refined in the Development Programme for 1970–75 (Matthew, Wilson and Parkinson (1970)) designated three main 'centres of accelerated growth': the Belfast area (including Craigavon and Antrim), Ballymena, and Londonderry. Eight other relatively important provincial towns were denoted as 'key centres' and significant expansion was contemplated in them. It was planned, however, that the main growth would take place in the centres of accelerated growth, and the population projections associated with the programme envisaged that the three centres would account for 62 per cent of the population of Northern Ireland by 1986 compared with 53 per cent in 1966.

Two features of the Development Programme are particularly noteworthy. First, the expansion planned for the three major centres involved a massive public investment programme: actual expenditure on the new town at Craigavon up to 1974, for example, was of the order of £70 million. Secondly, the physical strategy depended on the willingness of substantial numbers of people to move to the new centres: the programme required a high level of population mobility. To achieve the projected development even in favourable circumstances would have been a formidable task. The outbreak of civil disorder in 1968 made the task doubly difficult. The slowing down in the inflow of new industry reduced the impetus to growth, particularly in Craigavon; and the fears engendered by violence dramatically reduced the willingness of people to move.

In 1975 a further publication, *Northern Ireland: Discussion Paper: Regional Physical Development Strategy 1975–95,* considered a number of alternative approaches and outlined a preferred strategy. The document still places major reliance on a small number of major growth centres, but the main centres within the Greater Belfast Area are treated individually and emphasis is on their development separate from Belfast. Thus it is suggested that there should be four centres, Belfast, Londonderry, Craigavon and Antrim/Ballymena (considered as a single complex). At the second level the Discussion Paper adopts a more dispersionist tone, suggesting the planned development of a further eighteen towns as District Centres which would fulfil the functions of administrative, market and service centres. Many of these towns — for example, Larne — already have substantial amounts of

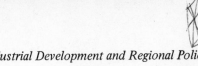

industry and it is recommended that more should be sought. It is envisaged that the smaller towns could also have an industrial role, for while they are not to be regarded primarily as locations for industry, they are urged to make themselves attractive to new small-scale enterprises.

In general the policy outlined in the Green Paper involves a considerable softening of the fairly vigorous growth centre strategy that had emerged from the previous Development Programmes. In this it is, in part, recognising the difficulties involved in implementing the amount of social engineering involved in that strategy in the present conditions in Northern Ireland. At the same time it is attempting to strike a fair balance between the necessity for economic efficiency and the desire to see that people are presented with a wide range of choices and considerable freedom in the ordering of their lives.

Like many other things on the economic scene in Ireland, the regional policies of the two economies appear to be drawing together with the passing of time. In Northern Ireland an early commitment to a fairly strong form of growth centre policy is in the process of being softened to take more account of the needs of smaller communities in remoter areas. In the Republic, although the current tone of regional strategy lays emphasis on the need for widely spread development, the population projections for the major centres suggest a considerable concentration of industrial growth, particularly in Cork and Limerick, during the next decade. Governments in both parts of Ireland are taking a somewhat eclectic view of the growth centre debate: both are willing to recognise that there must be some concentration of development in a limited number of centres; but both are also emphasising the need to take positive action to stimulate the growth of smaller communities. Neither is prepared to place all its eggs in a limited number of growth centre baskets and to rely on 'trickling-down' effects to stimulate activity elsewhere.

In the last analysis, however, regional strategies are significant only to the extent that they affect decisions. Rapid development of any centre, whether in Northern Ireland or the Republic, is certain to be very expensive in terms of public investment in housing, roads, power supplies, telecommunications and all of the other complex elements of infrastructure. The regional patterns that emerge in the two areas during the next two decades will depend upon the willingness of governments to concentrate public investment on those centres which enjoy rapid growth or show clear potential for rapid growth, possibly at the expense of investment elsewhere.

REFERENCES

Allen, K. J. and Hermansen, T. (1968): *Regional Policy in E F T A* (University of Glasgow Social and Economic Studies), Oliver and Boyd, Edinburgh.

Buchanan, C., and Partners (1968) in association with Economic Consultants Ltd: *Regional Studies in Ireland,* An Foras Forbartha, Dublin.

Buckley, P. J. (1974): 'Some Aspects of Foreign Private Investment in the Manufacturing Sector of the Economy of the Irish Republic', *Economic and Social Review,* Vol. 5, No. 3 (Apr.).

C I P (1973): *General Report* (Prl 2927), Stationery Office, Dublin.

Cuthbert, N. (1970): *The Northern Ireland Economy* (The Queen's University of Belfast New Lecture Series No. 55), Belfast.

Department of Commerce (1974): *Facts and Figures on Industrial Development in Northern Ireland,* Belfast.

Department of Housing, Local Government and Planning (1975): *Northern Ireland: Discussion Paper: Regional Physical Development Strategy 1975–95,* H M S O, Belfast.

Durkan, J. and Kelleher, R. (1974): in *Quarterly Economic Commentary,* E S R I (Oct.).

Economic Development in Northern Ireland (1965) (Cmd 479), H M S O, Belfast.

Jefferson, C. W. (1968): *A Method of Estimating the Stock of Capital in Northern Ireland Manufacturing Industry: Limitations and Applications* (E S R I Paper No. 44), Dublin.

McAleese, D. (1971a): *Effective Tariffs and the Structure of Industrial Protection in Ireland* (E S R I Paper No. 62), Dublin.

McAleese, D. (1971b): 'Capital Inflows and Direct Foreign Investment in Ireland 1952–70', *Journal of the Statistical and Social Inquiry Society of Ireland,* Vol. 32, Pt 4.

Matthew, Sir R., Wilson, T. and Parkinson, J. (1970): *Northern Ireland Development Programme 1970–75,* H M S O, Belfast.

N E S C (1975): *Regional Policy in Ireland* (Report No. 4) (Prl 4147), Stationery Office, Dublin.

N I E C (1967): *Report on Changes in Distribution* (Report No. 21) (Prl 9897), Stationery Office, Dublin.

O'Farrell, P. N. (1971): 'The Regional Problem in Ireland: Some Reflections on Development Strategy', *Economic and Social Review,* Vol. 2, No. 4 (Jul.).

O'Farrell, P. N. (1974): 'Regional Planning in Ireland – The Case for Concentration: A Reappraisal', *Economic and Social Review,* Vol. 5, No. 4 (Jul.).

O'Neill, H. B. (1971): *Spatial Planning in a Small Economy: A Case Study of Ireland,* Praeger, New York.

O'Neill, H. B. (1973): 'Regional Planning in Ireland – The Case for Concentration', *Irish Banking Review* (Sep.).

Slattery, D. G. (1973): 'Estimates of Capital Cost in Ireland'. (Mimeograph, Department of Economics, The Queen's University of Belfast.)

CHAPTER 3

The Labour Force and the Problem of Unemployment

B. M. WALSH

1 INTRODUCTION

Labour is the most important factor of production in the economic process. In almost all countries at least two-thirds of national income is paid out in the form of wages and salaries. Virtually every household contains a member of the labour force or someone receiving a pension due to years of service in employment. Only a minority of households obtain any significant non-labour or rentier income. Moreover, although the machinery and other equipment used in the productive process are very important, the skills, knowledge, and experience of the labour force are generally acknowledged as a major determinant of international differentials in productivity. The returns to this 'human capital' are, of course, part of wages and salaries as these are conventionally measured.

When an economy is producing less than the maximum output of which it is capable, the unused human resources in the form of unemployed men and women are recognised as a far more serious social problem than the unused capital equipment or excess capacity that exists at the same time. The socialist economies of Eastern Europe are organised so that such unemployment cannot exist; the 'mixed' capitalist-socialist economies of the industrial world have all developed elaborate systems of social insurance to maintain the income of unemployed workers. Most countries have schemes to retrain those whose skills are no longer in demand and to help young entrants to the labour market to gain access to the sectors where their contribution is most needed.

The problem of unemployment has been a dominant concern of economic policy in both parts of Ireland for many years. It is intimately linked with the development of the Irish economies and in particular the absorption of low-productivity farm-workers into the more productive non-agricultural sector. Emigration has been a more severe problem in Ireland than anywhere else in the world, and this, too, may be seen as an aspect of the employment problem, since young people will generally leave their native country in large numbers only because it does not offer them the prospect of employment at satisfactory wages.

In analysing the Irish labour force we shall therefore pay particular attention to the factors behind the related problems of unemployment and emigration.

2   MEASURING THE LABOUR FORCE

The labour force is usually defined as the total number of people who are in employment or looking for work. This concept is broader than the notion of the labour input to the productive process, as it includes that part of the supply of labour which is unsuccessful in getting work. Moreover, the labour force concept usually relates to the *number of people* who are economically active, whereas a measure of the labour input to the economy should take account of the *number of hours* worked.

Economists are generally willing to accept the concept of the labour force in the aggregate as meaningful, although in fact the number thus obtained relates to the sum of very varied types of labour inputs — men and women, young and old, clerical and production, skilled and unskilled. In some applications it is more meaningful to take a weighted sum of the different groups of workers, using relative wage rates as weights.

The definition of employment also poses problems. Economists are generally concerned with activity that can be related, directly or indirectly, to the measuring-rod of money. Thus employment refers primarily to paid employment. A major exception arises in an Irish context in connection with the self-employed, especially family farm workers. Furthermore, in recent years economists have devoted considerable attention to the decision-making process that governs allocation of time between producing 'market' and 'home' goods and services — a belated recognition that most women spend a great deal of time and energy in domestic duties, and that although this work may not contribute to national income, it is none the less part of the behaviour that should be studied by economists.

Data on Irish employment and unemployment can be found in the censuses of population and production, and national insurance records. These sources suffer from some defects: the population census relies on self-reporting and obtains fairly limited details of occupations. It is up to a respondent to decide whether he or she is 'out of work' or 'unemployed', as opposed to being 'economically inactive'. In the Northern Ireland census, the data collected on economic activity relate specifically to the respondents' status during the week preceding the census day; in the Republic the instructions specify only that details of one's 'principal occupation' should be given. Coverage by the Census of Industrial Production (Republic of Ireland) is limited to firms employing at least three people, and provides no information on unemployment. National insurance records provide a wealth of information on employment and unemployment, but relate only to the insured population. In the Republic before 1974 only manual workers and all those earning below £1,600 a year had to be insured. Since 1974 in the Republic, and since the early post-war years in Northern Ireland, the entire employee labour force is insured. The self-employed labour force is generally outside the compulsory insurance scheme in both areas.

The most widely quoted figures on unemployment are derived from the numbers registering for unemployment benefits or assistance. The widely quoted unemployment rate is calculated by dividing the numbers thus registered as unemployed by the insured labour force. This concept is similar to that used in Britain, but in the United States and some European countries the unemployment rate is calculated on the basis of survey data on the numbers looking for work in a particular week. In general, the U S approach to measuring unemployment includes as unemployed more people than the British or Irish approach: married women or school-leavers who do not qualify for benefits but who would work if suitable jobs were available tend to be excluded from the Irish measures of unemployment. On the other hand, there may be registrants for unemployment benefits who are not really 'willing and able to work' due to physical or psychological problems. On the whole, however, the net tendency in the official Irish unemployment data is towards understatement.

Census of population and national insurance data yield fairly similar unemployment statistics in Ireland, as may be seen in Table 3.1. If the Republic's figure from the census is expressed as a percentage of the employee labour force (only employees are recorded as 'out of work' in the census), the unemployment rate is 8·8 per cent, and the comparison between the two sources in each part of Ireland is very consistent, with a somewhat higher figure obtained from the self-reported data in the census.

Table 3.1: Unemployment Rates (%) in Northern Ireland and the Republic,
April 1971

	Population census	Registered unemployment
Northern Ireland	8·3	7·6
Republic	7·3 (8·8)	7·9

Note: The data for the Republic exclude farmers and assisting relatives, but include agricultural labourers. The figure in parentheses for the Republic is the rate per 100 employees.

Sources: Census of Population reports, 1971; N I: *Digest of Statistics*, No. 36 (Sep. 1971), H M S O, Belfast; R I: *Trend of Employment and Unemployment*, Stationery Office, Dublin.

The measurement of unemployment in the agricultural sector poses enormous problems, since most of the labour force is not employed on an hourly or daily basis, and underemployment among family farm workers is difficult to measure. One approach is to estimate, using input-output and linear programming methods, the number of man-days *required* in an optimal situation to produce the actual level of output, and to label any excess of the actual labour force over and above this requirement 'underemployment'. There are, however, objections to this approach, and hence the measurement of unemployed labour in agriculture is generally left aside.

From 1975 onwards a labour force survey based on EEC methodology will be conducted in the Republic. This will resemble the US survey on employment and unemployment and will provide standardised data on the labour force for all EEC countries. This will represent a great improvement over the existing situation, where reliance on national censuses and insurance records gives rise to problems of interpretation of the labour force statistics for the two parts of Ireland.

3　GENERAL TRENDS IN EMPLOYMENT IN IRELAND

In Table 3.2 the broad picture of employment and unemployment in Ireland in the period 1961–73 is summarised. The similarity of experience in both parts of Ireland is striking: in both areas agriculture declined by about the same percentage; total employment, and indeed total population, grew at similar rates. In both areas the numbers not in employment, whether unemployed or outside the labour force, grew more rapidly than the numbers in employment, and consequently the employed labour force as a percentage of the total population declined slightly, from 37·3 to 36·6 per cent in the Republic, from 37·8 to 37·4 per cent in Northern Ireland.

The expansion of non-agricultural employment in the Republic – by 18 per cent over the twelve years – is the most impressive figure in the table. Employment in manufacturing industry grew even more rapidly, by 21 per cent, and in 1973 exceeded the numbers in manufacturing in Northern Ireland by almost one-third. The relative stagnation of non-agricultural, and especially industrial, employment in the North needs, however, to be interpreted in conjunction with data on the decline of certain traditional industries: employment in 'shipbuilding and marine engineering' fell from 20,200 in 1961 to 9,800 in 1973, and employment in textiles fell from 56,300 to 39,400. Manufacturing industry outside these two declining sectors rose from 104,500 in 1961 to 114,900 in 1971 – or by 10 per cent. This figure understates the extent of the growth in new industrial employment because in the textile industry in particular some of the employment in traditional industries, such as linen, has been replaced by the rapid growth of new industries, such as man-made fibres.

Table 3.2: Trends in Employment, Unemployment, and Population, Northern Ireland and the Republic, 1961–73 (000s)

	Northern Ireland			Republic		
	1961	1971	1973	1961	1971	1973
		a	b			
Employment in Agriculture, Forestry, Fishing	73	53·3	56·2	379·5	273·1	261
Employment in Manufacturing Industries	181	179·9	169·7	179·4	213·6	217
Employment in Other Non-Agricultural sectors	285	324·4	321·8	493·6	568·1	574
Total in employment	539	557·6	547·7	1,052·5	1,054·8	1,052
Out of work (R I): Registered unemployment (N I)	33	37·0	30·4	55·6	64·7	66
Total labour force	572	594·6	578·7	1,108·1	1,119·5	1,118
Total not in labour force	853	941·5	968·4	1,710·2	1,858·7	1,933
Total population	1,425	1,536·1	1,547·1	2,818·3	2,978·2	3,051
Total net migration between dates[c]	−71	−15		−135	+2	

[a] Series based entirely on national insurance estimates (tends to overstate manufacturing employment due to inclusion of seasonal workers).

[b] Series takes into account the new census of employment.

[c] 1961–71 data are from the Census of Population reports; 1971–73 estimates are based on the natural increase and change in population data.

Note: The Republic of Ireland data relate to April; Northern Ireland data to June.

Sources: N I: *Digest of Statistics*, No. 41 (Mar. 1974), H M S O, Belfast, Table 7, and corresponding entries in earlier issues; R I: 1961 and 1971: Census of Population reports; 1973: *Review of 1973 and Outlook for 1974* (Prl 3774), Stationery Office, Dublin.

Despite these individual achievements, the overall picture remains one of inadequate employment creation in both parts of Ireland. The unemployment totals have not declined, and total employment has grown less rapidly than population. When viewed against a background of net emigration of 133,000 from the Republic and 86,000 from the North, equal to 13 per cent of the Republic's, and 16 per cent of Northern Ireland's, 1973 employed labour force, these trends show the serious labour surplus problem in Ireland today. This problem is, however, partly a structural problem in the sense that those available for work may lack the specific skills sought by employers. This question is discussed in more detail below (see also Chapter 2).

4   THE OPERATION OF THE LABOUR MARKET

In a simple model of macro-economic activity, the level of employment is usually determined by the interaction of the supply and demand for labour. The demand for labour is usually derived from a production function, which relates the physical quantity of production to the inputs of factors of production under a specified technology, on the assumption that firms attempt to maximise profits or net worth, taking factor and product prices as given. Under such assumptions, firms will hire labour up to the point where the marginal physical product of labour equals the real wage. The demand for labour is then the downward-sloping marginal product curve, holding technology and the level of non-labour inputs constant.

The supply of labour depends on the behaviour of individuals. They must decide about the allocation of time between work and leisure or, especially in the case of women, between work in the labour force, work at home, and leisure. The decision concerns how many hours per week will be supplied to the labour market: if none are supplied, the person is economically inactive or outside the labour force; if some hours are supplied, then the individual is in the economically active labour force. The individual decision-maker is assumed to maximise his utility, which includes income and leisure, given the constraint that there are only 168 hours in a week and that the wage rate he can obtain is in the short run beyond his own control. In the long run, however, his decisions about education and training affect his earnings potential. There is no unambiguous inference to be drawn about whether the amount of labour supplied will increase or decrease as real wages rise: this depends upon the nature of the individual's utility function, and perhaps also on the initial *level* of real wages. However, it is commonly assumed that the supply of labour is upward-sloping, at least over certain ranges, with respect to the real wage. In the case of women, this assumption is reinforced by the possibility that a rise in real wages can cause a substitution of market work not only for leisure, but also for work in the home.

Given the individual's decision about his supply of labour, the total labour supplied in an economy depends on the number of people of working age, as well as on the wage rate. In the short run, however, the population may be regarded as a constant (although in Ireland migration is an important consideration even in the short run), and our attention is generally confined to the influence of the real wage rate. Thus the conventional picture of equilibrium in the labour market is as in Figure 3.1. N, K, and T denote population, capital and technology respectively, and are written with bars to indicate that they are exogenous to the labour market. $(W/P)_E$ is the market-clearing wage rate. If this wage is established, no 'involuntary' unemployment exists. True, there are those who would accept work (or work longer hours) at a higher wage rate, but this does not constitute unemployment in the economist's meaning of the term. On the other side of the labour market there are no unfilled vacancies: true, there are employers who would hire more labour if the wage rate were lower, but this does not constitute a vacancy or a shortage of labour in our meaning of these terms.

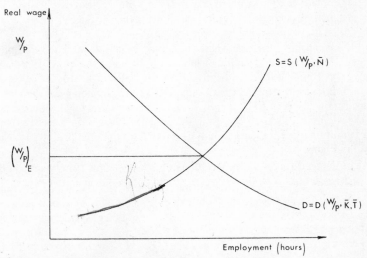

Figure 3.1: *Labour Market Equilibrium*

Even in the pre-Keynesian world this simple analysis was not accepted as telling the whole story. It was recognised that markets operate imperfectly: information about job opportunities and about available employees is not a free good. In the absence of full information there will be 'frictional' unemployment as employees and employers seek each other out. However, it seemed to Keynes that unemployment rates of 20 per cent and over could not be accounted for simply in terms of the gradualness of adjustment between supply and demand *at the equilibrium wage.* The debate that centred around this issue has been the most important concern of macro-economics since the publication of the *General Theory* in 1936.

The models presented in Chapter 1 are centred around the concept of aggregate demand. The demand for labour is essentially that amount required to create the output to match the aggregate demand — allowing for exports and imports. The supply of labour is given exogenously by demographic factors and the wage rate is influenced by the British wage rate. The Irish labour market is not assumed to be in equilibrium in the neo-classical sense. At prevailing wage levels labour supply exceeds demand. This is supported by the high levels of unemployment and emigration which both parts of Ireland have experienced over long periods.

The present consensus on the causes of unemployment has been summarised in a recent article by Lipsey (1974). His intention in this article was to provide the theoretical underpinnings for the empirically observed inverse relationship between the rate of increase in money wages and the unemployment rate. This relationship, known as the Phillips curve, is discussed in Chapter 5. Our present concern is with the insight that can be obtained into the problem of unemployment in Ireland using the syntheses of post-Keynesian theory provided by Lipsey.

Lipsey considers the case where the supply of labour is related to money wages. The demand and supply of labour can be made functions of money wages if the price level is held constant. A rise (fall) in the price level occasions a *shift* in the demand for labour, since at each money wage the real wage is now lower (higher) than before. If complete money illusion exists in the supply of labour, a change in the price level leaves the supply curve for labour unaltered. Lipsey's analysis is based on the relationship summarised in Figure 3.2.

The demand for labour reflects the number of people firms want to hire at each wage rate: it is, therefore the number of jobs available. Let us

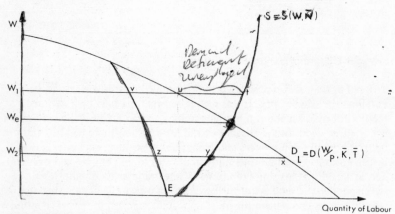

Figure 3.2: *Labour Market Money Illusion*

assume that actual employment will be the lesser of the quantities of labour supplied (q_s) or demanded (q_d). At wage rates $W \leqslant W_e$, there will be no unemployment. If $W = W_1$, unemployment is given by the distance ut as in Figure 3.2. This type of unemployment is referred to as *demand-deficient* unemployment, and is the type of unemployment whose existence Keynes strove to have recognised. It is possible that money wages will get stuck at values such as W_1 due to trade union resistence to wage cuts, and to the existence of a variety of factors which in fact set a minimum wage floor (e.g. minimum wage laws, income maintenance payments for the unemployed, public works employment at wages greater than W_e). The problem of demand-deficient unemployment can be overcome by any policy that will shift the demand for labour sufficiently far outward. One such possibility is a rise in the general price level (P) which causes a fall in the real wage (W/P) corresponding to each level of the money wage (W). This policy will succeed provided the supply of labour does not shift in an offsetting manner as the price level rises. Thus this solution is dependent on the existence of money illusion in the labour market and a 'Keynesian', as distinct from 'neo-classical', frame of reference.

To take account of frictional unemployment, consider the curve E, representing the number of people actually finding jobs. This may be less than the lesser of q_s and q_d, the number wishing to work and the number of jobs available, at any given wage rate. The possibility now exists that both unemployment *and* unfilled vacancies will coexist at a given wage rate: at W_1, for example, there are vu unfilled vacancies, and vt unemployment. Total unemployment is divided into demand-deficient (ut) and frictional (vu). Even at wage rates less than W_e, frictional unemployment persists.

The behaviour of unemployed workers has been analysed by economists in an attempt to understand the phenomenon of unemployment in greater depth. Mortensen (1970) has elaborated a model in which he sees the unemployed worker searching for job offers that must at least meet his reservation wage requirements. How long he continues to search depends on the cost of and returns to additional time spent searching. Income maintenance payments reduce the cost, while the proportion of vacancies open to him, which depends on his skill level, increases the prospective returns to job search. Thus the phenomenon of unemployment is not a simple dichotomy between having a job and not having one. The rational worker does not take any job open to him: he tries to maximise the present value of his future wages, and this may involve continuing to look for a job even when an offer of employment has already been received.

In analysing the problem of unemployment in any real-world economy, it is extremely difficult to disentangle frictional and demand-deficient elements. Moreover, in a developing economy, with a large subsistence agricultural sector, the phenomenon of non-agricultural unemployment has to be incorporated into a theory of the way in which the economy is developing, and in particular of the balance between the labour forces in the two sectors.

Harris and Todaro (1970) have developed a model applicable to an economy in which there is a considerable gap between the wage rates in the subsistence or rural and non-subsistence or urban sectors, with significant migration from the former to the latter despite the prevalence of high unemployment rates in the cities. The existence of an urban wage considerably above what would prevail in a free market, due to factors such as social security legislation, minimum wage laws, trade unions, can lead to substantial unemployment. Rural-urban migration will continue as long as the *expected* marginal real wage in the urban sector exceeds the value of the marginal physical product in the rural sector. The expected real wage in the urban sector equals the minimum wage times the employment rate (that is, 1 minus the unemployment rate). This model is particularly relevant to those sectors in the urban economy, such as casual labouring, to which the rural population has ready access. Harris and Todaro show that in this situation a limited wage subsidy in the urban sector and migration restrictions in the rural sector will lead to a higher standard of living for the population as a whole.

4.1 The Labour Supply

In the long run, demographic factors determine the supply of labour: the birth rate of fifteen to twenty years ago dictates how many school-leavers there will be looking for employment this year. A comprehensive view of economic-demographic interaction would lead us to try to explain part at least of the behaviour of marriage and fertility rates in terms of economic conditions: no doubt Ireland's very low marriage rate during the period 1840–1961 was due in part to religious, social and cultural influences, but the restricted non-agricultural economic opportunities and the constraints of a predominantly livestock-orientated agriculture also played a role. Similarly, the relatively low cost of additional children, due especially to the lack of employment opportunities for women, must be added to the more obvious explanations of the high Irish fertility. All of these factors played a greater part in the economic history of the Republic than in the North, where industrialisation modified the typically Irish demographic adjustment and resulted in a more normal, European population structure.

A notable feature of both parts of Ireland at the present time is the high potential growth rate of the population, due above all to a high birth rate. The 1973 situation is shown in Table 3.3, where comparative data for England and Wales are also presented. One special feature of the Republic's recent history has been the rapid decline in the proportion of each age group that is single. This rising marriage rate has counteracted the declining fertility rate, evident since 1963, with the result that the birth rate has increased slightly. In Northern Ireland, and even more markedly in Britain, the decline in fertility has led to a falling birth rate.

Table 3.3: Vital Rates per 1,000 Population, 1973

	Births	Deaths	Natural increase
Northern Ireland	18·7	11·4	7·3
Republic of Ireland	22·3	10·9	11·4
England and Wales	13·8	11·9	1·9

Sources: N I and England and Wales: *Monthly Digest of Statistics* (Oct. 1973), H M S O, London; R I: *Report on Vital Statistics 1973*, Dublin.

In view of the high birth rate characteristic of Ireland, it is not surprising to find an unusual age structure in comparison with Britain: the situation in 1971 is illustrated in Table 3.4. The age structure of the Irish population has implications for the provision of social services, and perhaps also for the rate of domestic savings, which tends to be depressed by a high dependency ratio.

Table 3.4: Age of Population, 1971 (Percentage Distribution)

	Under 15	15—64	Over 64
Northern Ireland	29·7	59·5	10·8
Republic of Ireland	31·2	57·8	11·0
England and Wales	23·9	63·0	13·1

Sources: Census of Population reports.

In the medium and short run the most obvious link between the population and the labour force is the level of migration. Both parts of Ireland have been net exporters of people for well over a century, and most of these emigrants have been of working age and would have entered the employed or unemployed labour force in Ireland had they not emigrated. Table 3.5, showing annual net emigration rates (per 1,000 average population) since the post-war period, gives an idea of the magnitude of this phenomenon. The rate was much higher in the Republic during the first decade, but about equal in both areas since 1961. In the years since 1971 there appears to have been a net inflow to the Republic, while emigration continues from Northern Ireland. These swings in the net migration rate illustrate its major role in adjusting the supply of labour to its demand, even in the short run. However, since migration is partly determined by economic conditions in the place of destination, for the most part Britain, this adjustment mechanism is only partial. None the less, the possibility and at times the actuality of large-scale emigration from Ireland has acted to place a floor on the real wage. Undoubtedly the gap between Irish and British wage rates could not move outside a fairly narrow band unless the unemployment rate in Britain were to rise to very high levels. This openness of the Irish labour market introduces an unusual degree of exogeneity in the determination of the wage rate (see Chapters 1 and 5).

Table 3.5: Annual Net Emigration Rates per 1,000 Population, Northern Ireland and the Republic, 1951–71

	Northern Ireland	Republic
1951–61	6·6	14·2
1961–66	5·2	5·7
1966–71	4·6	3·7

Sources: Census of Population reports.

The proportion of the adult population that is 'economically active' is an aspect of the supply of labour and is known as the participation or activity rate. Some major components of the overall participation rate change only slowly in response to long-term structural changes in the economy: it is unlikely, for example, that the participation rate among married women would rise steeply within a year or that the proportion of seventy-year-olds in the labour force would fall suddenly in response to demand shifts. In the long run, however, labour force participation among these groups does respond to economic forces. Cyclical fluctuations also occur, especially among married women.

In Table 3.6 we compare participation rates for Northern Ireland in 1966 and the Republic in 1971, using Census of Population data. (The 1971 Northern Ireland detailed census tables are not available at the time of writing.) The figures show the percentage of each population group that is in the labour force. The 1971 census of Northern Ireland reveals that the overall female participation rate had remained virtually unchanged (at 35·8 per cent), but the rate among married women had risen to 29·2 per cent. In Great Britain the participation rate among the population aged 15 and over was 79·6 per cent for males and 42·3 per cent for females in 1973.

It will be seen that with the exception of the 65 and over age group for males, and the 60 and over for females, the Republic's participation rates are uniformly lower than those found in Northern Ireland. The exceptions may be ascribed in part to the importance of family farming in the Republic, and the low rate of retirement from this occupation. The very marked contrast for the 15–19 age group is due to the high rate of participation in post-primary education in the Republic.

Table 3.6: Labour Force Participation Rates: Proportion of each Population Group that is 'Economically Active', Northern Ireland and the Republic, 1966 and 1971

Age	Males		Females (total)		Married Females	
	Northern Ireland 1966	Republic 1971	Northern Ireland 1966	Republic 1971	Northern Ireland 1966	Republic 1971
15–19	69·1	50·7	64·4	44·9	n.a.	n.a.
20–24	92·9	88·9	65·8	65·0	31·9	15·2
25–44	99·0	97·4	36·3	24·0	24·6	7·8
45–54	98·6	96·6	36·6	20·8	26·9	7·3
55–59	96·2	94·0	32·4	21·8	20·1	7·1
60–64	89·8	87·6	18·1	20·7	10·3	5·9
65+	20·8	36·6	4·9	11·3	2·6	2·9
Total, 15+	83·5	81·3	35·7	27·8	23·2	7·5

Sources: Census of Population reports.

There is a major contrast between the regions due to the low participation rate among married women in the Republic. Even if a liberal definition of 'economically active' is used, the Republic's rates remain substantially below those recorded in Northern Ireland: in a sample survey of women aged 15–64, Walsh (1973) found that inclusion of all part-time working women in his definition of the labour force raised the married female participation rate only to 15 per cent — not much more than half the rate recorded in the Northern Ireland census. The Northern Ireland rate, in turn, is significantly lower than that found in Great Britain, where in 1971 over 38 per cent of married women were economically active. If attention is confined to those married women who are full-time economically active in Northern Ireland, the participation rate obtained is 22·1 in 1971, three times the rate recorded in the census in the Republic. Thus although the participation rate among married women has been rising in the Republic, it remains very low by Western European standards. This aspect of the labour force in the Republic may be due to the absence, until recently at least, of an industrial and services sector requiring substantial numbers of women workers, and to the fact that whatever opportunities for female employment did exist were readily filled from the large reserve of unmarried females available for non-farm employment.

It is of interest to draw attention to the existing regional differentials within each part of Ireland: in Northern Ireland in 1971, for example, the married female participation rate varied from a low of 18·3 per cent in Fermanagh to a high of 32·1 per cent in Belfast County Borough. This factor, combined with the high rate of natural increase alluded to above, ensures that both parts of Ireland have a very high potential labour force growth rate. Furthermore, the proportion of the labour force still in agriculture is high (especially in the Republic), so that the growth in labour supply to the non-agricultural sector is very rapid.

In the short run, modern economic theory includes the level of income maintenance payments among the factors influencing the length of time a worker will spend unemployed. In both parts of Ireland an unemployed worker, if fully insured, qualifies for unemployment benefits and a pay-related supplement. The benefits take his family circumstances into account. In the Republic if he qualifies for redundancy pay, the rule is that his total receipts from benefits and redundancy pay must not exceed his pre-redundancy gross remuneration. Since income maintenance payments are not taxable, it is possible for net income to be higher while out of work than when in employment. These work-disincentive effects of the welfare system should be kept in mind in considering the short-run factors influencing the labour supply and the level of unemployment.

4.2   The Demand for Labour

This topic has already been explored in the chapters on the structure and development of the economies. The demand for a factor of production such as labour is derived from the production function, and it is usually expressed in terms of the levels of output to be produced and the ratio of factor prices. Neither of these is determined independently of what is happening in the labour market, so that the demand for labour interacts with the supply to determine wage rates. However, there are some major factors influencing the demand for labour that can be treated as external to the labour market. Chief among these is the changing structure of demand for final product, and in particular the long-run decline in the share of income devoted to agricultural products. The combination of this factor with the rapid rate of productivity growth in the agricultural sector has been behind the declining share of the agricultural labour force in the total. This has already been documented in Chapter 2.

In view of the slow expansion of non-agricultural employment in both parts of Ireland, the rate of contraction of the numbers in agricultural and related occupations has probably been slower than would otherwise have been the case. As will be documented below, the unemployment rate in certain unskilled manual occupations closely related to farming has been extraordinarily high in Ireland for a long time. Despite this, there is a net inflow of young people to these occupations each year. If this phenomenon is interpreted in the light of the persistent gap between the income of small farmers and those in non-agricultural employment, it could be concluded that the slow rate of growth of the demand for labour in the non-agricultural sector as a whole has been the constraint on the absorption of surplus labour from the agricultural sector. Both parts of Ireland have in recent years relied heavily on foreign investment to accelerate the rate of growth in the demand for labour in the non-agricultural sector.

Unquestionably, unemployment is the main problem of the Irish labour market. The allied phenomenon of emigration has declined in prominence in recent years. The problem may be put in perspective by attempting a comparison of unemployment rates in E E C countries. The available data are set out in Table 3.7. There obviously are problems involved in comparing these data: we have already discussed the conceptual issues arising from the attempt to measure unemployment. But the magnitude of the gap between the unemployment rate recorded in both parts of Ireland and that in the rest of the E E C leaves no room for doubt about Ireland's exceptionally severe unemployment problem. When these figures are combined with our earlier data on emigration, and it is recalled that, with the exception of Italy and the United Kingdom, the other E E C countries are areas of net immigration, it is very apparent that Ireland is a surplus labour area by E E C standards.

Table 3.7: Unemployment Rates (%) in EEC Countries, Average of 1970–72

Belgium	2·1	Netherlands	1·7
Germany (F R)	0·7	United Kingdom	2·8[a]
France	1·4	Denmark	0·9
Italy	3·4	Republic of Ireland	6·1[b]
Luxembourg	0·0	Northern Ireland	7·7

[a]Including Northern Ireland.

[b]Excluding agriculture, fishing and private domestic service: there are very high unemployment rates among agricultural labourers in the Republic.

Sources: Commission of the European Communities, *Report on the Development of the Social Situation in the Community in 1973,* Brussels, 1974; N I: *Digest of Statistics,* H M S O, Belfast, various issues.

The gravity of the unemployment problem is only partly conveyed by the data on unemployment rates. Many of those out of work in Ireland have been unemployed for a very long time: the average duration of unemployment is high. In Table 3.8 we summarise this aspect of the situation. There is a striking similarity in the duration of unemployment in the two areas. The slightly shorter average duration among females in the Republic may be due to the very small proportion of women who receive unemployment assistance: it seems that an unemployed woman who has exhausted her entitlement to benefits in the Republic is unlikely to remain registered as unemployed unless she is the head of a household.

Table 3.8: Percentage Distribution of Registered Unemployment by Duration, Northern Ireland and the Republic, 1973

Unemployed for:	Males				Females			
	4 weeks or less	4–13 weeks	Over 13 weeks	Total	4 weeks or less	4–13 weeks	Over 13 weeks	Total
N I	18·0	23·0	59·0	100·0	23·2	28·4	48·4	100·0
R I	16·0	22·9	61·1	100·0	24·6	31·5	43·8	100·0

Note: The N I and R I figures are based on monthly and quarterly data respectively. R I data exclude farmers and their relatives assisting, and all aged 65 years and over.

Sources: N I: *Digest of Statistics*, No. 42 (Sep. 1974), H M S O, Belfast; R I: *Trend of Employment and Unemployment*, Stationery Office, Dublin.

The fact that over half the unemployed men in Ireland have been out of work for at least three months is an index of the gravity of the problem. In the Republic there has been a sharp increase in the average duration of unemployment since 1966; at that date only 14 per cent of unemployed males had been out of work for over three months. It is possible that the rapid improvement in income maintenance payments in the Republic since the mid-1960s contributed to this lengthening of the duration of unemployment, but on the whole the evidence suggests that the long-term unemployed are part of the general unemployment problem and reflect the general slackness of the Irish labour market.

One of the key issues in any discussion of Irish unemployment is the division of the total into 'demand-deficient' and 'structural' components. In any region where there is so high an unemployment rate, and where so high a proportion of the unemployed have been out of work for so long, there is a natural tendency to dismiss much of the problem as 'non-economic' — due to the personal characteristics of the unemployed, rather than to a deficiency of aggregate demand. If emigration is, moreover, a major factor in the economy, there is another justification for suspecting that those remaining in long-term unemployment are really 'unemployable', namely, the possibility that migration is selective of the more able-bodied and enterprising from among the unemployed. Finally, the existence of some shortages of skilled labour (however defined) can be advanced as evidence that further expansion of the economy will not necessarily reduce the existing unemployment problem.

A detailed study of unemployment in the Republic has shown that, despite the magnitude of intersectoral differentials in unemployment rates, the rate in each industry, region, and demographic group is responsive to the overall level of aggregate demand. Moreover, even the very long-term unemployment rate shows some responsiveness to demand pressures (cf. Walsh (1974)). Thus structural and deficient demand elements undoubtedly coexist in the Irish unemployment problem: there are marked and persistent intersectoral disparities in unemployment rates, but none the less all sectors display a high degree of co-ordination in the cyclical behaviour of their rates. The role of manpower policy should be to reduce these sectoral imbalances, while fiscal and monetary policy should try to reduce (as far as is practical in an open economy) the cyclical swings in the aggregate level of economic activity. The topic of stabilisation policy is discussed in Chapters 6 and 7.

5   THE STRUCTURE OF UNEMPLOYMENT

5.1   Regional Imbalances

In Table 3.9 the unemployment rates by regions of Northern Ireland and the Republic are set out. It is of interest to compare the coefficients of variation (the standard deviation as a percentage of the mean), which were 29·8 per cent (Northern Ireland) and 26·6 per cent (Republic). Thus although the regional divisions used are arbitrary, the evidence suggests a markedly similar degree of regional imbalance in both parts of Ireland. In the Republic, however, the areas of very high unemployment (the three Ulster counties and North Connacht) are remote, sparsely populated areas where one would expect a permanently higher level of frictional unemployment due to the narrow labour market. In Northern Ireland, on the other hand, in addition to predominantly rural areas such as Tyrone and Fermanagh, there are sizeable urban centres, such as the city of Londonderry, with extremely high unemployment rates. Indeed, the regional disparity in the North is due above all to the low unemployment rates in counties Antrim, Londonderry and (if the Newry region is excluded) Down, compared with the southern and western regions. This pattern is associated with the regional concentration of certain industries which have experienced a long-run decline in employment. Partly because so much of its industrial employment is of recent origin, the Republic has not yet experienced this type of regional problem, and its greater industrial diversification may avert such a problem in the future.

Table 3.9: Regional Unemployment Rates (%), Northern Ireland, 1971, and the Republic, 1972

Northern Ireland, 1971		Republic, 1972	
Belfast Co. Boro'	9·6	Dublin	6·7
Londonderry Co. Boro'	14·2	North Leinster	9·1
Antrim	5·9	South Leinster	8·7
Armagh	9·6	North Munster	8·9
Down	6·2	South Munster	7·4
Fermanagh	9·2	North Connacht	12·2
Londonderry	9·8	South Connacht	8·3
Tyrone	12·6	Cavan, Donegal,	
		Monaghan	14·2

Note: Northern Ireland figures are based on Census of Population data for those 'out of employment' as a percentage of the total economically active. Republic of Ireland figures relate to the percentage of the insured labour force on the Live Register in each area.

Sources: N I: Census of Population report, 1971, H M S O, Belfast; R I: *Trend of Employment and Unemployment,* Stationery Office, Dublin.

5.2   Occupational and Industrial Imbalances

In most countries there are substantial differences in unemployment rates between occupations and industries. The decline of some major industry (such as linen) causes an excess supply of labour with skills specific to the declining industry. This is probably acknowledged as a major problem in

Northern Ireland, but the remarkable contraction of employment in shipbuilding may now be at an end, and employment in textiles has levelled off at the 1971 figure.

Certain occupations, regardless of the industry in which they are located, are typically characterised by high unemployment rates. In the Republic Geary and Hughes (1970) drew attention to the extremely high unemployment rates characteristic of a group of unskilled labouring occupations which they dubbed 'the depressed occupations'. They also commented on the fact that there was a net inflow of young persons to these occupations each year, despite their low wage levels and poor employment prospects. These unskilled labouring occupations may be transitional between agricultural and industrial employment, and the net in-movement in the face of the high unemployment rate is comparable to the continuing net movement of people in less developed countries to urban areas already characterised by high rates of unemployment. In Ireland, however, this process may be drawing to a close, due to the contraction of the relative size of the agricultural sector and the probable narrowing of the income differential because of the rapid rise in agricultural incomes in recent years. There is evidence that since 1966 the numbers in these 'depressed occupations' are falling.

Table 3.10 shows, as far as is practicable, a comparison of the unemployment rates by industrial sector in both parts of Ireland. Caution must be exercised in interpreting these data, since not only do the industrial classifications differ in some cases between North and South, but the coverage of the insurance scheme in the Republic in 1973 was more limited than was the case in Northern Ireland. The general similarity of the pattern of unemployment rates is striking: above all, the rates recorded in the building and construction sectors in both regions are extremely high and account to a considerable extent for the high aggregate rates. Unemployment in these sectors is also more seasonal than in most others and accounts for much of the increase in unemployment during the period January to March. If the two Northern Ireland sectors in which construction workers predominate — 'construction' and 'other services' — are merged, an unemployment rate of 14·3 per cent is obtained, which is very close indeed to the 14·8 per cent recorded in 'general building and other construction' in the Republic. At the other extreme, sectors such as 'professional and scientific services', 'gas, electricity and water', 'public administration and defence' have below average unemployment rates in both areas. The remaining sectors, which include the main industrial groups, have unemployment rates in the range of $4-5\frac{1}{2}$ per cent in Northern Ireland, 5—8 per cent in the Republic.

The importance of construction workers in the total pool of unemployment is illustrated by the fact that almost one-half of those out of work in Northern Ireland are in either 'construction' or 'other services', and about one-third of those out of work in the Republic are in 'general building and

Table 3.10: Unemployment Rates by Industrial Group, Annual Average of Monthly Rates, Northern Ireland and the Republic, 1973 (Percentage of Insured Labour Force Unemployed in each Sector)

	Northern Ireland	Republic
Mining and Quarrying	5·2	8·1
Food, Drink and Tobacco	4·9	6·2
Shipbuilding and Marine Engineering	2·5	0·0
Other Engineering (N I); Metals and Engineering (R I)	4·0	4·7
Vehicles	2·2	5·1
Textiles	4·3	5·8
Clothing and Footwear (N I); Clothing (R I)	5·3	7·9
Other Manufacturing Industries[a]	4·5	7·4
Construction (N I); General Building and Other Construction (R I)	16·5	14·8
Gas, Electricity and Water	1·7	4·6
Transport and Communication	5·1	8·2
Distributive Trades	5·3	6·4
Professional and Scientific Services	1·6	3·2
Other Services (incl. N I Housing Executive)[b]	12·5	
Public Administration and Defence	4·2	3·9
Total (excluding Agriculture, Fishing, Forestry and Private Domestic Service)	6·2	7·4

[a]Includes Chemicals, Paper, Bricks and several miscellaneous sectors.

[b]This group includes Insurance, Banking and Finance and 'Miscellaneous Services'. The N I H E is included as part of the latter. In R I, the unemployment rate in Finance is low (about 4·5 per cent).

Sources: N I: *Digest of Statistics,* No. 42 (Sep. 1974), H M S O, Belfast, Tables 8 and 11; R I: *Irish Statistical Bulletin* (various issues, 1973–74), Stationery Office, Dublin, tables on 'Unemployment among Currently Insured Persons'.

other construction'. The ratio of the unemployment rate in the construction sector to the overall rate is 2·3 in Northern Ireland, 2·0 in the Republic.

This emphasis on the high unemployment rates prevalent in the construction industry in Ireland needs to be modified by taking two points into consideration: (*a*) It has been shown that the *fluctuations* in the unemployment rate in the Republic follow quite closely the cyclical pattern displayed by the rest of the economy (Walsh (1974)). Thus while this sector's unemployment rate is persistently above average, it is influenced by the general level of aggregate demand in the economy. (*b*) In other countries also, the unemployment rate in the construction industry is typically higher than the overall rate. In Great Britain in 1973, for example, the rate for the construction industry was 6·3 per cent compared with a national rate of 2·4 per cent — the ratio of the rates was 2·6, slightly higher than that found in either part of Ireland. Thus the phenomenon of extremely high unemployment rates in the construction sector does not, of itself, point to a severe structural problem. On the other hand, manpower and labour market policy should be directed to the task of trying to reduce the persistently high level of frictional unemployment in this sector.

Given that high rates of unemployment are a commonplace feature of the construction sector, the question arises whether the high overall unemployment rate in Ireland is partly attributable to an exceptional importance of this sector in the economy. Construction accounts for a much higher proportion of the non-agricultural labour force in both parts of Ireland than in Britain. Thus the greater relative importance of construction as a sector in the Irish economies contributes to the high overall unemployment rate. Moreover, Ireland is the only E E C area, other than Italy, where the construction sector is not heavily dependent on immigrant workers.

We have no very reliable occupational data on unemployment. The available evidence is consistent with the picture that emerges from the industrial analysis, namely, very high unemployment rates among the unskilled, especially those in general labouring. In the 1971 Census of Population in the Republic the proportion of male employees recorded as 'out of work' was 18·1 per cent among builders' labourers, and 21·9 per cent among 'labourers and unskilled workers (not elsewhere stated)'.

These two occupational groups contained almost 19,000 out of a total of 44,000 unemployed men. At the other extreme, there were thirty-nine skilled and semi-skilled occupations, containing 23 per cent of the employee labour force, in which the unemployment rate was less than 3 per cent. There has, however, been a significant downward trend in the proportion of the labour force that is unskilled, and this has been accompanied by a decline in the proportion of the unemployed who are unskilled. These trends have been analysed more fully in Walsh (1974). Comparable data are not available for Northern Ireland for any date more recent than 1961, when 24 per cent of the male labourers recorded in the Census of Population were returned as 'out of employment', compared with an unemployment rate among male non-agricultural employees of 13·6 per cent.

The main theme of this subsection has been the particular unemployment problem experienced by the unskilled and those employed in the construction sector in Ireland. Allied to this is the fact that emigration from Ireland has been heavily concentrated among workers from this occupational group: 31 per cent of the economically active males who migrated from the Republic in 1965 and who were recorded in the 1966 British census were described as 'labourers'. Undoubtedly it is among this group that the most pronounced labour surplus exists. In his discussion 'Why has

Britain had Full Employment since the War?' Matthews (1968) drew attention to the dualistic nature of the labour market in Britain before 1914 and in the underdeveloped world today,

> with some workers [being] engaged in relatively capital-intensive industries such as manufacturing or railways, or else in privileged occupations such as government service, while the rest of the labour force remains outside the circle in low-productivity employment or else without any employment at all. This state of affairs had not entirely ceased to hold in Britain in 1914. The unskilled labour that jostled for jobs at the docks, on the building sites and in many other trades was the remnant of the chronic labour surplus associated with incomplete development. (Matthews (1968), p. 565.)

Harris and Todaro, in the article referred to earlier in this chapter, have provided a more analytical model of this situation. Undoubtedly Ireland, with a relatively high rate of natural increase, a large proportion of the total labour force still in low-income family farming, a high proportion of the non-agricultural labour force in the construction sector, and very pronounced differentials in unemployment rates between skilled and white-collar occupations on the one hand and unskilled occupations on the other, fits this model rather well. In particular, the unskilled labouring occupations may be seen as the sector through which the surplus agricultural labour force passes during the process of development and full absorption into the non-agricultural labour force.

6   MANPOWER POLICY

The unemployment problem in both parts of Ireland has influenced government policy in the whole area of industrialisation and development. The financial incentives given to industry have been discussed in Chapter 2. From the viewpoint of manpower policy, we should examine these incentives in the light of their probable effects on the level of employment. Undoubtedly, the amount of money made available by government for use as investment grants has a major impact on the rate of growth of new industries. Most of the grants available — initial grants, advance factories, accelerated depreciation, corporate profits tax relief (in the Republic) — involve subsidies to capital, and it may be questioned whether these types of subsidies are the most appropriate in dealing with economies where *labour* is the surplus factor. This point has been made in a recent study of the cost of capital to Irish industry, where it is shown that, in line with international experience, the ratio of wage to capital costs has fallen significantly and that the Republic's package of incentives to industry has added appreciably to this decline (Geary, Walsh and Copeland (1975)). The appropriateness of these incentives has also been questioned by the recent survey *Manpower Policy in Ireland* (O E C D (1974)):

> If the main problem is labour surplus, there are arguments for compensating directly for the differences between actual wages and some kind of equilibrium wage (the latter being lower) than [*sic*] to give subsidies for capital equipment. Without detailed control there will be a tendency for capital subsidies to create a bias towards more capital-intensive projects. (p. 32)

In Northern Ireland, however, two policies have been implemented that directly affect wage costs. First, the Selective Employment Tax (S E T), designed primarily to redistribute labour away from the services sector, was, up to September 1967, partially refunded in respect of male employees in certain activities for which British employees received no refund. This established a temporary subsidy on employment in Northern Ireland compared with the rest of the United Kingdom. S E T was abolished in April 1973. More importantly, Northern Ireland benefitted from the introduction of the Regional Employment Premium because the entire province was classified as a Development Area of the United Kingdom.

The Regional Employment Premium (R E P) was introduced in 1967. Employers in the Development Areas of the United Kingdom are entitled to a subsidy for each employee (initially £1·50 weekly per male employee, raised to £3·00 in 1974). This subsidy significantly lowers labour costs in manufacturing industry and reinforces the existing incentives for industry to locate in Development Areas. The R E P's effects have not yet been assessed by economists, but a survey by the Confederation of British Industry in 1973 is reported to have shown that abolition of the R E P would put between 20,000 and 50,000 men out of work in the Development Areas. 'It also found that R E P was particularly useful in Ulster. Half of Ulster firms said they employed more men because of it.' (*The Economist*, 27 Jul. 1974, p. 80) The absence of a similar measure in the Republic is a major difference between both manpower and regional policy, North and South.

6.1 Training and Retraining

The Republic has been expanding the scope and size of its training programmes. The body responsible for these programmes is An Comhairle Oiliúna (AnCO), which administers a levy/grant scheme. Each firm in an industry contributes a percentage of its wage bill to a fund and in return is awarded a grant if it fulfils certain conditions regarding staff training. AnCO also operates nine training centres with an annual through-put of about 4,000 trainees (as of 1974) and is currently planning a major expansion of these centres, with financial support from the E E C Social Fund.

In Northern Ireland, Government Training Centres capable of accommodating over 2,000 trainees have been in existence since the early 1970s. In 1973 4,700 trainees were trained in these centres, which concentrate on providing skills in those engineering occupations most in demand by new industry. Substantial training allowances are paid to trainees. Grants are also available to employers for on-the-job training. In addition, Industrial Training Boards have been set up in most industries to assess the individual sector's required apprenticeship intake and, working together with the Youth Employment and Technical Education Services, to undertake the training and placement of apprentices. Data for 1972 show that of the 14,300 young people entering employment in Northern Ireland in 1972, 5,600 were in apprenticeships or some type of planned training; an additional 1,700 girls entered clerical employment. In general, the resources devoted to industrial training in Northern Ireland appear to be greater not only than those available in the Republic but also than those provided in Great Britain. However, expenditure on this heading has risen very rapidly in the Republic in recent years, and further expansion is being planned.

7   CONCLUSIONS

In this chapter the Irish unemployment problem has received considerable emphasis. The size of the problem has been illustrated by reference to the chronically high unemployment rates in both parts of Ireland, as well as to the heavy emigration that has been characteristic of the whole island for many generations. The extent to which this surplus labour problem is 'demand-deficient' or 'structural' has been discussed, and the policy responses adopted in both parts of Ireland have been described.

Without doubt, one of the main indictments of economic policy in both parts of Ireland is the continuing failure to overcome the labour surplus problem. In part this is probably due to the restricted range of policy instruments that have been adopted, and especially to the heavy reliance on 'manpower policy' and subsidies to enterprises that would not otherwise locate in Ireland to solve a problem that may require more fundamental remedies.

Other policies have, in theory at least, been available in the Republic of Ireland. Among these is an independent exchange rate policy, which may offer an opportunity for a more relevant macro-economic policy and a radical attack on the endemic unemployment problem. Whatever the potential efficacy of an independent exchange rate policy, it is evident that the unemployment problem is an integral part of the macro-economic issues discussed in Chapters 6 and 7.

REFERENCES

Geary, R. C. and Hughes, J. G. (1970): *Certain Aspects of Non-Agricultural Unemployment in Ireland* (E S R I Paper No. 52), Dublin.

Geary, P. T., Walsh, B. and Copeland, J. (1975): 'The Cost of Capital to Irish Industry', *Economic and Social Review,* Vol. 6, No. 3 (Apr.).

Harris, J. R. and Todaro, M. P. (1970): 'Migration, Unemployment and Development: A Two-Sector Analysis', *American Economic Review,* Vol. 60, No. 1 (Mar.).

Lipsey, R. G. (1974): 'The Micro Theory of the Phillips Curve Reconsidered: A Reply to Holmes and Smyth', *Economica,* Vol. 41, No. 161 (Feb.).

Matthews, R. C. O. (1968): 'Why has Britain had Full Employment since the War?', *Economic Journal,* Vol. 78, No. 311 (Sep.).

Mortensen, D. T. (1970): 'Job Search, the Duration of Unemployment, and the Phillips Curve', *American Economic Review,* Vol. 60, No. 5 (Dec.).

O E C D (1974): *Manpower Policy in Ireland 1974,* O E C D Publications Office, Paris.

Walsh, B. M. (1973): *Women and Unemployment in Ireland: Results of a National Survey* (E S R I Paper No. 69), Dublin.

Walsh, B. M. (1974): *The Structure of Unemployment in Ireland* (E S R I Paper No. 77), Dublin.

Social Security

J. W. O'HAGAN

1   INTRODUCTION

To secure a livelihood, man has in principle two sources of income at his disposal, his assets and his working capacity. The great majority depend for a livelihood on the latter, i.e. on wages. However, only those participating in the production process earn wages and little more than one-third of the population takes part in production in Ireland, as was shown in Table 3.2. The remaining two-thirds — which includes the aged, the sick, the unemployed and children — are excluded from primary income distribution. It was, and is, largely in response to this fact that social security measures have had to be introduced in Ireland and elsewhere.

Narrowly defined, social security may be viewed as 'the result achieved by a comprehensive and successful series of measures for protecting the public (or a large sector of it) from the economic distress that, in the absence of such measures, would be caused by the stoppage of earnings in sickness, unemployment or old age and after death . . . and for subsidising families bringing up young children' (Paukert (1968), pp. 425—6). To meet these requirements social security measures must fulfil three functions: (a) income compensation, (b) risk compensation, and (c) income redistribution (Zollner, (1970)). Income compensation brings about a transfer of income from one stage of life to another and refers mainly to provisions for cessation of earnings in old age. The level of benefits is determined by the contributions previously paid either to a bank, an insurance company, one's employer, or the government. Risk compensation, which effects a transfer of income between different individuals, is rooted historically in private insurance. The price charged for coverage against a risk will depend on the likelihood of its occurrence, and benefits are paid, subject to contribution conditions, for the duration of the income loss. Income redistribution, which also brings about a transfer of income between different individuals, is the most contentious function of social security measures. Entitlement depends on the gap between one's income and one's needs as decided by statute.

Some or all of the functions of social security could in principle be performed by either private insurance companies, occupational welfare schemes, personal saving, National Assistance and/or compulsory National Insurance schemes. A combination of all of these schemes exists in Ireland. In the last twenty years or so, however, the number aided by National Assistance and/ or compulsory National Insurance schemes has dramatically increased so that today the state plays a very prominent role in ensuring social security.[1]

2 DEVELOPMENT OF STATE SOCIAL SECURITY SERVICES IN IRELAND

Before 1921 social security services in Ireland comprised two elements. The first, the Poor Law, arose from the extension of the machinery of unions, workhouses, Board of Guardians and local rating devised in England in 1834 to Ireland in 1838. The second, state provision, was of more recent origin as non-contributory old-age pensions and unemployment and disability insurance had been introduced in 1908 and 1911 respectively. These two acts, in fact, were as a result of the first real upsurge of public demand for government intervention to protect those impoverished by loss of earnings. Five reasons have been given for this change of attitude: the enfranchisement of the working class in 1867—85, the spread of socialist ideas, the paternalistic humanitarianism of the time, the realisation that the amelioration of poverty was of advantage to industrialists, and the social surveys that quantified the extent and causes of poverty. (See George (1973).)

Since 1921, state social security programmes in Northern Ireland and the Republic have developed in differing ways. Northern Ireland not only maintained the schemes of non-contributory pensions and unemployment insurance it inherited in 1921 but ever since has adopted every new social security measure introduced in Britain. (See Lawrence (1965), pp. 160—65.) On the other hand, although the Republic also retained the social security schemes it inherited in 1921, it has tended to introduce income maintenance measures similar to those in Britain only after a time lag, if at all. As the Republic's system, however, is to all intents and purposes a reflection of social ideas and policy in Britain and Northern Ireland, a chronological listing of developments in social security there, with some analysis of the thinking behind them, will be presented. The history of the developments which took place in the Republic should then complete the picture.

From 1911 to 1942 there was no major innovation in the field of social security in Britain and Northern Ireland. However, some alterations and extensions to the system took place. The state sickness and unemployment insurance schemes initiated in 1911 were extended and virtually covered

1 A useful discussion of the rationale for the prominent role of the state in the area of social policy is contained in Culyer (1973).

most of the working-class population by the outbreak of the Second World War. A contributory pensions scheme was introduced in 1925 to run alongside and eventually replace the 1908 scheme. Lastly, the Unemployment Assistance Board was established in 1934 in response to the increase in the number of long-term unemployed resulting from the depression.

The year 1942 saw the publication of the Beveridge Report, 'the *locus classicus* of British Social Security', which brought the processes initiated in 1911 to their logical outcome. It was the first-ever comprehensive piece of social planning in Britain and Northern Ireland and was based on four main principles, principles which were implicit in the 1911 act and/or the intervening legislation. The first was that of universality in that *every* adult citizen should be *compulsorily* insured against the main risks of income interruption, chiefly old age, unemployment and sickness. The second principle was that of insurance, in that payment of benefit depended on having paid the necessary number of contributions. From an actuarial point of view, however, it has little meaning, as a person's contributions never covered expected benefits. Contributions and benefits were, in fact, to be flat-rate (the third principle) and thus not related to risk or need. Besides, part of the cost was to be met by the employer and the balance by the government. The fourth principle was that of a national minimum, i.e. that everyone in need should receive a subsistence income, and only this, from the state. This would be payable of right, preferably through insurance benefits. The system of National Assistance, later called Supplementary Benefits, was seen only as a safety net to protect those in need who, for one reason or another, did not qualify under the insurance scheme or who found their insurance benefits inadequate. It was hoped that eventually there would be no need for this safety net. These four principles were enshrined in the National Insurance Act (U K) of 1946 and, with one notable exception, have dominated most thinking on state social security measures in Britain, Northern Ireland and the Republic to this day.

The notable exception just alluded to is the principle of flat-rate contributions and benefits. Beveridge had intended that anyone who considered the state benefits inadequate should make, and be encouraged to make, private provision. The reasons why many would, and did, became clearer over time, and arose from the increased understanding that relative poverty may be said to exist if one's standard of living is substantially lower at one point in time relative to a standard enjoyed formerly. The *stated* need for government action arose from the fact that such provision could reasonably only be made through occupational schemes, schemes which were not available to all. This need was intensified when workers needed to be placated to accept the large-scale redundancies which were anticipated as a result of industrial reorganisation in the 1960s and 1970s. As a result, since 1966 all the unemployed in Britain and Northern Ireland who are covered by unemployment and sickness insurance in particular receive a flat-rate benefit and an earnings-related supplement for a specified period of time.[2] This was the first and only major break with Beveridge to the present time.

Some other less notable developments since Beveridge were the Contracts of Employment Act (1963), the Industrial Training Act (1964) and the Redundancy Payments Act (1965). However, one scheme of potentially great significance, and of great practical significance in Northern Ireland, is the Family Income Supplement (F I S) introduced in 1971. One of the drawbacks, a point which is taken up again later, of the state social security system in Britain and Northern Ireland is that Supplementary Benefits cannot be claimed by persons in full-time employment even though their earnings are below the Supplementary Benefits level. F I S was designed partly to overcome this problem.

Although an unemployment assistance programme had been introduced in 1933 to replace Poor Law relief, the first major development in the provision of state social security in the Republic did not take place until 1952. The Social Welfare Act of that year led to the amalgamation of all insurance and assistance programmes to form one unified system. At the same time, the insurance schemes in operation were extended in coverage, but the act still excluded the higher-paid salaried workers and the large number of self-employed. The next major development took place in 1961 when old-age pensions were included under the National Insurance scheme, twenty-six years after such a move took place in Northern Ireland. The Industrial Training and Redundancy Payments Acts introduced in 1967 had objectives similar to the 1963—65 and 1964 acts in Northern Ireland. Perhaps the most important social security developments in the state's history took place in 1974. First, National Insurance was extended to cover *all* wage and salaried employees and, secondly, *pay-related* contributions and benefits, for unemployment and sickness in particular, were introduced, with conditions very similar to those prevailing in Northern Ireland since 1966.

By 1974, therefore, the two systems had become remarkably similar in general principle. The fundamental differences still remaining were that, unlike their Northern counterparts, the large number of self-employed people in the Republic do not have to be compulsorily insured and, arising from the relatively high level of Supplementary Benefits, that employed people in Northern Ireland can obtain a F I S. Moreover, the financial arrangements of the two systems still differ to a considerable extent.

Table 3A.1 outlines the trend in total expenditure on National Insurance and National Assistance expressed as a percentage of personal incomes and in the percentage of that total devoted to insurance payments. A number of interesting findings emerge. First, state social security expenditure accounts for a much higher proportion of personal incomes in Northern

2 Because of intense party-political controversy about the objectives of pension schemes and the means of achieving them, little fundamental change has taken place in UK state provision of pensions. (See Kaim-Caudle (1973), pp. 170—73.)

Ireland than in the Republic, a finding that can be largely explained by the differing coverage of the social insurance schemes and the somewhat higher National Assistance/Supplementary Benefits level in Northern Ireland. Secondly, and partly following from the above, National Insurance accounts for a much higher proportion of total expenditures in Northern Ireland than in the Republic, although this situation is changing somewhat and should alter appreciably with the introduction of the new social security measures in the Republic in 1974. Lastly, Supplementary Benefits have steadily increased as a percentage of total expenditure in Northern Ireland, in contrast to Beveridge's hopes, and this despite the fact that everyone is compulsorily insured.

Table 3A.1: Trends in National Insurance and Assistance Expenditure, Northern Ireland and the Republic, 1962—73

Time period[a]		1962—65	1966—69	1970—73
National Insurance and Assistance expenditure[b] as % of personal incomes	N. Ireland[c]	10·7	12·1	11·7
	Republic[d]	6·4	7·2	7·8
National Insurance expenditure[e] as % of total National Insurance and Assistance expenditure	N. Ireland	69·3	66·5	62·3
	Republic	45·0	48·2	50·8

[a] Financial years ending March 1962 to March 1973.

[b] Inclusive of expenditure on administration.

[c] Both the expenditure and income data are for the financial years ending March 1962 to March 1972.

[d] The expenditure data relate to the financial years ending March 1963 to March 1973 and the income data to the calendar years 1962 to 1972.

[e] Net of administration costs.

Sources: N I: *Digest of Statistics,* H M S O, Belfast, various issues and *Social Security Statistics,* H M S O, London, various issues; R I: *National Income and Expenditure,* Stationery Office, Dublin, various issues, and information supplied by the Department of Social Welfare, Dublin.

Table 3A.2 outlines the trend in the main National Insurance categories when expressed as a percentage of total National Insurance expenditure.[3]

3 With the exception of children's allowances, these are also the main categories of expenditure under National Assistance/Supplementary Benefits.

The relatively minor importance of unemployment benefits should be noted, as economists often tend to overlook this point when discussing the labour supply effects of state social security schemes as a whole. As might be expected from the previous remarks, old-age contributory pensions is the dominant category in Northern Ireland. There has been no marked change in the proportion of total expenditure going to each category.

Table 3A.2: Percentages of National Insurance Expenditure[a] Allocated to Different Purposes, Northern Ireland and the Republic, 1962–73

		1962–65	1966–69	1970–73
Unemployment benefits	N. Ireland	14·8	13·8	10·9
	Republic	17·8	18·2	18·1
Old-age contributory pensions[a]	N. Ireland	54·3	53·8	55·3
	Republic	27·7	26·9	26·5
Sickness/disability[b] benefits	N. Ireland	19·8	22·0	23·3
	Republic	31·1	31·0	30·9
Other	N. Ireland	11·1	10·4	10·5
	Republic	23·4	23·9	24·2

[a]The 1971 figure includes retirement pensions, introduced in 1970, which are payable at age 65 to insured persons who retire and satisfy the contribution conditions. Until July 1973 old-age pensions were only payable at age 70, but this is to be steadily reduced to 65 by 1977.

[b]The 1971 figure includes invalidity benefits, also introduced in 1970, which are payable to insured persons who are permanently incapable of work.

Note: The figures are for financial years and are net of administration costs.

Sources: N I: *Social Security Statistics,* H M S O, London, various issues; R I: Reports of the Department of Social Welfare, Dublin.

Table 3A.3 gives a comparison both of some of the more important National Insurance payments applicable in Northern Ireland and the Republic in April 1975 and of their growth over the period 1961–75. Some interesting points emerge from this table. First, payments have grown *considerably* faster in the Republic, to the point that by April 1975 they were nearly as high as in Northern Ireland for every category shown.[4] This is partly due to the relatively faster increase in living standards in the Republic (see Chapter 1). Secondly, up to 1972 payments in the Republic kept more or less in line with the rise in personal incomes whereas they fell

4 Maximum assistance rates in the Republic were still below the maximum Supplementary Benefit levels in Northern Ireland, but the gap between them has also closed appreciably in the 1961–75 period.

somewhat behind in Northern Ireland, especially between 1968 and 1972. However, in both parts of Ireland contributory pensions have kept sufficiently in line with living standards to enable it to be asserted that governments can and do provide pensions that are related to overall rises in money incomes.

Table 3A.3: Rates Payable April 1975 and their Growth, Northern Ireland and the Republic, 1961—75 (1961=100)

	Northern Ireland		Republic	
Contributory pension:				
Personal	£11·60	(288)	£10·50	(525)
With adult dependant	£18·50	(400)	£17·50	(511)
Unemployed or man on sick leave:	£ 9·80	(341)	£ 9·40	(579)
With adult dependant	£15·90	(344)	£15·50	(555)
Plus 4 children[a]	£23·80	(344)	£25·20	(611)

[a]Apart from the basic benefits, an unemployed man or man on sick leave can get pay-related benefits and children's allowances. However, the inclusion of these does not appreciably affect the picture emerging from the Northern Ireland/Republic comparison above.

Sources: N I: Department of Health and Social Services, *Family Benefits and Pensions in Northern Ireland,* Belfast 1975; R I: Department of Social Welfare, *Summary of Social Insurance and Assistance Services, 1974—75,* Dublin, and information supplied by the Department of Social Welfare, Dublin.

Although there are few direct implications arising out of E E C membership for the development of social security in Ireland, apart from the fact that benefits are paid to immigrant workers from other member states on the same basis as native workers, undoubtedly comparisons will be made between the social security provisions in existence in the member countries. Inevitably, this will bring pressure to bear on individual countries to alter their social security arrangements in line with overall community standards.

Table 3A.4 compares the social budget expenditures of the member states of the community both as a percentage of G N P and by category of benefit. Although probably only 50 to 70 per cent of this expenditure is strictly for social security purposes, the remainder largely consisting of health expenditure and public sector superannuation schemes, the comparison is still of considerable value.

First, it can be seen that the Republic devotes the lowest percentage of G N P to social budget expenditure. From Table 3A.1 it would seem likely that Northern Ireland is about average in this respect. However, as with

Table 3A.4: Social Budget Expenditure[a] in the Member States of the EEC

Country:	Belgium	Denmark	Germany	France	Republic of Ireland	Italy	Luxem- bourg	Nether- lands	UK
Total expenditure[b] as % of GNP:									
1972	18·3	20·2	20·2	17·6	12·9	20·3	18·8	22·4	16·1
1975[c]	18·4	22·3	20·7	18·1	14·7	21·0	17·4	25·5	15·8
% of total expenditure in 1972 devoted to									
Unemployment	5·4	3·6	0·8	1·1	5·7	1·6	0·0	4·1	5·1
Sickness	23·0	27·8	29·0	26·7	29·2	26·1	17·9	27·0	26·3
Invalidity/industrial injuries/occupational disease	13·6	14·9	12·1	5·8	10·9	18·0	13·4	17·6	9·3
Old age	36·6	35·6	45·6	38·5	37·1	35·9	57·0	38·4	47·5
Family benefits	16·7	15·0	8·1	17·2	13·1	8·4	10·9	12·3	7·4
Other	4·7	3·1	4·4	10·7	4·0	10·0	0·8	0·6	4·4

[a] The only major difference between the expenditure figures used here and those for total National Insurance and National Assistance expenditure looked at in Table 3A.1 is the inclusion of social security payments in kind (chiefly on health) and some public sector employee pensions. It should be noted that the German and French data include employers' voluntary benefits and that the figures for all countries, except Ireland, include bene- fits to victims of political events or natural disasters.
[b] Net of administration.
[c] Projection.

Source: Commission of the European Communities, *First European Social Budget: 1970–75*, Brussels 1974.

the comparison in Table 3A.1, the low ratio for the Republic can be partly explained by the limited coverage of National Insurance. Moreover, when account is also taken of the relatively low level of G N P *per capita* in the Republic, 'it would be extremely difficult to assert that Ireland compares favourably or otherwise with the other E E C countries in social security consciousness' (O'Hagan and O'Higgins (1973)).

Secondly, when the comparison of Table 3A.2 is extended to cover both *total* expenditure and *other* countries, the general findings remain unaltered. Provision for old age and sickness still dominates, with expenditure on un-employment not constituting more than 5·4 per cent of total expenditure in any country. In fact, it is interesting to note the marked similarity between the member states in the pattern of expenditure, especially given that the data are only comparable in a very general sense.

This completes this brief description of the development of state social security measures in Ireland. It remains to assess these measures in the light of the main role they are intended to play as set out in the introduction.

3   ASSESSMENT

In Northern Ireland and Britain parliament specifies a minimum level of income (Supplementary Benefit levels) below which it is considered un-desirable that any family's income should fall. As such, Supplementary Benefits provide a useful benchmark against which state social security pro-visions can be assessed. Unfortunately, the political process in the Republic does not produce any such yardstick.

It has been estimated that between 5 and 8 per cent of the population of the U K in 1969 were in 'poverty' (i.e. below the Supplementary Benefit levels),[5] and the figure for Northern Ireland is likely to have been consider-ably greater. The absolute number of people that these figures involve is staggering. Many have asked how this happened when everyone was either compulsorily insured and/or entitled to Supplementary Benefits. There are two main explanations for this situation.

First, ever since the end of the Second World War Supplementary Bene-fit levels, when rent allowance is included, have been *higher* than flat-rate unemployment and sickness benefits and, in particular, contributory old-age pensions. This has meant that a very large number of pensioners would have had to obtain *means-tested* Supplementary Benefits to avoid falling into 'poverty'. Many of these pensioners did not, in fact, claim these bene-fits and thus fell below the Supplementary Benefits level, thereby account-ing for a large percentage of those in 'poverty'. The low 'take-up' was partly

5 Using a 'proposed *ad hoc* poverty level somewhat below the Northern Ireland Supplementary Benefit levels, it has been estimated that 20 to 30 per cent of the population in the Republic were in 'poverty' in 1971. (See Ó Cinnéide (1972).)

due to ignorance of rights and partly to the stigma that the process imposes.[6]

Wage earners comprised a second general category of persons who fell below the Supplementary Benefit levels. As mentioned before, Supplementary Benefits *cannot* be paid to anyone in full-time employment even though many people's earnings, especially those with large families, fall below the official minimum standards. Moreover, if a man is out of work, he cannot receive an amount in state assistance that would bring his income within 15 per cent of that which he would receive at work. This is the 'wage stop' rule; and the lower level of earnings in Northern Ireland relative to the UK means that it was, and is, particularly affected by this rule. The F I S only partly alleviates this problem in that it does not fully make up the deficiency of family income below Supplementary Benefit levels, especially in the case of a family with above average rent to pay. Besides, the scheme involves yet another major means test and, partly as a result of this, not all of those families who are eligible actually apply.

These findings, even given that the situation has improved in the intervening years, point to the conclusion that, by the government's own standards, a position of social security does not exist in Northern Ireland and Britain. Taking U K standards as a yardstick, the situation is considerably worse in the Republic. Moreover, and of more importance, as indicated in the previous section, state social security payments in Northern Ireland have not kept pace with rising living standards over the last six years or so, thereby casting doubts on the adequacy of Supplementary Benefits as a minimum standard. In addition, the baffling array of small assistance payments and benefits in kind as well as the overlapping of income taxation and poverty alleviation programmes has frequently resulted in very high marginal tax rates and administrative chaos. This, then, is the background to the increasing demands for a radical reorganisation of state social security measures in Britain, developments which undoubtedly will have a profound influence on social security measures in Ireland.

REFERENCES

Culyer, A. J. (1973): *The Economics of Social Policy*, Martin Robertson, London.

George, V. (1973): *Social Security and Society*, Routledge and Kegan Paul, London.

Kaim-Caudle, P. R. (1973): *Comparative Social Policy and Social Security*, Martin Robertson, London.

6 National Assistance was renamed Supplementary Benefits in 1966 and improved this somewhat. In the Republic some evidence has been compiled on the views of Home Assistance recipients to the payment process. Although Home Assistance accounts for a small proportion of total National Assistance expenditure, it is the most means-tested transfer. (See Sheehan (1974).)

Lawrence, R. J. (1965): *The Government of Northern Ireland*, Clarendon Press, Oxford.

Ó Cinnéide, S. (1972): 'The Extent of Poverty in Ireland', *Social Studies*, Vol. 1, No. 4 (Aug.).

O'Hagan, J. and O'Higgins, M. (1973): 'Are Ireland's Social Security Payments Too Small? A Comment', *Economic and Social Review*, Vol. 5, No. 1 (Oct.).

Paukert, P. (1968): 'Social Security and Income Redistribution', *International Labour Review*, Vol. 98, No. 5 (Nov.).

Sheehan, M. (1974): *The Meaning of Poverty*, Council for Social Welfare, Blackrock, Co. Dublin.

Zollner, O. (1970): 'Relating Social Insurance Benefits to Earnings', *International Social Security Review*, Vol. 30, No. 2.

CHAPTER 4

The Foreign Sector

DERMOT McALEESE

1 INTRODUCTION

'Although Ireland is an island, this does not mean it is an economic unit.' (Matthew, Wilson and Parkinson (1970)) This statement serves as a useful starting-point to this chapter. For the most striking feature of the Irish economy, regardless of whether it is viewed as two separate units or as a whole, is its small size in economic terms. The combined G D P of the Irish Republic and Northern Ireland amounts to only a small fraction of that of most Western European countries.

One of the few safe generalisations in international economics is that the degree of a country's participation in the international economy varies inversely with the size of its domestic market. Small countries tend, *ceteris paribus,* to have higher ratios of imports and exports to G N P than large countries. As has been shown in Chapter 1, the Republic's trade ratios are nearly twice as high as those of the U K, and Northern Ireland's are even higher still.

The reason for small countries' greater dependence on international trade is that larger countries can avail of all the same advantages by trading internally. Thus what passes for interregional trade in a large country would be classified as international trade if that country were subdivided into a number of separate national entities. There is plenty of evidence substantiating the existence of large interregional trade flows. Indeed, trade at an interregional level appears to have reached a far more advanced state of specialisation in many areas than trade between countries of comparable size.

Countries engage in trade because it is mutually advantageous to do so. In this they are no different from regions within a country or, for that matter, from individuals within a region. The gains from trade arise because different countries enjoy a comparative advantage in different goods. The theory of comparative advantage or comparative costs is a familiar ingredient in basic economic textbooks and need not be explained here. Suffice it to say that comparative advantage arises for a number of reasons. Some have to do with natural endowments. This would explain, for instance, why Saudi Arabia has a comparative advantage in oil relative to the UK or Ireland. Others relate to factor proportions. Thus a labour-abundant country like India can produce labour-intensive goods much more cheaply than most West European countries. Economies of scale, product differentiation and market organisation also play an important part in determining comparative advantage, particularly in the case of manufactured goods.

In the case of the Irish Republic and Northern Ireland, the trade-dependence or openness of the economy, as reflected in high foreign trade to GDP ratios, and, more particularly, in a high marginal propensity to import, has a number of important implications for economic policy. First, the heavy leakage out of the economy through imports restricts the effectiveness of fiscal policy. A second consequence of high trade dependence is the limitation it sets on a small economy's ability to control domestic prices and insulate them from world trends. With fixed exchange rates, increases in world price tend to frustrate domestic price stabilisation policies by raising the price of imports and also by exerting strong upward pressures on export prices. In this way, world inflation is 'imported' into the economy from abroad. Thirdly, changes in the terms of trade (i.e. the ratio of export to import prices) exercise a very important influence on real income in a small open economy compared with larger economies. Thus the estimated 14 per cent decline in the Republic's terms of trade in 1974 involved a 6 per cent fall in real incomes (Durkan and Kelleher (1974), p. 16). Fourthly, cyclical swings in the economies of Ireland's major trading partners tend to be transmitted very rapidly to the Irish economies; and the ability of a small economy to insulate itself against them is strictly limited. Thus a fall in exports following a downturn in the world economy cannot be compensated for by an expansionary domestic fiscal policy without running into serious balance of payments difficulties. A final consequence of openness, which we shall discuss in more detail later, is that a strong self-correcting mechanism tends to be at work in the balance of payments in the sense that exogenous changes in exports (positive or negative) tend to be offset by a relatively high induced value of imports. These implications are incorporated in the formal model presented in Chapter 1.

This emphasis on the inherent openness of the Irish economies now seems quite unexceptional. A few decades ago, however, in 1932 a future Minister for Industry and Commerce in the Republic, just prior to taking up office, expressed an opinion regarding Ireland's potential viability which contrasts starkly with the opening quotation of this chapter: 'We believe that Ireland can be made a self-contained unit, providing all the necessities of living in adequate quantities for the people residing in the island at the moment and probably for a much larger number.' (Quoted in Whitaker (1974), p. 40.) This belief that Ireland could be made into a self-sufficient unit won few adherents in Northern Ireland. Indeed, the fear that an independent Ireland would resort to protection and thus weaken the ability of Northern industries to export, both by making imported inputs dearer and by inviting foreign retaliation, served only to strengthen many Northerners' already strong antipathy towards the idea of a United Ireland.

As it turned out, the Irish Republic opted for a policy of protection. In the 1930s, of course, almost every country in Europe was engaged in protecting its home industries. The efforts of the government in the Republic to do likewise earned widespread support, including that of no less eminent an authority than J. M. Keynes, who declared that he found 'much to attract' him in the 'economic outlook' of the government. The United Kingdom government also raised tariffs on imports; Ryan (1949) estimated that the UK tariff in 1937 was about 65 per cent of the corresponding tariff level in the Republic. Thus, by proxy, Northern Ireland also received a degree of protection, although the bulk of its trade (that with Britain) remained unaffected.

It is beyond the scope of this chapter to trace in detail the history, implications and development of the Republic's era of protectionism. The policy succeeded to a certain extent — a small industrial base of light consumer goods and intermediate goods was created and industrial employment rose rapidly, especially in the early stages. The difficulty, however, was that continuing growth proved progressively more difficult to achieve. By the 1950s it became clear that the attempt to make the Republic's economy more self-sufficient had achieved all it could achieve and that a change was necessary. Complete self-sufficiency was seen to be an unattainable goal without a drastic reduction in living standards. Gradually the Republic moved back towards a policy of free trade. In 1965 the Anglo-Irish Free Trade Area Agreement (AIFTA) was signed, and in 1973 the Republic joined the European Economic Community. The transitional period to full free trade with Western Europe is now well under way.

While both parts of the island therefore share many key features, one must keep in mind the fact that the economy of the Republic is now in the process of transition from protection to free trade, whereas Northern Ireland, by contrast, has remained fully integrated in the economic sense with Britain, its major trading partner, for the last century and a half. Naturally, much interest attaches to the question of how this contrasting experience influenced the present pattern of international trade and payments in the two parts of Ireland.

In order to place these issues in perspective, however, the composition and geographical distribution of Ireland's foreign trade must first be examined. This will be done in the next section. After that, the main features of the capital account and the 'invisible' items on current account will be discussed. An analysis of the trade policy options and trade prospects for the Republic and Northern Ireland is then undertaken. The final section of the chapter presents a brief summary of the discussion and of the major conclusions to be drawn from it.

2   THE STRUCTURE OF MERCHANDISE TRADE

2.1   Availability of Statistics

Statistics of merchandise trade for the Republic are available in considerable detail and have been systematically collected and published since 1924. The basis of compilation and the classification of commodity groups have changed a number of times since then, notably in 1935 and 1963, but consistent series for many aggregates are obtainable from 1924 onwards.

Northern Ireland's official trade statistics are much less satisfactory, and the compilation and classification suffer as regards quality and coverage. The compilation of regional trade statistics, however, involves special difficulties. In a sense we are lucky to have any trade data whatsoever for Northern Ireland. Northern Ireland fares much better in this respect than Scotland or Wales, as British regional economists have often observed.

Northern Ireland's trade is currently classified by S I T C two-digit groupings. Although information on trade flows with areas other than the U K is collected in the normal way, details on trade with Britain are obtained from the Harbour Authorities, whose data come solely in terms of the gross weight of the goods traded (i.e. in tonnes, kilograms, etc.). The Ministry of Commerce is thus left with the difficult task of assigning values to these physical quantities. This is done in three ways: (*a*) by using unit values of total U K trade, (*b*) by direct inquiry from the firms involved in the trade, and (*c*) by utilising Census of Production average values. Inevitably, as the ministry itself quite properly underlines, the translation of volume into value in this manner involves a wide margin of error, and the resulting statistics can be taken as no more than indicative of the broad magnitudes involved.

A further difficulty in dealing with Northern Ireland's trade statistics is that no distinction is drawn between ordinary trade and transit trade. Thus many of Northern Ireland's 'imports' from Britain are, in effect, destined for immediate transference to the Republic.[1] Similarly, many of its exports to Britain consist of goods which are in course of transhipment to other

---

1 Some indication of the magnitude of the discrepancies created by transit trade can be obtained by comparing the Republic's estimates of intra-Ireland trade with those of Northern Ireland. In 1972 the North imported £103·5m and exported £73·8m to the Republic, according to Ministry of Commerce statistics (*The Trade of Northern Ireland,* 1972). Figures for the same year from the Republic's Central Statistics Office show domestic exports to Northern Ireland as £62·5m and imports from Northern Ireland as £30·9m. The substantial difference between these figures confirms one's impression of a large volume of transit trade moving between Northern Ireland and the Republic.

countries. A final limitation that needs to be mentioned is the absence of a
constant price series for the North's total exports and imports.

2.2 Anglo-Irish and Intra-Ireland Trade Flows

The evolution of Anglo-Irish trade patterns must be viewed against a background of very rapid trade expansion, especially during the last decade. Thus
since 1960 the Republic's exports and imports have increased at an average
annual rate of 14·4 per cent and 12·8 per cent respectively, compared with
an average annual GDP growth rate of 11·4 per cent (all in current values).
Northern Ireland's external trade has also expanded rapidly since 1960,
with exports increasing by 8·7 per cent and imports by 7·8 per cent, but
the average GDP growth rate of 9·3 per cent exceeded the rate of increase
of trade flows. This rather unusual phenomenon can perhaps be explained
by the exceptionally large expansion of the services sector during the
period, much of it financed by government outlays.

In Table 4.1 data on certain aspects of trade between the Republic and
the United Kingdom are presented. The table illustrates clearly the important
role played by the UK in the Republic's international trade. Thus roughly
50 per cent of the Republic's imports are provided by the UK and 55 per
cent of the Republic's exports are sold to the UK. But there are other, and
perhaps less familiar, features of the Republic's trade with the UK which
must be emphasised.

First, Table 4.1 shows the very large and steady decline in the proportion
of the Republic's exports destined for the British market. In 1926 83 per
cent of the Republic's exports were purchased in Great Britain; by 1970
this percentage had fallen to 51 per cent; and by 1973 it was down to 45
per cent. Northern Ireland's share of the Republic's exports also fell steeply
during the same period, from 13 per cent in 1926 to 9 per cent in 1973, but
at a slower rate than Britain's. Northern Ireland has thus become, relatively
to Britain, a more important customer of the Republic now than it was
forty years ago.

Secondly, in contrast with the behaviour of exports, the proportion of
the Republic's imports coming from the UK has remained remarkably constant, at around 50 per cent, throughout the period since independence.[2]
Between 1950 and 1970 the average UK share of the Republic's imports
was 52 per cent, with a standard deviation of only 2·6 percentage points.

Closer investigation of imports from the UK reveals, however, that the
constancy in the level of the UK's aggregate share since 1950 conceals a

2 Import statistics, compiled on a country of consignment basis in 1926, show
76 per cent of imports coming from the UK. Investigations by the CSO a decade
later, however, suggested that about 25 per cent of imports consigned from the UK
were of non-UK origin. Hence imports of non-UK origin in the immediate post-
independence years probably amounted to somewhere between 50 and 60 per cent
of the Republic's total imports.

very sharp decline in its share of manufactured imports over the period 1950–70. The UK's share of the Republic's manufactured imports declined from 78 per cent in 1950 to 62 per cent in 1970, and further to 54 per cent in 1973. The aggregate UK share remained virtually unchanged, however, because both the share of manufactured goods in total imports into the

Table 4.1: Merchandise Trade of the Republic with Northern Ireland and Great Britain, selected years 1926–73

	1926	1936	1950	1960	1970	1973
Imports	£m current					
Total Republic imports c.i.f.	61·3	39·9	159·4	226·2	653·6	1,138·4
from Northern Ireland	6·5	0·5	2·4	7·4	30·2	42·7
from Great Britain	39·9	20·7	82·0	104·6	322·4	534·8
	Percentage shares					
Percentage of imports						
from Northern Ireland	10·6	1·4	1·5	3·3	4·5	3·8
from Great Britain	65·1	51·9	51·4	46·3	47·7	47·0
	75·7	53·3	52·9	49·6	52·2	50·8
Exports	£m current					
Total domestic exports	42·0	22·5	72·4	152·7	455·5	869·2
to Northern Ireland	5·7	2·3	8·5	20·3	53·5	82·2
to Great Britain	34·9	18·3	54·3	92·3	230·9	393·1
	Percentage shares					
Percentage of domestic exports						
to Northern Ireland	13·6	10·1	11·7	13·3	11·7	9·5
to Great Britain	82·7	81·4	75·0	60·4	50·6	45·2
	96·5	91·5	86·7	73·7	64·9	54·7

Note: Pre-1935 import figures are not comparable with later statistics since the former were classified by country of consignment rather than by country of origin. Also 1973 export figures refer to total exports, not domestic exports.

Sources: *Trade and Shipping Statistics, External Trade Statistics, Trade Statistics of Ireland,* all Stationery Office, Dublin, various issues.

Republic was rising throughout this period, and the share of the UK in this rapidly growing section of imports was higher than its share of non-manufactured imports.

Thirdly, the fall in the UK's share of total exports reflects a declining share of both agricultural and industrial exports. Although Britain still remains the chief market for the Republic's agricultural exports, absorbing about 70 per cent of the total, its share has fallen from 90 per cent in 1950. In the case of manufactured exports, however, the decline is even more pronounced, from 83 per cent in 1950 to 47 per cent in 1973.

Turning now to intra-Ireland trade, details of the commodity composition of North-South trade since 1959—60 are contained in Table 4.2. A brief commentary on some of the more important features of the table may be helpful.

One striking feature of Table 4.2 is the surprisingly high proportion of the Republic's domestic exports sold on the Northern Ireland market. Thus the North purchased no less than 14 per cent of the Republic's exports in 1959—60 and 10 per cent in 1972—73. This is well above what would have been expected if the North were to be regarded merely as another region of the UK. For, in that case, the North's 'expected' share of the Republic's trade with the UK would be roughly proportional to its share of the UK population or GDP, i.e. 2—3 per cent.[3] The North's expected share of the Republic's total trade would then be half that figure. Thus contiguity is obviously an important factor.

Exports to Northern Ireland are predominantly agricultural. Roughly half of the Republic's total exports to Northern Ireland consist of live animals and food, such as store cattle, dairy products and animal feeding-stuffs. Although the composition of the Republic's exports to Northern Ireland has shifted more and more towards manufactured goods, this has not prevented the latter's share of the Republic's total *manufactured* exports from falling by 6 percentage points, from 15 per cent to 9 per cent, in the course of the last decade. This is a substantial share decline which is, as we have seen, replicated for the UK as a whole. In attempting to explain this decline, account must be taken of the small base from which the growth in the Republic's manufactured goods exports started in 1959—60. Thus one could argue that Northern Ireland's 25 per cent share of chemical exports in 1959—60 tells one more about the small value of total exports of this type from the Republic (£0·6m) than about the importance of the Northern Ireland market to the Republic's exporters.

Table 4.2 also shows that rather less than 4 per cent of the Republic's imports originate in Northern Ireland, a percentage which has changed only marginally since 1959—60. The commodity composition of these imports has, however, altered significantly. Whereas only 22 per cent of the Republic's

3 Northern Ireland's population and GDP amount to 2·7 per cent and 2·0 per cent of the UK total respectively.

Table 4.2: Trade of the Republic with Northern Ireland, 1959–60 and 1972–73

SITC	Description	Exports from the Republic				Imports into the Republic			
		1959–60 Av. (£000)	(%)	1972–73 Av. (£000)	(%)	1959–60 Av. (£000)	(%)	1972–73 Av. (£000)	(%)
0	Live animals and food	12,359	15·8	33,881	10·9	5,231	15·4	15,969	14·8
1	Beverages and tobacco	1,471	20·6	6,405	28·6	23	0·0	718	3·6
2	Raw materials	568	5·9	2,220	5·1	608	3·1	2,013	3·4
3	Fuels and lubricants	212	7·0	1,257	19·7	19	0·0	196	0·0
4	Animal and vegetable oils	104	39·0	336	13·7	33	2·1	454	8·6
0–4	Total non-manufactured	14,714	15·0	44,099	11·4	5,913	6·8	22,080	7·3
5	Chemicals	164	25·4	2,370	5·0	43	0·0	1,501	1·4
6	Manufactured goods, classified by material	1,896	14·6	15,824	13·2	1,548	3·7	9,935	4·6
7	Machinery and transport equipment	1,102	19·5	3,526	4·6	133	0·0	1,774	0·0
8	Manufactured articles n.e.s.	694	10·4	6,356	7·9	72	0·7	3,283	3·6
5–8	Total manufactured	3,856	14·9	28,076	8·7	1,795	1·6	19,990	2·4
0–9	Grand total	18,876	13·8	74,609	9·9	8,157	3·8	36,828	3·8

Note: Percentages refer to the share of exports (imports) to Northern Ireland in the Republic's total exports (imports). Total non-manufactured and total manufactured trade do not add up to the grand total as category 9 has been omitted.
Source: Trade and Shipping Statistics 1959 and 1960, Stationery Office, Dublin and Trade Statistics of Ireland (Dec. 1973), Stationery Office, Dublin.

imports from Northern Ireland consisted of manufactured goods in 1959—60, a decade later this share has risen to 54 per cent. In absolute values, imports of manufactured goods from Northern Ireland increased eleven-fold compared with a less than four-fold increase in non-manufactured goods imports. Nevertheless, despite this rapid increase in absolute terms, the North's share of imports of manufactured goods into the Republic, at 2 per cent, still remains exceedingly small.

As in the case of exports, it is clear from Table 4.2 that the bulk of non-agricultural goods entering the Republic from Northern Ireland consist of live animals and food. Of these by far the most important element is imported live animals, chiefly fat cattle. Thus the large volume of two-way cattle trade takes the form of store cattle being sent from the Republic to Northern Ireland and fat cattle being imported from Northern Ireland by the Republic's meat processing and slaughtering industries. This two-way trade in live animals and goods is highly sensitive to the structure of price subsidies in the two parts of the island.

On the manufactured goods side, imports from the North are heavily concentrated in textiles and textile products (carpets, table linen, synthetic yarns). Non-metallic mineral manufactures are also significant items in the import bill, as are miscellaneous manufactured goods (Table 4.2, row 8) consisting of a wide range of clothing products, furniture, newspapers, plastic bags, etc.

A curious feature of intra-Ireland trade is that, throughout the 1960s, the more industrialised North has exported a lower value of manufactured goods to the Republic than the Republic exports to Northern Ireland. In 1972—73 a trade balance of £13m in favour of the Republic existed in these products. Perhaps the comparatively low level of Northern Ireland exports can be attributed to the historically high level of protection in the Republic against manufactured imports. Alternatively, the level of specialisation in the North may be such as to exclude the possibility of the Republic's market being significant for Northern Ireland exporters. Whatever the cause, it is clear that FitzGerald's observation that 'something of a paper curtain seems to have cut off the North from the Republic as far as many manufacturers in the South are concerned' (FitzGerald (1972), p. 75) applies with as much if not greater force to Northern manufacturers as to those in the Republic.

2.3 Geographical and Commodity Composition of Irish Trade

So far various features of Anglo-Irish trade flows and intra-Ireland trade flows have been discussed. Attention can now be turned to the composition and structure of Ireland's trade with the rest of the world. The Republic's trade is examined first, and the relevant data are presented in summary form in Table 4.3.

Looking at the pattern of the Republic's imports, one immediately observes the substantial increase in the share of manufactured goods in the

Table 4.3: Trade of the Republic by Area and Commodity Composition, 1959–60 and 1972–73

	Imports			Exports		
	£m	% distribution		£m	% distribution	
	1972–73	1959–60	1972–73	1972–73	1959–60	1972–73
Area						
UK	503·3	50·6	50·8	434·9	73·8	57·8
Other EEC	196·6	13·4	19·7	147·4	5·9	19·1
US and Canada	82·8	9·8	8·4	86·1	8·3	11·4
EFTA	59·1	4·2	6·0	20·7	1·1	2·7
All other areas	148·7[a]	22·0	15·1	68·8[a]	10·9	9·0
Total	990·5	100·0	100·0	757·9	100·0	100·0
Commodity Composition						
Manufactured goods (SITC 5–8)	683·4	52·0	68·9	322·2	19·0[b]	42·3
Non-manufactured goods (SITC 0–4)	265·5	42·0	26·8	387·4	74·9[b]	51·3
Other	41·6	6·0	4·3	48·3	6·1[b]	6·4
Total	990·5	100·0	100·0	757·9	100·0[b]	100·0

[a]Figures for 1972 include re-imports and temporary domestic exports.
[b]Domestic exports only.

Sources: *Trade and Shipping Statistics 1959* and *1960*, Stationery Office, Dublin, and *Trade Statistics of Ireland* (various issues, 1972 and 1973), Stationery Office, Dublin.

total import bill. In 1959–60 52 per cent of the Republic's imports consisted of manufactured goods; little more than a decade later, this share has
risen to 69 per cent. All this, of course, reflects the effect of the rapid industrialisation of the country and the accompanying rise in standards of living.

Associated with these changes in commodity composition, and in part
caused by it, have come changes in the geographical origin of the Republic's
imports. The share of imports supplied by Other E E C (E E C six plus
Denmark) countries has risen from 13 per cent in 1959–60 to 20 per cent
in 1972–73. E F T A's share has also increased during this period, from 4
per cent to 6 per cent. All Other Areas and the Dollar Area, by contrast,
have experienced a share loss, largely because of the heavy preponderance
of raw materials and primary products in imports from these areas. Although
the U K's share of the Republic's imports has remained constant, we have
already noted that its share of manufactured goods imports fell continuously
throughout the decade.

The causes of this observed decline in the U K's share of the Republic's
manufactured imports are not easy to identify. One must remember, however, that the U K was losing its share of the world market for manufactures
throughout the post-war period, so there is nothing particularly exceptional
about the Republic's experience in this regard. Also, it is interesting to note
that the U K's share losses, especially in the latter half of the 1960s, were
concentrated in a small number of product groups, in particular motor
vehicles and electrical engineering products. Loss of competitiveness in
both price and non-price terms relative to other European manufacturers,
combined with the translation of higher living standards in Ireland into increased demand for product variety, were important factors in explaining
the U K's declining share of these products. Although the preferential treatment given to UK imports under the Anglo-Irish Free Trade Area Agreement
gave a significant competitive edge to U K exporters in the Republic's
market, this was evidently not sufficient to outweigh the negative influences
which were simultaneously at work. (See McAleese and Martin (1973).)

The commodity composition of the Republic's exports also changed substantially during the last decade. Here also a sharp increase in the share of
manufactured goods in the total can be observed. Whereas in 1959–60
manufactured exports amounted to 19 per cent of total exports, by 1972–73
this share had increased to 42 per cent. The annual growth rate in value
terms of manufactured exports averaged 20 per cent during the 1960s,
roughly twice the growth rate of total exports. During the last few years
growth rates of 30 per cent and over in manufactured exports have been
achieved.

Again, as in the case of imports, changes in export commodity composition have been associated with changes in geographical distribution. Exports
to Other E E C countries, the United States and Canada increased very rapidly
– their combined share of total exports rose from 14·2 per cent in 1959–60

to 30·5 per cent in 1972—73. On the other hand, the UK's share fell markedly during the period from 74 per cent to 58 per cent. Only part of this fall, however, can be attributed to the high concentration of agricultural goods in total exports to the UK. Account would also have to be taken of the comparatively slow growth of the UK market during the last fifteen years and of the influx of new industrial projects into the Republic from countries other than the UK.

A few further features of the Republic's trading pattern may be noted, namely, the large deficit in merchandise trade amounting to over £233m in 1972—73, the adverse trade balance with every area except the United States and Canada, and the marked increase in the degree of diversification of the Republic's export markets during the last decade.

Evidence of greater market diversification also exists for Northern Ireland, although data limitations make a detailed analysis of this trend very difficult. This is because the North's trade statistics are classified on a country of consignment basis. No differentiation is made therefore between goods exported to Britain as the place of final destination and goods sent there from the North in transit for other countries: and likewise, *mutatis mutandis,* in the case of goods imported into Northern Ireland from Britain. By ignoring transit trade, these statistics, no doubt, underestimate the true value of the North's *extra*-UK trade flows. More reliable data on the geographical distribution of the North's trade are available from the Census of Production, but these cover only manufactured exports, and no comparable figures for manufactured imports or non-manufactured trade flows are available.

In Table 4.4 census figures for the external sales of industrial goods from Northern Ireland are classified according to commodity group and area of destination. Northern Ireland's heavy dependence on the British market is immediately apparent. More than four-fifths of its industrial exports are sold there, as compared with the Republic's fraction of one-half. During the 1960s, however, the share of other countries increased slightly from 11 per cent in 1959—60 to 14 per cent in 1969—70. As in the Republic, the North shows signs of developing a more diversified set of export markets than hitherto; but the strength of this tendency is much less strong than in the Republic.

A very important feature of the North's trade in comparison with that of the Republic emerges when exports are examined not on their own but in relation to total output. Although 1970 is the latest year for which broadly comparable data are available, one sees very clearly that the percentage of industrial output destined for export in Northern Ireland is nearly three times that of the Republic, 70 per cent as against 26 per cent respectively.[4] The recent publication of an input-output table for North-

4 Figures taken from the 1970 Census of Production report and *Review of 1973 and Outlook for 1974* respectively.

Table 4.4: External Sales of Manufactured Goods from Northern Ireland, 1959–60 and 1969–70

Sales to:	Textiles £m		Clothing £m		Engineering £m		Other £m		Area total £m		Share of total external sales %	
	1959–60	1969–70	1959–60	1969–70	1959–60	1969–70	1959–60	1969–70	1959–60	1969–70	1959–60	1969–70
North America	6.6	8.4	0.1	0.3	1.2	3.8	0.4	2.6	8.3	15.1	2.5	2.1
EEC[a]	2.2	6.3	0.2	0.2	2.1	7.5	1.1	3.1	4.9	17.1	1.5	2.4
EFTA (excluding Britain)	1.0	10.2	0.1	0.2	2.9	2.7	0.4	6.3	4.3	19.5	1.3	2.7
Other	5.9	12.7	0.2	0.7	12.5	26.8	0.7	10.0	19.9	50.2	6.0	7.0
Total	15.7	37.6	0.5	1.4	18.7	40.8	2.6	22.0	37.4	101.9	11.3	14.2
Great Britain	32.0	100.1	21.3	41.1	48.6	74.0	193.9	401.2	295.8	616.4	88.7	85.8
Total external sales	47.7	137.7	21.8	42.5	67.2	114.8	196.5	423.2	333.2	718.3	100.0	100.0
British share of total external sales	67.1	72.7	91.7	96.7	72.2	64.5	98.7	94.8	88.7	85.8		

[a] The six original members.

Note: Figures exclude value of work done.

Source: Census of Production reports, 1960 and 1969–70.

ern Ireland for the year 1963 makes an even closer comparison, on an industry-by-industry level, possible. The present author has examined these figures in some detail in a separate publication (McAleese (1976)). Dividing the manufacturing sector into twenty-nine groups, it was found that twenty industries in Northern Ireland had export ratios greater than 50 per cent in 1963 compared with only two industries in the Republic in 1964 and three in 1971. Even allowing for the fact that the Republic's domestic market is larger than the North's, these contrasting export ratios provide impressive evidence of the effects of protection in the Republic which systematically distorted production towards serving the domestic market rather than foreign markets. The dramatic expansion in the Republic's exports in recent years shows that the pendulum has begun to swing the other way. But even in 1974 one can guess that the Republic has much leeway to make up before its export ratios approach the size of those in Northern Ireland's industry. Thus the similarity in the form of the foreign sector equations for Northern Ireland and the Republic in Chapter 1 must not blind one to the fact that the values of the basic parameters are probably quite different.

3 INVISIBLES, CAPITAL FLOWS AND THE BALANCE OF PAYMENTS

3.1 What is the Balance of Payments?

The balance of payments is, by definition, the record of all commercial transactions between residents of one country and residents of another. There are a number of ways of classifying these transactions, but for simplicity, three basic concepts only are considered here. First, there is the *balance of trade,* representing the difference between the value of merchandise exports and imports. Secondly, the *balance on current account* is obtained by adding 'invisible' items such as net tourism receipts, emigrants' remittances, income earned on capital held abroad, transportation charges, etc. to the balance of trade. It is customary nowadays to divide invisibles into two groups: services and international transfers. Thirdly, there is the *balance of autonomous transactions,* which equals the current account balance plus net long-term capital inflows. Thus if the current account registers a deficit of £100m and net long-term capital inflow equals £150m, the balance of autonomous transactions is in surplus to the value of £50m. In deciding whether a country has a balance of payments 'problem' or not, the balance referred to ought, in most normal circumstances, to be the balance of autonomous transactions.

The remaining items on balance of payments account include changes in external reserves and short-term capital movements. These are referred to in the literature as *accommodating* items, on the grounds that they react passively to changes in the balance of autonomous items. Thus if a country has a deficit on the balance of autonomous payments, equality between supply and demand for foreign exchange can be brought about either by a reduction in the level of external reserves or by short-term foreign borrowing. The change in accommodating transactions is viewed as the direct consequence of the deficit in the balance of autonomous payments.

In Table 4.5 the balance of payments account for the Republic in the year 1973 is presented in summary form in order to illustrate more clearly the practical importance of these various balance of payments concepts.

Starting from a balance of trade deficit in 1973 of £271m, the gap between receipts and earnings of foreign exchange is lessened by virtue of

Table 4.5: Balance of Payments of the Republic, 1973 (£m)

	Credit	Debit	Balance
Current Items	(+)	(−)	
Merchandise			
(1) Goods[a]	848·6	1,119·5	−270·9
Invisibles			
(2) Services	269·5	176·2	+ 93·3
(3) International transfers	101·0	10·7	+ 90·3
(4) Other	9·2	0·0	+ 9·2
Balance on Current Account	1,228·3	1,306·4	− 78·1
Capital Items			
(5) Long-term government and state-sponsored bodies (net)			+ 61·5
(6) Private (net)			+ 21·8
Balance of Autonomous Items[b]			+ 5·2
(7) Short-term capital (govt)			− 2·1
(8) Change in reserves (−) = increase (+) = decrease			− 3·1
Total			0·0

[a]Adjusted for balance of payments purposes.
[b]This is an approximate figure, since certain short-term capital movements (accommodating items) are included in the total and cannot be separately distinguished.

Source: *Irish Statistical Bulletin* (Dec. 1974).

a substantial £193m surplus in invisibles, split roughly half-and-half between services and international transfers. Among the service items, the tourist trade is an important net earner of foreign exchange. In 1973 inflows of foreign exchange under the heading 'tourism and travel' amounted to £83m compared with outgoings of £59m. The major items included in the international transfer category are E E C transfers, emigrants' remittances and pensions and allowances.

The addition of the surplus on invisible account of £193m to the deficit in the balance of trade of £271m leaves a net deficit on current account of £78m. This deficit must be financed by a net capital inflow and/or by a reduction in the level of official reserves.

Details of capital flows in Table 4.5 indicate how important a role these items play in the Republic's balance of payments. Net foreign borrowing by the government and semi-state bodies amounted to £61m, and a further net capital inflow of £22m is attributable to the private sector. It must be emphasised, however, that most private capital transactions are valued on a *net* basis in the balance of payments statement. Net increases in private capital inflow could occur for a variety of reasons, including the following three: (a) foreigners decide to invest more in the Republic, (b) citizens of the Republic decide to send less capital abroad, and/or (c) citizens of the Republic repatriate existing holdings of foreign assets. As yet, sufficient statistics are not available to identify these separate elements.

It is always difficult to distinguish in practice between autonomous and accommodating items in the balance of payments. In the case of the Republic, the difficulty is compounded by the absence of a clear division between long-term and short-term capital movements on private account in the balance of payments statement. For the sake of convenience, the total net private inflow is included as an autonomous item, but the reader must be warned of the essentially approximate nature of this estimate.

Adding the autonomous items on capital account to the balance on current account, the Republic ends with a surplus on autonomous transactions of £5m. The fact that current account deficits so frequently co-exist with autonomous account surpluses underlines the importance of distinguishing clearly between these two types of transactions. Equally, it is important to keep in mind the often quite close functional relationship between current account transactions and autonomous capital transactions. For example, suppose that a foreign investor wishes to establish a subsidiary manufacturing enterprise in the Republic for which most of the equipment has to be imported. One could, in crude terms, visualise this project as involving two types of transactions: (a) a transfer of funds to the subsidiary in the Republic (long-term capital inflow), and (b) the use of these funds to import capital equipment (merchandise imports on current account). If it were not for the capital inflow, in other words, the rise in the import bill would not have occurred. This same interdependence can be observed in cases where purchases by state-sponsored bodies of foreign equipment is directly financed by a long-term loan from the company or country from which the equipment is purchased.

The balance of payments statement is completed by the inclusion of £2m short-term capital outflow on government account and by the increase in reserves of £3m. The balance of these accommodating items must necessarily be equal, and opposite in sign, to the autonomous transactions balance.

3.2 Balance of Payments of the Republic

The behaviour of certain key components in the Republic's balance of payments in recent years is examined in Table 4.6. From this table five important and strikingly persistent features of the Republic's balance of payments position during the last two decades can be discerned: (*a*) a large deficit on balance of trade, (*b*) a surplus on invisibles account, (*c*) a current account deficit, (*d*) a net capital inflow in excess of the current deficit, and (*e*) an increase in the level of official reserves. Since 1969 these characteristics have become further accentuated and the absolute magnitude of the sums involved has increased markedly both in money terms and in real terms. Thus the average current account deficit has risen from £13·4m in 1959—68 to £67·8m in 1969—73. The annual net capital inflow averaged over £98m in 1969—73 compared with an average annual inflow of £21m for the decade to 1969. In the course of the five years 1969—73 the total net capital inflow amounted to almost £500m. Preliminary figures for 1974 suggest that the deficit in this year alone will add a further £360m to the total.

The largest single identifiable source of the net capital inflow in recent years has been official foreign borrowing, i.e. foreign borrowing both by the government and by semi-state enterprises. Official foreign liabilities are estimated by the Central Bank to have increased from £63m in 1966 (much of which would have been accounted for by Marshall Aid contracted just after the Second World War) to some £300m at end-March 1974 (*CBR* (1974), p. 39; see also Chapter 7, p. 258). Between 1969 and 1973 slightly over £200m, or 40 per cent, of the total net capital inflow was accounted for by official borrowing abroad.

Data limitations unfortunately prevent any clear identification of the various sources of the remaining three-fifths of the net capital inflow. Direct foreign investment in new enterprises, foreign investment in the mining industry, takeovers of firms in the Republic by foreign interests, investments in land and property have all undoubtedly contributed in some degree to the net inflow on private sector account. The Republic operates an 'open-door' policy as far as most foreign investment is concerned and no official control is exercised over capital transactions between Dublin and London. It is scarcely surprising, therefore, that statistical records of these capital inflows are a good deal less than comprehensive.

Table 4.6: Balance of Payments of the Republic, 1959–73 (£m)

Year	Balance of Trade	Balance of Invisibles	Current Balance of Payments	Changes in Official Reserves	Net Capital Inflow
1959	− 82·3	73·6	− 8·7	+ 4·4	+13·1
1960	− 73·8	73·0	− 0·8	− 0·3	+ 0·5
1961	− 81·8	83·0	+ 1·2	+14·6	+13·4
1962	−100·2	86·8	−13·4	+ 9·5	+22·9
1963	−111·2	89·1	−22·1	+ 2·9	+25·0
1964	−127·8	96·4	−31·4	+ 5·2	+36·6
1965	−147·1	105·3	−41·8	−17·2	+24·6
1966	−124·5	108·4	−16·1	+22·4	+38·5
1967	−100·1	115·3	+15·2	+46·3	+31·1
1968	−153·2	136·9	−16·3	− 7·9	+ 8·4
1969	−211·3	142·2	−69·1	+ 5·9	+75·0
1970	−213·0	147·7	−65·3	+ 2·4	+67·7
1971	−217·3	146·3	−71·0	+90·8	+161·8
1972	−192·0	136·2	−55·8	+51·1	+106·9
1973	−271·0	192·8	−78·1	+ 3·1	+81·2
Average 1959–68	−110·2	+ 96·8	−13·4	+ 8·0	+21·4
Average 1969–73	−220·8	+153·1	−67·8	+30·7	+98·5

Source: *Irish Statistical Bulletin*, various issues, and *C B R*, various issues.

The explanation of the increased rate of capital inflow poses as many problems as the identification of its source. One important factor, however, has been the rapid increase in the level of total government expenditure, particularly in recent years. In the period 1969–73 government expenditure (capital and current) increased by 17·2 per cent per annum compared with an average GNP increase of 14·5 per cent. It goes without saying that this expansion of the public sector has many important economic implications, not alone for the capital account of the balance of payments, but also for monetary policy and anti-inflation policy. As far as the balance of payments is concerned, the need for extra finance has forced the government to an increasing extent to have recourse to foreign borrowing rather than to increase further its already large liabilities on the domestic market. Furthermore, it has led to intensified pressure being placed on semi-state bodies to finance their capital expansion by direct borrowing abroad rather than by seeking assistance from the government.[5]

A second factor relates to the rapid growth of IDA-sponsored foreign manufacturing enterprises during the last five years. Although the gross capital inflow directly attributable to these enterprises during the 1960s was estimated by McAleese (1972) as no more than one-quarter of the total net inflow during the same period, there are reasons to believe that the relative importance of this source has expanded considerably in recent years. IDA new industry job approvals have jumped from 11,000 in the financial year 1969–70 to 22,000 in 1973–74. Furthermore, the average grant received as a percentage of total fixed asset expenditure by these enterprises has declined steadily in recent years to its present level of 26 per cent. This suggests that the proportion of funds provided by the foreign enterprises has tended to increase over time, a fact which should be reflected in the capital inflow figures.

Being a large net capital importer is not a particularly unusual phenomenon, and there are many countries, e.g. Israel, Taiwan, Greece, Spain and Cyprus, which rely heavily on foreign borrowing for their continued growth. Unlike many other countries in the same debtor category, however, the Republic has experienced a heavy capital inflow and, simultaneously, benefited from an increase in its official reserves which have risen from £210m in 1959 to £288m in 1969 and to £495m in 1974.[6] At end-1974 the Republic's official reserves corresponded in value to about three and a half months' imports at 1974 levels, an adequate ratio by international standards. Furthermore, the Republic's net capital inflow has not yet been associated

5 Kennedy and Bruton (1975) show that the share of state-sponsored companies' net borrowing in the net capital inflow rose from 6·9 per cent in the period 1961–68 to 17·2 per cent in 1969–72.

6 The composition of these reserves at mid-1975 was as follows: gold (1 per cent), IMF reserves (7 per cent), sterling (26 per cent), other currencies (66 per cent). The last decade has seen a significant rise in the share of non-sterling balances in the total.

with any especially severe foreign debt-servicing problems such as those which currently afflict many less developed countries. But this satisfactory state of affairs is not guaranteed to last indefinitely. The rise in oil prices since the end of 1973, combined with the gradual erosion of competitiveness relative to European and U S markets during 1974 and 1975, suggests that there are no grounds for complacency as far as the Republic's balance of payments is concerned during the next five years.

3.3   External Transactions of Northern Ireland

As a region of the U K, Northern Ireland has no separate balance of payments statement nor can it have a balance of payments 'problem' in the accepted sense of the term. Information on certain components of a balance of payments statement for the North is, however, available. Also, since differences between total regional receipts and expenditure must inevitably tend to arise on an interregional no less than on an international level, it is of interest to examine the mechanism by which equilibrium is restored in the former situation. This is a particularly topical issue nowadays in view of the widespread concern over problems of economic and monetary integration between independent nations.

Although the value of Northern Ireland's trade increased steadily since 1959, at 7·9 per cent on average per year, the balance of trade has displayed no noticeable trend. The balance of trade deficit in Northern Ireland has, however, tended to be much smaller relative to both total imports and G D P than that of the Republic. Northern Ireland's average trade deficit amounted to 6·5 per cent of total imports and 6·2 per cent of G D P in the years 1969–72 compared with corresponding statistics in the Republic of 29·3 per cent and 14·0 per cent respectively.

To get from the balance of trade to the balance on current account, estimates are required of the balance on invisibles account, comprising both services and transfer payments. As far as services are concerned, there is little to be said that is not educated guesswork. One suspects that tourism and transportation are net deficit items in the last few years, especially since the outbreak of civil disturbances. Income from capital, on the other hand, probably yields a net surplus to Northern Ireland, as it does still in the Republic (despite the massive capital inflow during the last decade) and as it did for much of the nineteenth century for the whole island.[7]

The other major heading in the invisibles account, after services, is official and private international transfers. The net direction of flows under this heading is almost certainly in Northern Ireland's favour, the predominant factor being the transfer of official funds from Westminster. Various estimates have been made of the magnitude of the net official transfer, after

---

7 Dowling (1975), however, suggests a *deficit* on income from capital account of £30m in 1972. He points out that the cost of servicing the rapidly increasing debt from the U K has risen considerably in recent years.

allowing for revenue attributed to Northern Ireland and excluding borrowing transactions. It has been officially estimated at £161m in 1972—73 and £313m in 1973—74. The net transfer has risen rapidly in recent years from a level of about £50m in the mid-1960s.

It is clear, therefore, that Northern Ireland's balance of payments could well have been, and very probably was, in current account surplus throughout much of the post-war period. Small deficits in merchandise trade and services were counterbalanced by transfer payments from the UK exchequer. It must be remembered, of course that the North's receipts of income transfers from Britain are contingent on its position as part of the UK.

Information on capital account transactions for Northern Ireland is even more sparse and uncertain than that on current account items, and the limited statistics available relate almost exclusively to the 1950s.

Outflow of capital occurs in a number of ways from Northern Ireland. Some capital is exported through the commercial banks, some through building societies. The transfer of life assurance premiums to Britain and their subsequent investment there is another source of leakage.[8]

Investment by Northern Ireland citizens in UK government bonds and public shares also constitutes an important medium of capital outflow. Northern Ireland, like the Republic, has tended in the past to be a net exporter of capital on *private* account. Isles and Cuthbert (1957) estimated that the cumulative net export of capital from Northern Ireland amounted to £330m in 1950, and Dowling (1975) concluded, following an interesting investigation of the Northern Ireland banks' balance sheets, that *net* capital outflow on private account could have amounted to as much as £140m in 1972 alone. But quite clearly there is a large two-way traffic in private capital flows. Thus investment in Northern Ireland by external interests is also well established. The Discussion Paper (Northern Ireland Office (1974)) shows that 78 per cent of the capital of all manufacturing firms in Northern Ireland with a workforce of over 500 persons is owned by external residents. This figure also accords closely with an estimate for the year 1947 (Isles and Cuthbert (1957)). They found that 76 per cent of the assets of a sample of public companies in Northern Ireland were owned by residents outside the province.

As far as public capital transactions are concerned, the major item consists of borrowing by the Northern Ireland authorities from external sources. The most important item under this heading are borrowings from the National Loans Fund, which, during the year 1973—74 alone, amounted to £64m. Indeed, again drawing on the Green Paper, roughly two-thirds of Northern Ireland's total debt of over £600m represents direct borrowing from the UK treasury.

8 In the Republic this type of outflow is limited by an agreement whereby insurance companies from outside the state reinvest a large proportion of their premium income collected in the country.

While much interesting information is available on individual facets of the North's balance of payments, the statistics are still insufficient to enable a comprehensive statement of the payments situation to be drawn up. The balance of probability suggests the existence of a balance of payments surplus on current account, provided inter-governmental transfers are included, as they should be, among the invisible items along with services. On capital account, there is no way of distinguishing *a priori* between autonomous and accommodating items. In any case, this distinction in an interregional payments context has very little analytical significance. If the predicted sign on the current account balance is correct, however, it follows logically that Northern Ireland must have an opposite but equal balance on capital account, i.e. there must be a net capital outflow, either long-term or short-term. Furthermore, since there is a net inflow of funds on government account, the net outflow must consist of private capital flows. Unfortunately, it is not possible to go any further than this: no satisfactory description of the actual composition of this outflow can be provided.

3.4 Balance of Payments Adjustment

Consideration of the balance of payments statement of Northern Ireland and the Republic naturally leads on to a discussion of the balance of payments *adjustment mechanism* in each area. This entails an examination of the processes whereby *ex ante* imbalances between the supply and demand for external funds are brought into *ex post* equilibrium. To simplify the analysis, we begin by assuming that (*a*) only current account transactions exist, and (*b*) prices remain constant, implying the existence of unemployed resources. These assumptions will be relaxed later on.

Starting from a position of initial current account balance, consider the effects of, say, a £100 increase in the value of manufactured exports caused by an exogenous shift in foreign demand. Two factors are immediately set into operation which tend to reduce the £100 surplus thereby created. First, the import content of these extra exports will, in small economies like Northern Ireland and the Republic, tend to be very high.[9] So the extra demand for exports automatically creates a proportionately large increase in the demand for imports required as inputs for their production. Secondly, the increase in aggregate demand generated by the rise in export demand (i.e. exports *minus* imported inputs) percolates through the economy according to a multiplier process of the kind described in Chapter 1. The amount of extra income generated in this way hinges crucially on the value of the

9 Henry (1972) has calculated that the total average import content of manufactured goods in the Republic amounts to 41 per cent. That is, each £100 of output entails the purchase of £41 of imported inputs on average. The *marginal* imported input ratio is probably much higher than this. Examination of the North's input-output table suggests that the import content of industrial output in Northern Ireland is at least as high as in the Republic.

marginal propensity to import, the marginal savings propensity and the marginal tax rate. The higher the marginal import propensity, the greater is the extent to which the extra export demand will be translated into increased import demand. In Ireland, on both sides of the border, we can expect marginal propensities to import to be extremely high. To give a concrete example, Henry and Copeland (1975) have estimated that a £100 increase in final demand for the output of the chemicals industry in the Republic would generate, directly and indirectly, a rise of £59 in demand for imports. Leakages through savings and taxation would amount to £18 and £23 respectively and disposable income would rise by only £45. Of course, as the same authors illustrate in their paper, different types of expenditure have quite different multiplier effects. But the point to keep in mind is the basic strength of the automatic adjustment process in small open economies in response to changes in most expenditure categories (see Whitman (1967)). Note, however, that the adjustment mechanism is still only a partial one. The initial surplus is greatly reduced but not totally eliminated. Consequently, other mechanisms must come into play in order to restore equilibrium.

At this stage, capital account transactions can be introduced into the analysis. In both Northern Ireland and the Republic the net surplus will appear in the form of additional deposits held in the domestic banking system, offset by credit balances against external banks or external branches of domestic banks. The balance of payments surplus, in other words, increases the domestic money supply and, at constant prices, the value of real balances. If it is accepted that households maintain a constant relation between their cash balances and levels of expenditure, further changes in income and imports must occur in order to preserve monetary equilibrium.

There are a number of ways in which this adjustment could occur. Increased cash balances could be viewed as leading to extra consumption, which directly stimulates import demand. Alternatively, these balances may be invested in bonds, in which case bond prices tend to rise, interest rates fall and expansion in investment demand may occur, leading again to a rise in import demand. Financial intermediaries can also be introduced into the analysis: the adjustment process might be viewed as leading from increased reserves in the banking system, to reductions in bank interest charges, to increased borrowing for investment and/or consumption. The increase in aggregate demand, by whatever process it comes about, must continue until full equilibrium can be restored.

The automatic adjustment mechanism described above stresses the link between the net surplus on current account, the improvement in the liquidity position of individuals and/or domestic banks, and the translation of the latter into an increased level of advances and, eventually, increased aggregate demand. While relatively simple in theory, in practice the process may take a long time to work through the system. Moreover, various institutional factors may also delay the adjustment process.

In Northern Ireland most commercial banking business is carried out by subsidiaries of British banks. The improved reserve position of their Northern Ireland branches may exert little pressure on them to expand lending in Northern Ireland as opposed to anywhere else in the U K. Moreover, since the North constitutes only a tiny fraction of an integrated U K capital market, changes in the liquidity position of Northern Ireland have no effect on the U K market interest rates. Thus while a net current account surplus in Northern Ireland *may* be used to expand credit in the region, there may not be any automatic forces at work to make this happen, at least not in the short to medium term. It could well be that the surplus accruing to the North is, in fact, re-lent on the British mainland, in which case the commercial banks could be viewed as acting as intermediaries in a net capital outflow transaction. Many less developed regions assist the development of the richer regions of the country in this way.

The situation regarding the disposal of a net surplus in the Republic is somewhat different to that in Northern Ireland. While interest rates in the Republic must also be taken as determined exogenously by those in Britain, the commercial banking system is nevertheless not free to dispose of its increased liquidity as it wills. Accumulated foreign balances must be transferred to the Central Bank, where they become part of the country's official reserves, in exchange for domestic balances. By adjusting its liquidity ratios the Central Bank can attempt to 'sterilise' the potential expansionary impact of the commercial banks' increased liquidity on advances and credit. The effectiveness of the Central Bank's control is a subject which is considered in detail in Chapter 7. It is clear, however, that the Central Bank's powers over the domestic money supply are limited, particularly in the long term.

So far a *rigid* price system has been assumed. Suppose this assumption is replaced by that of a fully employed *flexible* price economy, how would the adjustment process work?

An increase in foreign demand for exports, in those circumstances, would lead not to an increase in real output but to a rise in prices. Initially export prices would rise and a surplus on current account would appear. This would, in due course, attract resources from the import-competing and services sectors into the export sector, which tends to raise price levels in these sectors also. A further boost to the rise in the domestic prices would be provided by the additional cash balances and the improvement in the banks' liquidity position which the initial balance of payments surplus created. As domestic prices increase, imports become more competitive and domestic demand for imports increases. At the same time the rise in export prices due to domestic cost increases tends to reduce the increased foreign demand for exports. In this way balance of payments equilibrium is automatically restored by changes in the price level rather than by changes in real expenditure. This account of balance of payments adjustment has a long history, dating back to the eighteenth-century philosopher David Hume, whose work has provided a starting-point for the modern monetary approach to balance of payments adjustment.

The above description of the adjustment process permits a temporary divergence to exist between Irish prices and world prices. This assumption, while in conformity with the model in Chapter 1, conflicts with the orthodox 'small country' model often found in textbooks, where infinite elasticities of export demand and import supply ensure that the small country's price level is always determined by world prices. The textbook model, however, is a long-run model; in the short run, it is quite permissible, and more realistic, to assume that some divergences between Irish prices and world prices can occur.

For the sake of simplicity the textbook convention of keeping income and price effects in two separate compartments has been followed. In reality, of course, this type of rigid separation is not possible and models have been constructed which attempt to dispense with this assumption. The real world contains no truly rigid-price economy as postulated in the orthodox Keynesian model of income determination. Changes in the level of real output inevitably involve price effects also, and in applying balance of payments adjustment theory to practical situations this fact must be borne in mind. Provided this is done, the framework outlined in the previous paragraphs will prove helpful and instructive in analysing real world situations.

So far, automatic adjustment mechanisms have been considered. Government policy can encroach upon the automatic process of adjustment not only by sterilising the monetary effects of balance of payments disequilibrium, as already described, but also in a number of other ways.

To take a simple example, suppose that the Republic runs a net current account deficit with the UK of £100 per annum, that accounts with all other nations exactly balance, that there are no autonomous capital movements, and that the fall in money supply caused by the deficit is promptly counteracted by offsetting action on the part of the Central Bank. The result will be a de-cumulation of official reserves. Since reserves are finite, this state of affairs cannot continue indefinitely.

To solve the financing problem, a country like the Republic must resort to other policy instruments. First, commercial policy can be used to affect trade flows directly, subject, of course, to limitations placed by free trade agreements. Secondly, the exchange rate can be changed. Thirdly, fiscal policy can be used to reflate (deflate) the economy, thereby increasing (reducing) the volume of imports. Fourthly, measures can be taken to establish an independent prices and incomes policy designed to preserve balance of payments equilibrium. Although the Republic has not, so far, chosen to change its exchange rate *vis-à-vis* sterling, it has on a number of occasions resorted to commercial and other policy instruments, notably in 1956–57 and again in 1965, in order to restore balance between autonomous payments and receipts. By contrast, none of these policy measures, with the exception of fiscal policy where some room for discretionary action exists, can be taken by the Northern Ireland administration under its present constitutional powers.

Because of their small size and the openness of their economies, the similarities in the basic payments adjustment process between Northern Ireland and the Republic are very striking. In both areas a close link exists between exports and income and between income and imports. Exogenous changes in export receipts or the import bill automatically set in motion a series of offsetting forces. While Northern Ireland has less problems associated with the financing of its balance of payments balance, this does not mean that sudden shifts in its propensity to export or import have no bearing on its level of economic activity. On the contrary, these shifts have much the same consequence as in any other economy of comparable size. On the other hand, to counterbalance the disadvantage of having financing problems, an independent country has discretionary policy instruments which not only help to overcome the problem of financing but also help to cushion the economy against possible undesirable side-effects of certain exogenous changes in the external sector. Thus a temporary shortfall in export demand can be compensated for by an expansionary budget which helps keep real income constant. The adverse effects on the level of activity following an increase in the propensity to import, can theoretically at least, be offset by an appropriately designed package of import restrictions, etc. To discuss in detail the practical effectiveness of these policy instruments in the context of a small economy would require more space than can be afforded here. But a brief indication of the main constraints on their use can be gleaned from the next section which deals with trade policies and prospects.

4   TRADE POLICIES AND PROSPECTS

4.1   Economic Integration

The degree of world economic integration has increased steadily throughout the post-war period. Measures of trade liberalisation, particularly as regards industrial goods, taken in the framework of free trade areas and customs unions, have been prominent features of this new development. The (in part resultant) rapid growth of world trade has made separate national economies more interdependent than ever before. Countries as small as the Republic of Ireland and as large as the United States have all been affected. Thus even for the United States the ratio of imports to G N P has risen from 4·6 per cent in 1953 to 7·4 per cent in 1973, and trade has become an increasingly important ingredient in that nation's economic prosperity (Eckstein (1974)).

The closer integration between the two parts of Ireland itself, between Ireland and Britain, and between Ireland and the rest of the world, sketched earlier in statistical terms, has been accompanied by, and associated with, a number of formal international agreements. The Republic applied for E E C membership in 1961, but this move collapsed when negotiations between the UK and the EEC broke down in 1963. The Anglo-Irish Free Trade Area Agreement (A I F T A) was negotiated in 1965 and provided for the gradual establishment of free trade in most industrial commodities between the Republic on one hand and Northern Ireland and Britain on the other. Provision was also made for improving the Republic's access to the U K market in agricultural goods. In 1967 the Republic became a member of G A T T, and in 1973 both parts of Ireland, together with Britain, became partners in the European Economic Community. This momentous decision was preceded in the Republic by a referendum, the results of which showed an 83 per cent majority in favour of amending the Constitution to permit E E C entry. The prospect of E E C entry was somewhat less enthusiastically received in Northern Ireland.

The predicted economic gains to Northern Ireland of membership of the Community were considerably less impressive than those held out for the Republic. Thus, as part of the U K, the North already benefited from a highly developed system of protection for agriculture. The prospect of higher food prices under the E E C's Common Agricultural Policy (C A P), which proved so attractive to farmers in the Republic, offered little in the way of extra income to their counterparts in Northern Ireland, taken as a group. Small gains expected to accrue to cereal producers and extensive beef producers had to be offset against the prospective losses of intensive livestock producers whose profit margins were likely to be squeezed by higher feeding-stuff prices.

On the industrial side, the possible benefits of entry were viewed as being of minor importance. As we have seen, the E E C (six) market absorbs directly only a small fraction of the North's exports. While free access to this market gives extra scope to the North's export industries, it was not clear how significant an advantage this would turn out to be, especially when weighed against the loss of the North's preferential position in the British market. Also it was argued that a free trade agreement with the E E C, on the lines subsequently negotiated with other E F T A members, would confer the same benefits of market access without incurring the obligations of full E E C membership. In contrast with the Republic, however, the prospect of increased competition from foreign producers in the domestic market gave rise to no apprehension in Northern Ireland, since its industry had long been exposed to competition from Britain and elsewhere.

It was hoped in Northern Ireland, as in the Republic, that the establishment of a Regional Fund by the E E C would bring further financial assistance to its less developed regions. Already, of course, the North was a recipient of substantial sums, which could have been classified as a form of regional aid, from the U K exchequer. Nevertheless, the E E C Regional

Fund would have been an ideal vehicle for setting up growth centres in the relatively neglected and underdeveloped North-West of the island. This type of project required the sort of intergovernmental co-operation on both sides of the border which a neutral body could have done much to initiate and foster. However, at the time of the entry negotiations in 1972 the E E C's regional policy had yet to be converted into significant concrete measures and could not be expected to have been a decisive factor in people's minds.

4.2   Transition to Free Trade

For the Republic entry into the E E C represented the culmination of a pro-cess which had begun in the mid-1950s. Throughout this period, policies of protection and resistance to foreign ownership of companies in the Republic had been giving way to a new set of industrial policies which took the form of encouragement to exports through tax and marketing aids, the provision of grants to new industries (irrespective of the nationality of their owners), and the gradual dismantling of import barriers and restrictions. E E C entry occurred at a time when the Republic's economy was undergoing a profound structural change.

In discussing the reasons for and consequences of the Republic's entry into the E E C, it must be kept firmly in mind that the Republic's choice, in sharp contrast with that of the U K, was not one between maintaining the status quo and entering the Community. Rather the choice was between entering the E E C alongside the U K or staying out of the E E C while the country's major trading partner, the U K, went in. Either way, a fairly radi-cal change in the environment of the Republic was bound to occur (see McAleese (1975)).

On the positive side, the C A P offered the prospect of relatively high and stable prices for the produce of farmers in the Republic. In the years pre-ceding entry, C A P prices for dairy products looked particularly attractive. More important still, as a member of the E E C, the government was assured a strong say in all aspects of policy making which were likely to affect the agricultural sector. Prior to that, the Republic was more or less at the mercy of the vagaries of U K and European agricultural policy, in the formulation of which the government of the Republic played no part. The adverse effects of these factors had been seen in the high volatility of agricultural export earnings in the post-war period (see Kennedy and Dowling (1975)).

Added to these agricultural gains was the prospect of further industrial growth following from the improved access to the European market which E E C membership promised to provide. The Common External Tariff and the various non-tariff barriers raised by E E C countries made profitable exporting to these areas a difficult task for producers in the Republic. They also created a degree of insecurity as to the permanence of market access to which, according to the Industrial Development Authority, foreign investors were extremely sensitive. E E C membership was expected to enhance the

Republic's attractiveness as a secure base from which to export to the European market. As in Northern Ireland, financial benefits were also anticipated to emerge from the Community's regional policy.

Against these proposed benefits had to be weighed the dangers of exposing the Republic's domestic market to further competitive pressure. Tariffs had already been reduced early in the 1960s in the form of two unilateral across-the-board 10 per cent reductions. Further reductions had taken place under the terms of A I F T A, and complete free trade with the U K in industrial goods, with some exceptions such as motor vehicles, was scheduled to occur by mid-1975 and with Northern Ireland one year earlier. Surprisingly, especially in view of the extremely high initial levels of protection from which the Republic started,[10] the process of adjustment to freer trade had, by the early 1970s, proved relatively smooth. Although industrial imports from the U K increased both relative to non-U K imports and relative to supplies from domestic sources, the employment effect of A I F T A was estimated as involving a net loss of 2,000 jobs, a significant but by no means catastrophic consequence (McAleese and Martin (1973)).[11] The fact that there was a net job loss at all, of course, reflects the 'unbalanced' nature of the Agreement. Since producers in the Republic had enjoyed virtually unimpeded access to the U K market prior to A I F T A, the U K had few concessions on the industrial side with which to reciprocate those offered by the Republic; and the agricultural concessions offered by the U K proved in retrospect to be both less valuable than had been expected and also of little consequence as direct employment creators. In both respects the E E C promised more favourable prospects in that it offered a significant improvement in market access for industrial goods and large gains in the agricultural sector.

Studies of the overall effect of the E E C on the Republic's balance of payments therefore suggested that the overall comparative static effect would be at worst neutral and very likely positive, in the sense that balance of payments equilibrium at this higher level of trade would be maintained at the existing exchange rate. This conclusion is of considerable importance for, if correct, it meant that the much vaunted but difficult to quantify 'dynamic' gains from free trade could come into operation without being choked off by short-term balance of payments problems. The fact that trade liberalisation in manufactured goods coincided with high prices for agricultural goods played a key role in the above analysis, and also in the attendant conclusion that the transition to free trade could be effected smoothly and with tolerably small adjustment costs. By the end of 1974, however, events

10 In 1966 the average effective tariff on industrial goods in the Republic was estimated at 79 per cent, one of the highest in Europe. The comparable U K figure was 28 per cent (McAleese (1971)).

11 Job losses are not the same, nor as socially undesirable as redundancies. Thus many of the 'lost' jobs take the form of non-replacement of retired staff.

had altered radically. World beef prices fell dramatically, and with them the price of cattle in the Republic, the oil crisis substantially altered the balance of payments position of the Republic, and the conjunction of worldwide inflation and balance of payments difficulties in many Western countries engulfed both parts of Ireland in the most serious recession in the Western world since the 1930s.

4.3   Beef Crisis, Oil Prices and Inflation

Two years' experience of membership of the E E C has exposed its new members to many of the weaknesses of the Community which the prosperity of the previous decade had hitherto kept undisclosed. E E C membership was expected to provide not only high, but also stable, prices to farmers in the Republic. Yet throughout much of 1974 they were selling calves and store cattle at ruinously low prices. To many in the farming community the situation was more reminiscent of the 1930s than of the bold and prosperous future they had supposed themselves to be entering.

A number of things went wrong simultaneously to bring about this state of affairs. First, the rapid expansion of cattle herds following the record price levels of 1972 was translated into increased beef supply just at the time when demand was beginning to falter as a result of the slower growth of real incomes. Secondly, the C A P provides a minimum price for beef of a certain quality only. Not all farmers in the Republic, certainly not those holding calves and store cattle, could avail of the intervention prices. Thirdly, high feeding-stuffs prices and escalating input costs (e.g. of fertilisers) made the holding of the existing cattle stocks a difficult and potentially very unprofitable exercise, just at a time when stocks were at unprecedently high levels. Finally, exports of cattle to the continent were impeded by the imposition of special levies as a result of the continuing weakness of sterling.

All these factors combined to make 1974 generally a bad year for farming in the Republic, with certain types of farmer, notably the small stockowner in the Western regions, being particularly badly affected. Although efforts were made in September 1974 to improve the position, by the adoption of the so-called 'Green Pound' (see Attwood (1974)), as well as by significant overall C A P price increases for dairy products, it became clear that the C A P system was a highly imperfect one and in bad need of a thorough overhaul. In particular, the C A P's inability to operate effectively in a world of constantly fluctuating exchange rates proved especially damaging.

Difficulties in the agricultural sector were accompanied by a new and potentially more serious set of problems towards the end of 1973, when oil producers demanded and received an enormous increase in oil prices. The immediate implications of this increase for the Republic's economy were (*a*) a sharp increase in the current balance of payments deficit, and (*b*) a dramatic fall in real income as a result of the adverse terms of trade effect.

The cost of oil supplies consumed by the Republic in 1974, a year of comparatively slow economic growth, rose by about £150m as a result of increased oil and oil-substitute prices. The cost to Northern Ireland in the same year was about half this sum. This rise in the import bill has had a pronounced deflationary impact on the Republic's economy. Moreover, the fall in real incomes caused by the terms of trade effect has been poorly understood and has led to an inflationary round of income increases as each group has tried to preserve its level of real income in a situation where aggregate real incomes had fallen by a significant percentage.

To counter the deflationary impact of the oil price rise by an expansionary fiscal policy raises many of the problems mentioned earlier in this chapter. Because of the Republic's high propensity to import, a policy of fiscal expansion inevitably entails more imports.

The Republic is thus in the extremely difficult position of finding that the achievement of one target (a reduction in the rate of unemployment) tends to diminish its chances of attaining the other (a reduction in the balance of payments deficit). Scope for expanding government expenditure in a selective, deliberately import-minimising way exists but cannot be expected to exert anything more than a marginal influence.

It has been proposed that, since oil producers can translate only part of their extra income into demand for goods and services, each oil-consuming nation should try to finance part of its 'oil deficit' by borrowing directly or indirectly from the oil producers. The difficulty lies in converting this general advice into practical guidelines for the borrowing and lending nations. Does the 'oil deficit' refer to the extra cost of oil supplies (*a*) at current import levels, (*b*) at the level they would be at in a full-employment situation, or (*c*) at the level they would be at if all reasonable steps were made to reduce the quantity of oil consumed? Clearly there are tremendous difficulties inherent in the definition of the oil deficit. It is also a moot point whether the oil deficit can be viewed independently of all the other elements in the overall balance of payments situation. These ambiguities mean that oil producers will continue to fear that borrowing countries will use the funds to finance inflation. Present rates of inflation in the UK and the Irish Republic suggest that the oil producers' fears are not altogether unfounded.

Thus even if the desire to borrow were there, together with the determination to use the borrowed funds to expand investment, it may prove more difficult than it appears at first sight. For the Republic this difficulty might take the form of reluctance of foreigners to lend to the government; for the North the difficulty would be manifested in a reluctance by Westminster to transfer funds on the scale required to offset the autonomous deflationary impact of the oil deficit. If the borrowing constraint were to prove binding, of course, the Republic has at least two policy options not open to the North — the imposition of direct import controls or devaluation.

Import controls, however, would create trouble for the Republic with its EEC partners, as well as inviting retaliation. As far as devaluation is concerned, its effectiveness would depend very much on the package of policy instruments accompanying the change in the exchange rate. Looking at the problem in a partial equilibrium framework, the rise in the domestic price of imports and the fall in the foreign price of exports could undoubtedly be expected to achieve some improvement in the current account of the balance of payments. But research into the Republic's economy has shown that the amount of devaluation required to obtain even a small improvement in the balance of payments is large because (*a*) the import content of the Republic's industrial exports tends to be very high, and (*b*) the elasticity of demand for many categories of imports tends to be low, owing to the absence of domestic substitutes.

If the framework is broadened to include the effects of induced real income changes on the import bill, assuming under-full employment, the effectiveness of a given percentage devaluation would be further reduced. In a full employment situation, by contrast, the devaluation would have to be accompanied by some deliberate absorption-reducing policies to be effective at all. Over and above all these factors would be the danger that increases in the internal price level following devaluation would spark off an inflationary round of wage and salary claims whose net effect might be to neutralise completely the initial benefits of devaluation. Thus devaluation may help, but it is obviously no panacea. In present circumstances it can only be successful if the community is prepared to accept some fall in real living standards.

5   CONCLUSIONS

The openness of the economies of Northern Ireland and the Republic has been stressed on a number of occasions in this chapter. The rapid economic growth of the island has accentuated this dependence on the world economy further. Both Irish economies have, it is true, reduced their dependence on the British economy by diversifying export markets, but only at the cost of increasing their dependence on the markets of Western Europe and the United States. Political independence and economic independence are two separate things, and one does not presuppose the existence of the other.

The current world recession forces one to focus attention once again on the problem of Ireland's vulnerability to external factors. The immediate issue is that of maintaining export growth in the face of adverse market developments abroad. If exports fail to maintain their past rate of expansion, the prospects for Ireland recovering its past GNP growth rates are very slim. An additional problem will centre around the foreign-owned industrial enterprises which have contributed so much to the economic prosperity of the two parts of Ireland during the last fifteen years. With world markets in a state of decline, the task of attracting new foreign enterprises to Ireland becomes progressively more difficult. For much the same reasons, domestic entrepreneurs are also reluctant to invest. Many Irish manufacturers, particularly those in the textile, clothing and footwear sectors, have been hit simultaneously by a reduction in demand for their products generally, due to lower incomes, and by increased foreign competition, due to the removal of protection. Their problems have been further compounded by the exceptionally high rate of inflation currently being experienced in both Irish economies. Indeed, it could be argued that the control of inflation is the most important prerequisite for a restoration of a satisfactory external position, as well as for the resumption of high growth rates and increased employment.

The prosperity of the Irish economies will also depend on developments within the E E C. The establishment of a properly functioning regional policy, with the financial backing needed to be effective, is an objective whose attainment is of vital economic interest to people on both sides of the Irish border. The development of a common E E C energy policy will also have important implications for Ireland. Finally, although the prospect of European economic and monetary union appears a long way off at this stage, progress towards this objective will undoubtedly take place during the next decade and will bring with it new opportunities and problems for the Irish economies.

REFERENCES

Attwood, E. A. (1974): 'The Agricultural Situation 1974', *Irish Banking Review* (Dec.).

Dowling, B. R. (1975): 'Some Economic Implications of a Federal Ireland' in N. J. Gibson, ed., *Economic and Social Implications of the Political Alternatives that may be Open to Northern Ireland,* New University of Ulster [Coleraine].

Durkan, J. and Kelleher, R. (1974): in *Quarterly Economic Commentary,* E S R I (Jun.).

Eckstein, O. (1974): 'A Plethora of Lessons from the Recent Expansion', *American Economic Review, Papers and Proceedings,* Vol. 64, No. 2 (May).

FitzGerald, G. (1972): *Towards a New Ireland,* 2nd ed., Gill and Macmillan, Dublin 1973.

Henry, E. W. (1972): *Irish Input-Output Structures 1964 and 1968* (E S R I Paper No. 66), Dublin.

Henry, E. W. and Copeland, J. (1975): *Irish Input-Output Income Multipliers 1964 and 1968* (E S R I Paper No. 82), Dublin.

Isles, K. A. and Cuthbert, N. (1957): *An Economic Survey of Northern Ireland,* H M S O, Belfast.

Kennedy, K. A. and Bruton, R. (1975): *The Irish Economy* (Commission of the European Communities, Economic and Financial Series, No. 10), Brussels.

Kennedy, K. A. and Dowling, B. R. (1975): *Economic Growth in Ireland: The Post-War Experience,* Gill and Macmillan, Dublin.

McAleese, D. (1971): *Effective Tariffs and the Structure of Industrial Protection in Ireland* (E S R I Paper No. 62), Dublin.

McAleese, D. (1972): 'Capital Inflows and Direct Foreign Investment in Ireland 1952 to 1970', *Journal of the Statistical and Social Inquiry Society of Ireland,* Vol. 22, Pt 4 (1971–72).

McAleese, D. (1975): Ireland in the Enlarged E E C: Economic Consequences and Prospects', in John Vaizey, ed., *Economic Sovereignty and Regional Policy,* Gill and Macmillan, Dublin.

McAleese, D. (1976): 'Industrial Specialisation and Trade: Northern Ireland and the Republic', *Economic and Social Review,* Vol. 7, No. 2 (Jan.).

McAleese, D. and Martin, J. (1973): *Irish Manufactured Imports from the U K in the Sixties: The Effects of A I F T A* (E S R I Paper No. 70), Dublin.

Matthew, Sir R., Wilson, T. and Parkinson, J. (1970): *Northern Ireland Development Programme 1970–75,* H M S O, Belfast.

Northern Ireland Office (1974): *Northern Ireland: Discussion Paper: Finance and the Economy,* H M S O, London.

Ryan, W. J. L. (1949): 'Measurement of Tariff Levels for Ireland, for 1931, 1936, 1938', *Journal of the Statistical and Social Inquiry Society of Ireland,* Vol. 18 (1948–49).

Whitaker, T. K. (1974): 'From Protection to Free Trade – The Irish Experience', *Administration,* Vol. 22, No. 4 (Winter).

Whitman, M. von N. (1967): *International and Interregional Payments Adjustment: A Synthetic View* (Princeton Studies in International Finance, No. 19), Princeton University.

CHAPTER 5

Wages, Prices, Income and Wealth

P. T. GEARY

1   INTRODUCTION

This chapter deals with a broad set of topics. Section 2 consists of a discussion of the determination of prices and wages in the models in Chapter 1 and
an examination of the data on prices and wages in the Republic of Ireland,
Northern Ireland and the United Kingdom. Section 3 contains an analysis
of personal expenditure data for the Republic and Northern Ireland; a lack
of data for Northern Ireland restricts the discussion of savings to the Republic only. This section is related to the consumption functions of the
models of Chapter 1. The personal distribution of income and wealth, which
is the subject of Section 4, has little direct connection with the highly
aggregated models of the two economies. On the other hand, the functional
distribution of income in each economy, i.e. the distribution of income
among the owners of factors of production, is, strictly speaking, implied by
the models. The issues which this raises, referred to in Chapter 1, together
with a discussion on the data on functional distribution, form the content
of Section 5.

2   PRICES AND WAGES

2.1   Price and Wage Determination in the Spencer-Harrison Model

The price and wage determination aspects of the models of the Republic and
Northern Ireland presented in Chapter 1 are identical and involve strong
assumptions. Prices are determined together with income, unemployment
and the level of employment. Once unemployment is determined, the wage
level is determined; if the wage level is changed due to a change in an exogenous variable, in this case the British wage rate, there are no feedbacks
through the system. Thus as the models are specified, wages in both
economies do not affect prices; this point is discussed in Chapter 1. Prices,
however, do affect wages. A change in the British price level changes more

than the domestic price level: exports and imports, and through them, income and unemployment are also affected, which leads to a change in wages. This may be seen in equations (5.1) to (5.5) which contain the price and wage determination system of the Spencer-Harrison model (taking the Republic version for convenience).

$$Q = C + I + G_1 + x\,(P_{GB}, P, \ldots) - m\,(P_{GB}, P, \ldots) \tag{5.1}$$
$$Q = h\,(N) \tag{5.2}$$
$$P = \theta\,(P_{GB}) + \bar{\theta}\,(u^*), \; u^* = U/\bar{N} \tag{5.3}$$
$$U = \bar{N} - N \tag{5.4}$$
$$W = \psi\,(W_{GB}) + \bar{\psi}\,(u^*) \tag{5.5}$$

The model clearly recognises external influences on prices and wages, but identifies these as the levels of the corresponding British variables. The appropriateness of this for Northern Ireland is self-evident; for the Republic it may appear less so, given the declining importance of Britain in the external trade of the Republic. This point applies with much greater force to the role of British income in the model of the Republic's economy than to prices and wages. In the case of the latter, there are obvious reasons why British labour market conditions should be the main external influence on the Republic's labour market. The dominant influence on the Republic's prices, too, should be British prices, given the absence of barriers to trade in goods and factors, the difficulty of operating restrictions on financial transactions, and the existence of an exchange rate with sterling which has not altered in over a century. These points are discussed in more detail below.

Alternative formulations of the price and wage determination mechanism spring readily to mind, but their consequences for the structure of the model would require analysis. A simple method of bringing the wage rate more directly into the model would be to include a wage term in the price equation, i.e.

$$P = \theta(P_{GB}) + \pi(W) + \bar{\theta}(u^*) \tag{5.6}$$

where $d\pi/dW > 0$. This would make the first eight equations in the full system (for Northern Ireland; seven for the Republic) fully simultaneous without making the properties of the model too complicated. In the restricted system, with (5.6) replacing (5.3), signing the results of the comparative statics would present few additional difficulties. The logic of the wage term is straightforward. The same would be true of introducing a price term in the wage equation, but to do this alone would not alter the original structure of the model.

The only market in the models of the two economies which is not assumed to be in equilibrium is the labour market; this is clear from the way unemployment enters both models. In these circumstances it might be argued that it is more appropriate to express the price and wage equations in terms of *changes* in prices and wages, rather than levels. This could be done very simply, without complicating the comparative static analysis of the models, as follows:

$$\Delta P = \theta(\Delta P_{GB}) + \bar{\theta}(u^*) \qquad (5.7)$$

$$\Delta W = \psi(\Delta W_{GB}) + \bar{\psi}(u^*) \qquad (5.8)$$

where ΔP and ΔW are the differences between current and last period's prices and wages. Such a formulation clearly draws attention to the assumed disequilibrium in the labour market; it has similarities to the wage-price models of the inflationary process which were developed in the late 1950s and have been extensively applied since then (see, for example, Lipsey and Parkin (1970)).

If a wage difference term is added to (5.7), which would give

$$\Delta P = \theta(\Delta P_{GB}) + \pi(\Delta W) + \bar{\theta}(u^*) \qquad (5.9)$$

the similarity to the price equation of these models is striking. It is usually written in terms of proportionate first differences, as follows:

$$\frac{\dot{P}}{P} = a_0 + a_1 \frac{\dot{W}}{W} + a_2 \frac{\dot{Pm}}{Pm} + a_3 \frac{\dot{Z}}{Z}, \quad a_1, a_2 > 0, a_3 < 0 \qquad (5.10)$$

where the dot on a variable denotes its time derivative (or first difference), Pm is import prices and Z is a measure of productivity. More recent versions of (5.10) have added a variable to allow for the effect of demand pressure on prices; as it stands the equation states that the rate of change of prices depends only on cost considerations. There are various possible ways of measuring demand pressure (see the essays in Eckstein (1972)). One would be the rate of unemployment, since the greater the level of demand, *ceteris paribus*, the greater the demand for labour, and hence the lower the unemployment rate. If this variable were added to (5.10) and import prices treated as equivalent to British prices, the only substantive difference between (5.9) and (5.10) is the presence of the productivity term in the latter.

The basic form of the wage equation of the wage-price models is

$$\frac{\dot{W}}{W} = b_0 + b_1 u^* + b_2 \left(\frac{\dot{P}}{P}\right)^e, \quad b_1 < 0, b_2 > 0 \qquad (5.11)$$

where $\left(\frac{\dot{P}}{P}\right)^e$ is the expected rate of price inflation. This is known as the augmented Phillips curve. The rate of change of u^* is often included as an independent variable, with the sign of its coefficient predicted to be negative, while u^* is often replaced by $1/u^*$. The coefficient of the price expectations term is sometimes restricted to be unity, so that (5.11) would state that the proportionate rate of change of the *real* wage depends on excess demand in the labour market, measured by unemployment. Such a restriction rules out money illusion in the labour market.

Occasionally the expected rate of *wage* inflation replaces the price expectations term in (5.11). Equation (5.8) is similar to the latter formulation, where the term involving the change in British wage rates is interpreted as measuring wage expectations. If the British wage rate term is replaced by a function of the change in British or Irish prices, this could similarly be interpreted as measuring price expectations. The latter may be measured in various ways. A simple expectations hypothesis would be that the current rate of change of prices equals the expected,

i.e. $\left(\dfrac{\dot{P}}{P}\right)^e = \left(\dfrac{\dot{P}}{P}\right)$ or $(\Delta P)^e = \Delta P$. In this case (5.8) would become

$$\Delta W = \Delta P + \bar{\psi}(u^*) \tag{5.12}$$

The relation to (5.11) is clear.

As already observed, while external influences on both prices and wages are recognised in the Spencer-Harrison model, domestic influences enter through the rate of unemployment. When the price equation is expressed in terms of rates of change rather than levels, the role of domestic factors suggests that the equation should be interpreted as a short-run relationship. The Republic of Ireland and Northern Ireland economies clearly qualify for the description of small open economies maintaining fixed exchange rates with their major trading partner, and it is the unambiguous conclusion of economic analysis that such economies, in the long run, experience the rate of inflation of the major trading partner. In other words, the long-run rate of inflation is externally determined; only in the short term are domestic influences relevant. The arguments in support of this conclusion and the qualifications that surround it are summarised in Geary (1974) and McDowell (1975); both contain references to more detailed analyses. The conclusion, of course, provides support for the assumption that it is British prices which are the relevant external influences on Irish prices. Its implications for the model, however, are important. If the price equation were stated in terms of rates of change and if unemployment were deleted, there would be *no* connection between the price equation and the real sectors of both economies. It should be noted that the above statement concerns the convergence of inflation rates, not price levels. Some convergence of price levels between Ireland and Britain seems inevitable, but domestic factors may exercise a long-term influence on them.

In the case of the wage equation, labour mobility between the Republic and Britain would suggest a long-term tendency for *real* wage levels in the two economies to converge. The closer relationship of the Northern Ireland economy to Britain's would suggest a stronger tendency in the same direction. In the long run, domestic unemployment could be a *consequence* of the process of real wage equalisation and would almost certainly be accompanied by migration. As far as (nominal) wages are concerned, the long-term behaviour of real wage levels and rates of price inflation just outlined would suggest that the rate of wage inflation in the Republic's economy initially exceeds that in Britain. Wage levels would initially diverge, but eventually convergence would occur. When the wage equation is expressed in terms of rates of change it may again be argued that the influence of domestic excess demand is essentially short-run.[1] Deletion of the unemployment term in the wage equation would mean that the Irish wage level in each model was simply determined by the British level.

Evidence on the role of domestic excess demand in the wage and price inflationary process in the Republic of Ireland may be found in studies by Geary and Jones (1975); evidence for Northern Ireland may be found in Geary (1975b). Variants of the wage-price model referred to above were estimated for the Republic of Ireland, using annual data for the post-war period. Domestic excess demand was found to play only a small part in the inflationary process. An augmented Phillips curve was estimated for Northern Ireland for the same data period, yielding a very small and statistically insignificant coefficient of the unemployment rate. In the estimates for both the Republic and Northern Ireland, the coefficient of the price expectation term in the wage equation was very close to, and not significantly different from, unity.

2.2 Prices

Price data are readily available for the Republic of Ireland, either in the form of fixed weight indices such as the Consumer Price Index (CP I) and the Wholesale Price Index (W P I), or variable weight indices such as the deflators of the Gross National Product (GN P), Gross Domestic Product (G D P) and other elements of the national accounts. Northern Ireland, on the other hand, has no equivalent to the C P I or W P I. The Retail Price Index (R P I) is compiled for the U K as a whole and not on a regional basis. There is, however, a deflator for G D P at factor cost, which may claim to be the only regional price index in the U K. It is derived from a combination of United Kingdom and Northern Ireland data. For some sectors U K sectoral deflators are employed. For others the deflators are based on the Index of Production produced by the Northern Ireland Department of Commerce, which is itself compiled from both U K and Northern Ireland data. Individual calculations from Northern Ireland data are made for the remaining sectors. The index is presented in Table 5.1(a), together with deflators of G D P at

---

1 The terms 'short run' and 'long run' should not be interpreted to imply fixed periods of time. For example, as is apparent from the data in Subsections 2.2 and 2.3, the 'long run' in which Irish and British inflation rates converge is much shorter than that in which price levels and real wages tend to equalise.

Table 5.1(a): Price Indices for Northern Ireland, the Republic and the
United Kingdom, 1961–74 (1960 = 100)

Year	Northern Ireland GDP deflator	Republic of Ireland GDP deflator	CPI	UK GDP deflator	RPI
1961	102·20	104·01	102·74	103·28	103·43
1962	103·99	108·80	107·09	106·88	108·11
1963	110·67	112·85	109·74	109·17	110·24
1964	110·83	121·05	117·09	112·06	113·57
1965	114·34	127·31	122·99	116·63	119·29
1966	119·15	131·13	126·67	121·36	123·65
1967	121·95	137·14	130·68	125·02	126·73
1968	128·37	144·52	136·84	128·88	132·68
1969	136·85	158·90	147·01	133·79	139·89
1970	151·00	173·00	159·06	144·00	148·81
1971	162·02	185·96	173·33	158·81	163·23
1972	182·56	211·01	188·20	173·68	174·39
1973	n.a.	237·39	209·40	189·51	190·42
1974	n.a.	n.a.	245·30	n.a.	220·98

Sources: N I: *Digest of Statistics*, H M S O, Belfast, various issues; R I: *Irish Trade Journal* (continued as *Irish Statistical Bulletin*), various issues; U K: *Department of Employment Gazette*, H M S O, London, various issues.

factor cost for the Republic of Ireland and the UK, the Consumer Price Index of the Republic and the Retail Price Index of the UK; the deflators are illustrated in Figure 5.1.

The graphs show that prices, as measured by the GDP deflators, have risen by more since 1960 in the Republic than in the UK or Northern Ireland. A comparison of the CPI and RPI in the table leads to the same conclusion. This point is discussed below. The Northern Ireland and UK deflators are very similar, as would be expected, though some differences exist. The main source of year-to-year differences is probably the difference between the sectoral composition of GDP in Northern Ireland and the UK as a whole. For example, agriculture etc., accounted for just over 8 per cent of GDP in Northern Ireland in 1972 and just under 3 per cent in the UK. It is of interest that the increase in the rate of inflation which occurred late in the 1960s appears to have started earlier in Northern Ireland; why this should be so is hard to say.

It is clear that the GDP deflator in the Republic of Ireland has risen by more than the Consumer Price Index, while in the UK the corresponding indices are very similar. The indices are constructed in different ways, of course, and the deflator covers a much broader set of goods and services;

unlike the CPI, it is exclusive of the effect of indirect taxes and subsidies. The difference may be largely attributable to the big rise in the cost of goods and services bought by the public sector, which accounts for a growing share of GDP. The rise may be due in part to the fact that many public sector activities have a rather high labour content and the price of labour relative to other inputs has risen sharply since 1953 (see Geary, Walsh and Copeland (1975)). It has also been suggested that a relative increase in the earnings of public sector employees might have contributed to the rise. The difference between the two indices should not conceal their essential similarity, both clearly reflecting the acceleration of inflation after 1967.

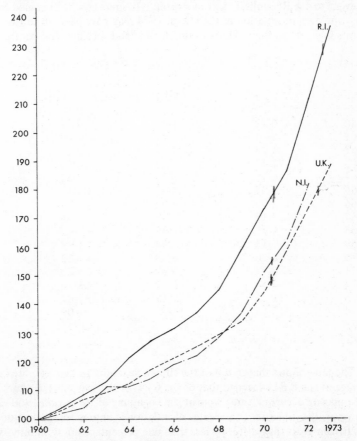

Figure 5.1: *GDP Deflators of Northern Ireland, the Republic and the United Kingdom, 1960–73 (1960 = 100)*

Source: Table 5.1(a).

The relationship between the two price indices of the U K is much closer, with only one point separating them in 1973, as compared with the eighteen-point difference in the Irish indices. Of greater interest, however, is a comparison of the cost of living indices of the U K and the Republic, i.e. the R P I and C P I respectively. The percentage rates of change of these indices, usually identified as *the* rate of inflation, are presented in Table 5.1(b). It is worth pointing out that these indices include the effects of the government's indirect tax and subsidy policies, so that a policy of shifting the base of taxation from income to expenditure would raise their levels, while one of subsidising commodities would lower them. This point is relevant to the Republic/U K comparison; it has recently been argued that the 'true' rate of inflation in the U K in 1974 may have been up to five points higher than the published rate, due to food subsidies and controls.

Table 5.1(b): Percentage Rate of Change of C P I and R P I, 1960—74

Year	C P I	R P I	CPI − RPI
1960	0·43	1·00	−0·57
1961	2·74	3·44	−0·70
1962	4·24	4·52	−0·28
1963	2·47	1·97	+0·50
1964	6·70	3·38	+3·32
1965	5·04	4·67	+0·37
1966	2·99	3·93	−0·94
1967	3·17	2·49	+0·68
1968	4·71	4·69	+0·02
1969	7·43	5·44	+1·99
1970	8·20	6·38	+1·82
1971	8·97	9·69	−0·72
1972	8·58	6·84	+1·74
1973	11·26	9·19	+2·07
1974	17·14	16·05	+1·09

Source: Calculated from data in Table 5.1(a).

The table shows that in ten of the fifteen years the percentage rate of change of the R P I exceeded that of the C P I; of the five years in which the opposite occurred, three were at the beginning of the period 1960—74. However, the similarity of the rates of inflation is impressive. In nine of the fifteen years they differ by less than one percentage point; in only two cases are the differences more than two percentage points. The average of the differences in column 3 is 0·7. The greatest difference between the two rates occurred in 1964, a year of fairly rapid growth of real G D P in the Republic, but in which there was also a sharp increase in agricultural prices and increased indirect taxation. Since 1967 the rate of increase of the C P I has almost always exceeded that of the R P I, although, as mentioned above, there are reasons for believing that in 1974 the rate of increase of the R P I understated the U K inflation rate. It is difficult to say exactly what accounts for the differences, i.e. whether they are largely a consequence of different tax policies, the structure of the two economies, or other factors. It should be noted, though, that in no year since 1967 have the rates of inflation moved in the opposite direction; most economists would regard the evidence of Table 5.1(b) as supporting the view, stated in Section 1 of this chapter, that a small open economy maintaining a fixed exchange rate with its major trading partner can achieve only short-term deviations of its rate of inflation from the rate set by that partner.

2.3 Wages

Data on industrial wages and earnings are available for Northern Ireland; in the Republic wage data are scarce, but earnings data are adequate. In Table 5.2(a) average hourly earnings for Northern Ireland, the Republic and the U K are presented. The data for the Republic refer to workers, male and female, aged eighteen years and over, in transportable goods industries. They refer to the month of October up to 1968; from 1969 onwards they refer to September of each year. The data for Northern Ireland and the U K refer to male manual workers aged twenty-one years or over, for 'all

Table 5.2(a): Average Hourly Earnings of Industrial Workers in Northern Ireland, the Republic and the United Kingdom, 1960–74 (in new pence)

Year	Northern Ireland	Republic	U K	Col. 1 ÷ Col. 3	Col. 2 ÷ Col. 3
1960	26·3	16·7	30·3	0·87	0·55
1961	26·5	17·9	32·4	0·82	0·55
1962	28·0	20·0	33·8	0·83	0·59
1963	29·0	21·0	35·2	0·82	0·60
1964	31·7	23·5	38·0	0·83	0·62
1965	34·9	24·6	41·7	0·84	0·59
1966	37·8	27·4	44·1	0·86	0·62
1967	40·3	29·1	46·3	0·87	0·63
1968	43·1	32·3	49·5	0·87	0·65
1969	46·1	36·5	53·4	0·86	0·68
1970	53·3	42·7	61·4	0·87	0·70
1971	62·0	49·8	69·2	0·90	0·72
1972	70·5	55·9	79·6	0·89	0·70
1973	81·0	69·2	89·7	0·90	0·77
1974	100·2	n.a.	107·8	0·93	n.a.

Source: As Table 5.1(a).

industries', and relate to October of each year. These data are graphed in
Figure 5.2. Note that they are not indices (they are denominated in new
pence) and, in comparing levels, that they are not defined for identical
groups of workers. The earnings data for the Republic of Ireland reflect the
system of wage rounds that operated in the 1960s. The small peaks that
occur in the graph in Figure 5.2 in 1962, 1964 and 1966 indicate a much
more rapid rate of increase of earnings in those years than in 1961, 1968,
1965, and 1967; in fact, the percentage rate of increase was over 11·5 per
cent in each of these years, as compared with increases of 7·5 per cent, 5

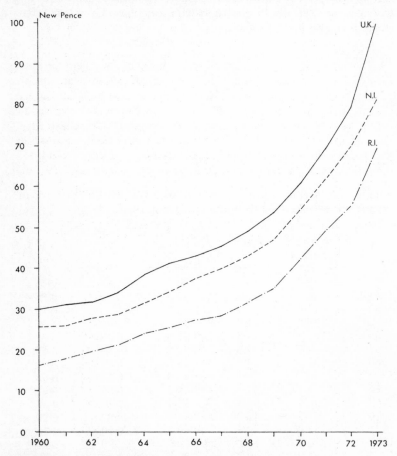

Figure 5.2: *Average Hourly Industrial Earnings in Northern Ireland, the
Republic and the United Kingdom, 1960–73*

Source: As Table 5.1(a).

per cent, 4·8 per cent, and 6·1 per cent in the odd-numbered years. Since then, however, the general increase in the rate of wage inflation that occurred all over the world is observed. Changes in the earnings rates for Northern Ireland and the UK exhibit somewhat different patterns up to 1967; from then on, the similarity dominates.

Table 5.2(a) includes the ratio of earnings in the Republic and Northern Ireland to UK earnings. The Northern Ireland/UK ratio fell in the early 1960s but by 1968 had regained its 1960 level and since then has risen slightly. The Republic of Ireland/UK ratio, on the other hand, has risen steadily, from 0·55 in 1960 to 0·77 in 1973 (the Republic/Northern Ireland ratio has risen from 0·63 in 1960 to 0·85 in 1973). The convergence of ratios, however, has not been sufficient to prevent increases in the absolute differences between the earnings rates. The difference between the Republic of Ireland and UK earnings rates has increased by seven pence, and that between Northern Ireland and UK rates by five pence. Thus while the earnings levels have not converged in the period 1960—73, the more rapid growth of earnings in the Republic would, if maintained, eventually lead to such a convergence.

Data on agricultural wages in both Northern Ireland and the Republic refer to *minimum* wages; they are presented in index form in Table 5.2(b). Data for the Republic relate to October of each year up to and including 1968; from 1969 onwards they relate to September. The Northern Ireland data relate to the end of June of each year. It should be emphasised that

Table 5.2(b): Index of Minimum Rates of Male Agricultural Workers in Northern Ireland and the Republic, 1962—74 (1961 = 100)

Year	Northern Ireland	Republic
1962	106·0	105·5
1963	110·1	111·6
1964	120·1	132·3
1965	126·9	146·4
1966	133·6	164·5
1967	136·2	164·5
1968	146·3	182·9
1969	157·7	210·7
1970	167·8	265·9
1971	189·9	296·5
1972	210·0	323·8
1973	254·4	360·9
1974	313·4	n.a.

Sources: N I: *Digest of Statistics,* H M S O, Belfast, various issues; R I: *CBR* (1975), Table 58.

these data refer to *minimum* wages and thus do not provide information on wage rates actually paid or on actual earnings.

The table shows that minimum wage rates have risen more in the Republic than in Northern Ireland. The actual wage rates in 1960 were £5·50 in the Republic and £7·45 in Northern Ireland. By 1973, however, the rates were £19·85 in the Republic and £18·95 in Northern Ireland. In 1974 the Northern Ireland rate rose sharply to £23·35; data for the Republic are not yet available. Thus there has been a convergence of the minimum wage levels of agricultural workers in the Republic and Northern Ireland. Comparison of Tables 5.2(a) and 5.2(b) is inappropriate, for the reasons already mentioned.

3   PERSONAL EXPENDITURE AND SAVINGS

3.1   Personal Expenditure

The analysis of personal expenditure involves disaggregating, by commodity group, the consumption variable in the models of Chapter 1, and relating expenditure on each commodity group to total expenditure. Savings are considered in Subsection 3.2. The study of personal expenditure was pioneered by Ernest Engel in the mid- to late nineteenth century in Germany. Using data from family budget surveys, he examined the relationship between total expenditure and expenditure on food, clothing, housing and so on; Prais and Houthakker (1955) contains an account of his work. The relationships are known as Engel functions and are discussed at greater length below.

Detailed analysis of personal expenditure is possible for both the Republic of Ireland and Northern Ireland, due to the existence of a substantial body of data. In the Republic of Ireland the national accounts include estimates of personal expenditure and its components at current and constant prices. In addition, three extensive surveys of expenditure patterns in *urban* areas, the Household Budget Inquiries, have been carried out since 1946, the first in 1951—52, the second in 1965—66, and the third in 1972—73; the last of these has not yet been published. [Since this was written, the first volume of the Household Budget Inquiry 1973 has been published. Unlike the previous HBIs, it includes rural as well as urban households; see below.— *Eds.*] The 1951—52 and 1965—66 surveys were used to revise the weightings of the Consumer Price Index. There are no national accounts data on personal expenditure for Northern Ireland. However, since 1967 a Family Expenditure Survey has been conducted annually, using the same procedures as employed in the UK Family Expenditure Survey, which has been conducted annually since 1957. The latter contained a small number of Northern Ireland households, but separate data were not released due to the small sample size.

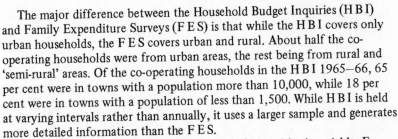

The major difference between the Household Budget Inquiries (HBI) and Family Expenditure Surveys (FES) is that while the HBI covers only urban households, the FES covers urban and rural. About half the co-operating households were from urban areas, the rest being from rural and 'semi-rural' areas. Of the co-operating households in the HBI 1965—66, 65 per cent were in towns with a population more than 10,000, while 18 per cent were in towns with a population of less than 1,500. While HBI is held at varying intervals rather than annually, it uses a larger sample and generates more detailed information than the FES.

The quality of the data obtained in household inquiries is variable. Expenditure data, in general, are good, with the notable exception of expenditure on alcoholic drink, which tends, in the Republic, Northern Ireland and the UK, to be understated by 50 per cent. Income, on the other hand, tends to be underestimated systematically, in the 1965—66 HBI by an estimated 10 per cent. The data will be examined under two headings: (*a*) average expenditure proportions of the main categories of expenditure, and (*b*) expenditure elasticities for these categories.

(*a*) The shares of the main categories of expenditure in total expenditure are given in Table 5.3. For the Republic of Ireland these data are given for 1951—52 and 1965—66 from the HBIs. In addition, shares calculated from national accounts data for 1965 and 1973 are presented. Northern Ireland data for 1967 and 1973 are included. It is emphasised that the data in columns 5 and 6 are not strictly comparable with other data on the same rows; these two columns are calculated from national accounts data.

The most striking characteristics of columns 3 and 4 are the fall in the share of food, from a very high 37·7 per cent to 31·55 per cent and the rise in the share of transport expenditure. In the national accounts data the share of food expenditure continues to fall to 27·9 per cent by 1973. The discrepancy between the share of declared expenditure on alcoholic drink in the HBI 1965—66 and its share in the national accounts data is remarkable; otherwise where comparison is possible, the two sets of data are very similar. A comparison between the HBI 1965—66 results and those of the Northern Ireland FES 1967 shows that the expenditure shares of most commodity groups are similar. The food share in Northern Ireland is slightly lower and the transport share somewhat higher, due in part, perhaps, to the higher level of income per head in Northern Ireland. In addition, the presence of rural households in the FES would be expected to raise the share of transport expenditure, and data in the 1972 FES confirms this: rural households devoted 5 per cent more of total spending to transport than did urban households. The main difference between the sets of results lies in the services category. This arises partly due to classification differences and partly to the nature of the system of social services. Expenditure on health insurance, life assurance and pension funds are included in the services category in the HBI but are excluded from expenditure in the FES. They alone

Table 5.3: Average Expenditure Proportions, Northern Ireland and the Republic, various years 1951–73

Commodity	Northern Ireland		Republic of Ireland			
	1967	1973	1951–52	1965–66	1965	1973
Housing	7·0	9·0	7·13	8·09	6·0	6·1
Fuel and light	6·8	6·8	7·13	5·29	4·5	4·1
Food	30·0	27·9	37·70	31·55	33·6	27·8
Alcoholic drink	2·8	3·9	6·17	3·72	9·7	11·1
Tobacco	6·1	4·6		6·18	7·9	5·4
Clothing and footwear	13·1	11·2	13·02	9·10	10·8	10·6
Durable household goods	5·0	6·9	2·62	4·10	5·2	5·7
Transport and vehicles	12·3	16·5	4·39	9·59	9·2	10·6
Services	9·5	7·0		18·00		
Other goods	6·1	5·8	21·83		13·1	18·6
Miscellaneous	1·2	0·4		4·39		

Sources: N I: *Northern Ireland Family Expenditure Surveys 1967 and 1973*, H M S O, Belfast; R I: *Household Budget Inquiries 1951–52* and *1965–66*, and *National Income and Expenditure 1973*, all Stationery Office, Dublin. (At the time of writing only summary results of the 1973 F E S were available.)

accounted for 3·7 per cent of total expenditure in the H B I 1965—66. Expenditure on health and education is included in both the H B I and F E S under the services category, but in the Republic of Ireland in 1965—66 it absorbed 2·9 per cent of total expenditure as opposed to 0·6 per cent in Northern Ireland in 1967. Income tax and national (or social) insurance payments are excluded from expenditure in both areas.

An international comparison of the composition of personal expenditure is presented in Table 5.4. The data are from the national accounts of various countries as published by O E C D. The classifications differ from those in Table 5.3 so that data for the Republic of Ireland are included. The table also includes G D P per head in U S dollars for each country in 1971. The first commodity group is obviously dominated by food, and there is a clear negative association between income per head and the share in personal expenditure of this commodity group. The same relationship arose in Table 5.3, thus providing more support for Engel's Law (see below). Other interesting features of the table are the relatively small variations across countries in the share of the clothing and transport categories and the large variation in the share of medical care. In comparing the Republic of Ireland with the other countries, the outstanding difference is in the large share of food, drink and tobacco. This is due, of course, not merely to the share of food, which has been declining, but also to the relatively large share of alcoholic drink in total expenditure.

(*b*) The Household Budget Inquiries of 1951—52 and 1965—66 have been extensively studied, the former by Leser and others, the latter by Pratschke (1969), who includes detailed references to the other studies. The main purpose of these studies was to estimate Engel functions. The Engel function is a relationship between household income, appropriately defined, and expenditure on individual commodities or groups of commodities. It is assumed that prices are constant, so that the function may be derived from the household's indifference map by parallel shifts of the budget constraint. It may be regarded as the precursor of the modern consumption function which is a relationship between expenditure on all commodities, i.e. total consumption, and income, for a given price level. The selection of the appropriate income variable raises some problems. Most frequently total expenditure is chosen, in the tradition of the one-period theory of consumer behaviour which usually ignores the savings decision. However, expenditure data in household budget studies include outlays which may be relatively large and infrequent, i.e. consumer durable expenditure. This and related difficulties are encountered in choosing the appropriate income variable in studies of the consumption function, although concepts such as relative and permanent income, so prominent in work on the consumption function have had less impact on Engel function (or demand function) studies.

The studies already cited used total expenditure as their income variable, and from their estimated Engel functions, calculated expenditure elasticities

Table 5.4: International Comparison of Expenditure Proportions, 1971

Commodity	Country						
	USA	Germany	Sweden	Norway	UK	Portugal	Rep. of Ireland
Food, drink and tobacco	18·2	28·8	28·9	35·1	32·5	50·9	46·9
Clothing and footwear	8·5	11·3	7·6	12·9	8·5	n.a.	10·1
Rent, fuel and power	18·5	14·6	21·3	11·9	17·3	5·2	10·8
Durable goods	8·6	13·5	6·2	11·0	8·9	n.a.	8·2
Medical care	7·7	2·9	4·2	3·4	0·4	n.a.	1·1
Transport and communication	15·7	12·5	12·7	11·8	13·1	n.a.	10·9
Other	22·8	16·4	19·1	13·9	19·3	n.a.	12·0
GDP *per capita* US $	5,129	3,551	4,409	3,349	2,428	763	1,526

Source: OECD, *National Accounts of OECD Countries*, Paris 1973.

for the various commodity groups. There have been no comparable studies of the Northern Ireland data, so expenditure elasticities have been estimated from the 1967 data and are presented here. These results may be regarded as the initial stage of a more detailed study (see Geary (1975a)). Pratschke estimated functions of the linear, log-linear and other forms and, in addition to total expenditure, he added household size, i.e. the average number of persons per household in each income group, as an independent variable. Household size and composition may be expected to exert an influence on consumption independently of income. For example, one would expect food consumption to vary with household size and composition for a given level of income. Pratschke (and Leser) tested different hypotheses about the effects of household size. A common one is that expenditure on a commodity per person is a function of income per person, which implies constant returns to scale in consumption. In some of his estimation this condition was *imposed,* but the results are not reported in detail. However, his published results do allow the role of household size to be evaluated.

The Engel functions estimated from Northern Ireland data were of the linear and log-linear forms and included household size as an independent variable. Formally,

$$v_i = a_{0i} + a_{1i} v_0 + a_{2i} n, \quad i = 1, \ldots, m \tag{5.13}$$

$$\log v_i = b_{0i} + b_{1i} \log v_0 + b_{2i} \log n, \quad i = 1, \ldots, m \tag{5.14}$$

where v_0 is total expenditure, v_i is expenditure on commodity group i, n is household size and m is the number of commodities. The expenditure elasticities implied by these forms are $a_{1i} v_0/v_i$ and b_{1i} respectively. These elasticities are constrained by the fact that the sum of expenditure on all commodity groups must equal total expenditure, i.e. $\sum_i v_i = v_0$. In terms of the theory of consumer demand, the household is always on, not below, its budget constraint. It can easily be shown that the sum of the expenditure elasticities, weighted by the expenditure proportions of the commodity groups, is 1:

$$\sum_i s_i e_i = 1 \tag{5.15}$$

where s_i and e_i are the expenditure proportion and elasticity of commodity group i. This condition is called the Engel aggregation condition. Equation (5.14) implies that the expenditure elasticity of each commodity group is a constant ($b_{1i}, i = 1, \ldots, m$). But constant elasticities will violate (5.15) unless all the elasticities are unity, i.e. they are, in general, inconsistent with the theory of consumer behaviour. To see this, suppose there are two goods, one with an expenditure elasticity of 2 and an expenditure share of 0·2, the other with an elasticity of 0·75 and an expenditure share of 0·8. Then multiplying the elasticities by the shares gives 0·4 + 0·6 = 1, so that (5.15) is satisfied. Now suppose that total expenditure doubles, from £1,000 to £2,000. Expenditure on the first good must now quadruple, since the expenditure elasticity is 2, and becomes £800; expenditure on the second good rises by a factor $2^{0.75} = 1.68$ and becomes £1,345. But this means expenditure of £2,145, exceeding total expenditure. Thus constant elasticity estimates must be applied carefully and especially so in situations involving large percentage changes in income. The linear function (5.13), on the other hand, does not imply constant elasticities; they depend on v_i and v_0. The Engel aggregation condition in this case reduces to $\sum_i a_{1i} = 1$, i.e. the sum of the slopes of the Engel curves must be 1. However, linear Engel curves have other implications.[2]

The expenditure elasticities for the Republic of Ireland for 1951–52 as estimated by Leser, and for 1965–66 by Pratschke, are summarised in Tables 9–17 of Pratschke's paper. The results are reproduced in Table 5.5, together with estimates for Northern Ireland for 1967. Pratschke's estimates of the expenditure elasticities are his preferred estimates, and in all cases but one they are derived from equation (5.14), i.e. the log-linear form. For Northern Ireland, elasticity estimates from both the linear and log-linear forms are presented, the elasticities in the former case being evaluated at the mean values of s_i, v_i. Only in the cases of housing and household durable goods do the alternative estimates differ very much, and in both cases the log estimates are not significantly different from zero at the 10 per cent level.

The results for the Republic in 1965–66 and Northern Ireland reveal a considerable degree of similarity, which perhaps is not surprising in the light of Table 5.3. In both areas the transport, services and alcoholic drink categories have elasticities well above 1, while the elasticities for food and fuel and light were well below 1. The food elasticity estimates are very close to each other; the zero elasticity for fuel and light in the case of Northern Ireland is surprising. It may simply be a peculiarity of the sample: preliminary estimates from the 1972 survey suggest an elasticity of about 0.35, very close to the Republic's elasticity for 1965–66. The elasticities of tobacco are not significantly different from 1 at the 5 per cent level in both areas, and while the same is true of clothing and footwear in Northern Ireland, the elasticity in the Republic is significantly different from 1 at the 5 per cent level. As far as housing and household durables are concerned, the estimates for the Republic of Ireland are similar to the Northern Ireland estimates from the linear Engel curves. Neither housing elasticity is significantly different from 1, but the Republic's household durable elasticity, unlike that of Northern Ireland, is.

2 Linear Engel curves are implied by certain types of utility function. Among these are the Stone-Geary function, which gives rise to the widely applied linear expenditure system, the quadratic utility function and the direct addilog model. Another widely applied model, the Rotterdam model, also involves linear Engel curves. See, for example, Brown and Deaton (1972).

Table 5.5: Expenditure Elasticities for Various Commodity Groups, Northern Ireland, 1967; Republic of Ireland, 1951–52, 1965–66

Commodity	Northern Ireland, 1967		Republic of Ireland	
	Linear	Log-linear	1951–52	1965–66
Housing	0·90	0·54	0·93	0·98
Fuel and light	0·00	0·00	0·50	0·32
Food	0·52	0·56	0·61	0·51
Alcoholic drink	1·94	2·16	0·87[b]	1·79
Tobacco	0·83	0·82		0·59
Clothing and footwear	0·89	1·17	1·49	1·14
Durable household goods	1·5	0·86[a]	2·00	1·20
Transport and vehicles	2·02	1·81	2·13	2·00
Services	1·85	1·87	1·54	1·52
Other miscellaneous	0·60	1·08	1·30	1·33

[a]The coefficient is not significantly different from zero at the 10 per cent level.

[b]This is the elasticity for alcoholic drink and tobacco; expenditure data for drink and tobacco as separate categories were not published in the HBI 1951–52.

Sources: Pratschke (1969); Geary (1975a).

It is of interest to compare these findings with those of Ernest Engel. He found that (a) food was the largest item of expenditure in the family budget, (b) the proportion of expenditure accounted for by food falls as the living standard of the household increases, and (c) the proportions of expenditure on housing and clothing are relatively constant while that of 'luxury' items increases with living standards. The second of these results has proved so durable that it has become known as Engel's Law; and the results presented above provide further strong confirmation of it. Of his other results, (a) holds in the Republic of Ireland and Northern Ireland and in several other countries, but not everywhere (see, for example, the data for the USA in Table 5.4). Engel himself recognised that this result would not prove durable. The third result, that the expenditure elasticities of housing and clothing should be close to 1 is borne out in the Republic and Northern Ireland, but international evidence on this point, as presented by Parks and Barten (1973), is variable.

The influence of household size is now briefly examined. The results for the Republic of Ireland for 1965—66 showed that household size had a significant influence on expenditure for the following commodity groups: food, housing, transport services, and other goods. For Northern Ireland, however, household size was significant only for food, at the 10 per cent level, fuel and light and services. The hypothesis of constant returns to scale in consumption was rejected for most commodity groups.

One conclusion which emerges from the foregoing analysis of personal expenditure is that when commodities are grouped into categories such as food, clothing, etc. there is a considerable degree of stability in patterns of expenditure, not merely across countries but also over long periods of time within countries. Even though the composition of populations change, tastes change, and new commodities emerge, the broad patterns of expenditure appear not to fluctuate very much. Obviously some major changes occur, as is instanced by the growth of expenditure on transport and communication, but overall the stability is noteworthy. When the commodity groups are disaggregated, however, it is far less apparent.

3.2 Personal Savings

The relationship between aggregate personal income and savings has been thoroughly investigated by economists, both theoretically and empirically. The most widely accepted theories, i.e. the permanent and normal income hypotheses and the endogenous income hypothesis, imply a proportionate relationship, in the long term, between the level of personal income and personal savings. In the short term, however, the relationship is not proportionate: a rise in income is accompanied by a more than proportionate rise in savings, and a fall in income by a more than proportionate fall in savings. Further, these theories imply that when income is growing, the ratio of savings to income tends to be stable as long as the growth rate of income is stable. If it is not, an increase in the growth rate of income is accompanied by an increase in the savings ratio, and a fall in income by a fall in the savings ratio. These results are derived and discussed in Johnson (1971). It is interesting to compare this result with the results of many growth theories, which imply that the growth rate of income is positively related to the savings ratio; see, for example, the chapter on economic growth in Dernburg and McDougall (1960).

The savings ratio may also be affected by the rate of interest, although the direction of the effect is not clear. Other relevant variables include the taxation system and variables arising from the fact that it is the ratio of *aggregate* savings to income that is being considered, e.g. changes in the demographic structure and changes in the occupational structure of the population.

The ratio of personal savings to personal disposable income, i.e. the personal income less taxes on personal income, in the Republic of Ireland for the period 1960–73 is presented in Table 5.6; the corresponding data are not published for Northern Ireland. The table shows that the savings ratio in the Republic of Ireland has increased, reaching the exceptionally high level of 18·1 per cent in 1973.

Table 5.6: Personal Savings as Percentage of Personal Disposable Income, Republic of Ireland, 1960–73

Year	%
1960	7·0
1961	9·4
1962	9·0
1963	8·1
1964	10·5
1965	10·9
1966	10·2
1967	10·1
1968	10·3
1969	10·3
1970	11·8
1971	11·7
1972	14·5
1973	18·1

Source: *National Income and Expenditure,* Stationery Office, Dublin, various issues.

There is some evidence that the growth rate of income has affected the savings ratio; in each year from 1970 to 1973 the growth rate of real income increased and the savings ratio behaved similarly. However, this by no means provides a complete explanation of the increase in the savings ratio. In fact, an empirical study of the determinants of the personal savings ratio in the Republic for the period 1949–68 by Kennedy and Dowling (1970) concluded that the growth of real income did not have a statistically significant effect on the savings ratio, a finding which differed from that in other countries. The variables that did have such an effect included the level of real income per head and tax variables, while variables which explicitly recognised aggregation difficulties, such as demographic characteristics and the ratio of farmers' income to personal disposable income also contributed to the explanation of the savings ratio. However, the Kennedy-Dowling result concerning the role of the rate of growth of income does not constitute a refutation of the theories outlined above, since the equation they estimated was not that implied by those theories; in particular, it did not include the lagged savings ratio (see Johnson (1971)).

4   THE PERSONAL DISTRIBUTION OF INCOME AND WEALTH

4.1   Theoretical Background

The distribution of income and wealth among persons has long been studied by economists but, as with other distribution issues, views as to its importance have varied both historically and among economists at any given time. The last decade has witnessed a strong revival of interest in distribution, and the questions of a contradiction between political equality and economic inequality and between social justice and economic efficiency are currently much discussed. In this section, following a brief outline of economists' work on personal distribution, the available data on the extent of economic inequality among persons, as measured by the distribution of income and wealth, in the Republic of Ireland and Northern Ireland are presented and compared with data for other countries. It should be noted that wealth refers to the stock of 'non-human' assets, e.g. physical and financial assets, and thus excludes a valuation of 'human' assets such as knowledge or skill. Income, of course, includes the return to such human assets, which economists describe as 'human capital', and the observed difference between wealth and income distributions is in part due to this.

The first major study of the personal distribution of income was done by Pareto (1897). He used the income tax data then available from various countries and cities at various times (including fifteenth-century Augsburg). He observed that not merely were incomes unequally distributed, but that there was a regularity in the *shape* of income distributions, which has become known as Pareto's Law. Roughly, this states that the number of persons earning at least a given income falls by a fixed percentage for every one per cent rise in that income level. The fixed percentage is usually referred to as Pareto's α. Subsequent studies have led to the rejection of Pareto's Law as a general description of income distributions, but it retains its applicability to the higher reaches of most income distributions.

A number of statistical explanations of the shape of income distributions have been formulated. Some of these show that, starting from a given distribution, the application of random changes in income (for example, due to capital gains or losses) can, over time, generate distributions of the type commonly observed. Attempts to explain the shape of the personal distribution of income have also been based on the distribution of ability, educational opportunity and attitudes to risk-bearing, as well as on assumptions about hierarchial pay structures in organisations. Detailed expositions of all the work just referred to may be found in the books by Pen (1971) and Bronfenbrenner (1971).

Statistical explanations apart, the personal distribution of wealth has been attributed to such influences as the laws of inheritance and demographic factors. A much discussed example of the former is the practice of primogeniture, which will obviously be associated with greater inequality than the practice of dividing an estate equally among all heirs. The relevance of age structure is strongly suggested by economic theories of the consumption function, such as the well-known life-cycle hypothesis of Modigliani and Brumberg and the endogenous income hypothesis of Clower and Johnson; both of these and other theories are discussed in Johnson (1971). They imply a *more* unequal distribution of wealth than income independently of the human capital issue. There is argument about how much of the observed inequality of the wealth of individuals is attributable to life-cycle factors, i.e. how important is age in explaining the distribution of wealth, as opposed to other factors such as inheritance (see, for example, Atkinson (1972)). But general theories of the personal distribution of income and wealth combining assumptions about savings behaviour with assumptions about inheritance laws, demographic factors and the availability of opportunities or skills are rare; Stiglitz (1969) provides one of the few examples. He presents a simple model of accumulation in which there is, under certain assumptions, a long-run tendency towards equalisation of the distribution of income and wealth and then shows how changed assumptions about inheritance, abilities, etc. affect this tendency.

The growth of interest in the distribution of income and wealth among individuals has led to discussion of the problems that arise in the measurement of inequality. The usual approach to the problem of comparing two frequency distributions of income or wealth is to use some summary statistic of inequality, such as the variance or the Gini coefficient, without discussing the reasons for the choice in any detail. However, each measure implies some concept of social welfare, and it is important to be aware of this; as Atkinson has written,

> The use of these summary measures often seems to obscure the fact that a complete ranking of distributions cannot be reached without fully specifying the form of the social welfare function. Further examination of the social welfare functions implicit in these measures shows that in a number of cases they have properties which are unlikely to be acceptable, and in general there are no grounds for believing that they would accord with social values. (Atkinson (1970), p. 244)[3]

In short, it is important to know exactly what is meant by inequality before trying to measure it. In the discussion that follows summary measures of inequality will not be employed. However, the Lorenz curve, which shows the percentage of income or wealth received or owned by the bottom *x* per cent of the population, will be used to compare distributions. In the paper

3 Reprinted in Atkinson (1973). For a discussion of Atkinson's work and more recent contributions to this literature, the reader should consult Sen (1973).

from which the preceding quotation was taken, Atkinson showed that if
two Lorenz curves do not intersect, the distribution, be it of income or
wealth, associated with the higher of the two curves is socially preferable
to that associated with the lower of the curves, when the social welfare
function is of a particular, rather restrictive type. However, this result has
been generalised to a much broader set of social welfare functions, defined
over incomes. When the Lorenz curves intersect, as is the case in Figure 5.1,
the social ranking of the distributions is not automatically known.

4.2 Personal Distribution of Income

In most countries the available statistical evidence on the personal distribution of incomes consists of the distribution of the incomes (before tax) of
taxpayers. Remarkably, in the Republic of Ireland not even these data are
published. The only evidence that is available is of an indirect kind, and
any conclusions which are drawn from it must be regarded as tentative.
The source of this evidence is the Household Budget Inquiry of 1965—66,
published in August 1969. The main purpose of the inquiry was to obtain
detailed information on the pattern of households' expenditure in urban
areas, i.e. towns and villages, but it contains one of the few pieces of
published evidence on the distribution of the weekly household income in
the Republic. Gross weekly income refers to *all* income received by the
household, including pensions and other payments, and it is gross of direct
tax. It also includes an imputed income for owner-occupied dwellings. The
distribution is presented in Table 5.7.

Table 5.7: Distribution of Gross Weekly Income among a Sample of Households, Republic of Ireland, 1965—66

Gross weekly income (£)	% of households	% of income
Less than 10	21·5	6·0
10 − 19·9	38·3	28·0
20 − 29·9	21·1	25·1
30 − 39·9	10·8	18·2
40 − 49·9	4·3	9·4
50+	4·0	13·3

Source: Calculated from *Household Budget Inquiry 1965—66*, Stationery Office,
Dublin 1969.

In interpreting this evidence, a number of points should be borne in mind.
First, the households were chosen from urban areas, thus excluding a large
part of the farming community. Secondly, as often occurs in such inquiries,
there appears to have been a systematic understatement of income by the
co-operating households of about 10 per cent. If the understatement was

systematic, i.e. uniform across all income groups, the shape of the distribution will be affected only in a simple and predictable way, but if summary measures such as the variance were being used for purposes of comparison with other distributions, it would be crucial to know the extent of the understatement. Thirdly, the data relate to households rather than to individuals. As will be noted below, this may have advantages when the concentration of incomes is being considered. Fourthly, the coverage of households at the lower end of the income scale is better than that achieved in a distribution based on tax returns; in the latter individuals with incomes less than their tax allowances are excluded. The nature of the distribution in Table 5.7 is clearly revealed by the fact that the top 8 per cent of the sampled households accounted for almost 23 per cent of income, while the bottom 60 per cent accounted for only 34 per cent. Unfortunately, the trend in the distribution of income in the Republic cannot be ascertained, since the Household Budget Inquiry of 1951–52 did not contain enough data to enable a distribution to be calculated, while the Inquiry of 1972–73 is not published at the time of writing.

Northern Ireland is better endowed with data on income distribution than the Republic, as the United Kingdom government publishes the distribution of personal incomes before tax on a regional as well as a national basis. Furthermore, since 1967 the Northern Ireland Family Expenditure Survey has been published annually. This survey, similar in character to the Household Budget Inquiry, also contains data on the distribution of income. It should be remembered, however, that it did not restrict itself to *urban* households. The evidence on the distribution of income from the survey is contained in Table 5.8, and it may be regarded as roughly comparable with Table 5.7.

A comparison of the income levels of the sampled households in Northern Ireland with those of the Republic shows a much lower percentage

Table 5.8: Distribution of Gross Weekly Income among a Sample of Households, Northern Ireland, 1967

Gross weekly income (£)	% of households	% of income
Less than 10	17·9	5·2
10 – 19·9	28·6	18·1
20 – 29·9	28·0	28·9
30 – 39·9	12·9	18·5
40 – 49·9	7·3	13·4
50+	5·3	15·8

Source: Calculated from *Northern Ireland Family Expenditure Survey 1967*, H M S O, Belfast.

(46·5 per cent) of households with weekly incomes of less than £20 in the North than in the Republic (59·8 per cent), while 12·6 per cent of the Northern sample had incomes above £40 as compared with 8·3 per cent in the Republic. It is clear that these differences cannot be accounted for by the later date of the Northern Ireland survey. However, when the proportions of income received by the bottom x per cent of households, i.e. the Lorenz curves, are compared, there is a very close similarity between them, as may be seen in Figure 5.3. The curves are plotted from the data in Tables 5·7 and 5.8. If income were distributed equally, the Lorenz curve would lie along the 45° line; since it is not, the curves lie below this line. However, they are so close to each other that, given data considerations, further comparison is unlikely to yield meaningful conclusions.

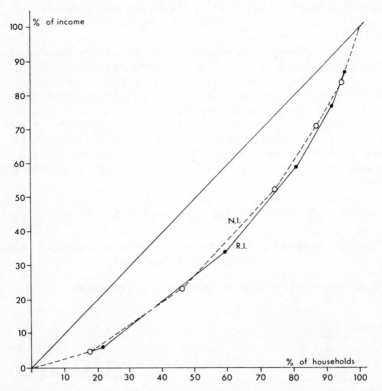

Figure 5.3: *Lorenz Curves of Gross Weekly Income for a Sample of House-holds, Northern Ireland, 1967, and the Republic, 1965—66*

Source: Tables 5.7 and 5.8.

The distribution of personal incomes before tax, as published by the Inland Revenue for Northern Ireland and the UK for the tax year 1971–72, is shown in Table 5.9. Income includes all personal incomes, including pensions, which are liable for income tax, i.e. in excess of £420 in 1971–72; certain interest, insurance benefits and income received in kind are excluded. The data relate to 'tax units', e.g. a married couple counts as a single unit for tax purposes. The growth of money incomes over the period 1965–66 to 1971–72 is evident from the table. Apart from the restricted coverage of low income units and the exclusion of imputed income to owners of dwellings, Inland Revenue data may understate the concentration of incomes if, say, the son of a wealthy father has an independent income treated separately for tax purposes. Household inquiry data do not suffer from this difficulty, since the household is the basic unit. On the other hand, the response rate among higher income groups in household inquiries may be lower than that of other groups, thus reducing the coverage of the upper end of the income distribution. The general impression given by Table 5.8 is confirmed in Table 5.9. The bottom 46·5 per cent of tax units accounted for approximately 21·8 per cent of income in Table 5.9; in Table 5.8 the bottom 46·5 per cent of households accounted for 23·3 per cent of income.

Table 5.9: Distribution of Personal Incomes before Tax, Northern Ireland and the United Kingdom, 1971–72

Income (£)	% of tax-units		% of income	
	NI	UK	NI	UK
420 – 999	40·2	27·8	17·1	10·6
1,000 – 1,499	21·1	23·7	15·8	15·9
1,500 – 1,999	16·1	21·4	16·9	20·1
2,000 – 4,999	21·3	25·2	44·7	47·4
5,000+	1·5	1·9	5·4	6·0

Source: Calculated from *Abstract of Regional Statistics 1974*, HMSO, London, Table 80.

At the upper end of the distribution, the top 12·6 per cent of tax units accounted for 28·7 per cent of income as opposed to the top 12·6 per cent of households accounting for 29·2 per cent of income. The comparative figures for the UK are that the bottom 46·5 per cent of tax units received approximately 23 per cent of income while the top 12·6 per cent received approximately 27 per cent. It should be noted that some of these data are estimates, the published figures being insufficiently disaggregated to allow direct calculation; the same is true of Table 5.10.

Table 5.10: Distribution of Gross Weekly Incomes for a Sample of Northern Ireland Households, 1967 and 1972

Group of incomes	% of income	
%	1967	1972
Top 5	14·9	13·9
10	24·4	23·4
Bottom 30	12·9	11·2

Source: Calculated from *Northern Ireland Family Expenditure Surveys 1967* and *1972*, H M S O, Belfast.

While there is no evidence on the trend of the distribution of income in the Republic of Ireland, the Northern Ireland Family Expenditure Survey for 1972 allows changes between 1967 and 1972 to be considered. As is evident from Table 5.10, the change in the distribution, though slight, is in the direction of greater equality. The trend in the distribution of income (before tax) in the U K over a long period has been towards greater equality, although there is some dispute over the magnitude of the change (see Atkinson (1973) and Polanyi and Wood (1974)).

International comparisons of the distribution of personal income before tax are difficult to make, because of the problems of availability and comparability of data. However, a recent study by Roberti (1974) presented data for a large number of countries. Some of these are given in Table 5.11, together with an estimate for the Republic of Ireland, using the Household

Table 5.11: International Comparison of Shares in Personal Income before Tax (in Percentages)

Country	Year	Income group	
		Top 10%	Bottom 30%
Norway	1967	21·4	10·2
Sweden	1967	26·4	9·2
Finland	1967	30·9	5·4
Netherlands	1967	29·6	8·9
France	1962	36·8	4·8
West Germany	1964	41·4	10·0
U K	1967	26·3	9·9
U S A	1967	25·7	8·2
Republic of Ireland	1965–66	25·6	12·2

Sources: Roberti (1974); 1965–66 estimate from same source as Table 5.6.

Budget Inquiry data. The share of the top 10 per cent of income recipients in Germany and France is appreciably higher than in other countries, while it is lowest in Norway; the share of the bottom 30 per cent is extremely low in France. Caution must be exercised in using the table for detailed cross-country comparisons, since the basis of collection of the data may not be the same in all countries, but the general picture makes it clear that the concentration of income in the Republic of Ireland and the United Kingdom is not exceptionally high.

4.3 Personal Distribution of Wealth

Measuring the personal distribution of wealth (the stock of non-human assets) is much more problematic than measuring the distribution of income. Information is gathered on people's incomes at frequent intervals, annually or even more often, but in most countries at present no information is collected on their wealth except at the time of death. This is true in the United Kingdom, and at the time of writing in the Republic of Ireland, although the introduction of a wealth tax and the abolition of estate duties will alter this situation. But estate duty returns currently constitute the main source of information on the distribution of wealth; as Atkinson (1972) remarks, 'In effect, they allow us to use the dead as a sample of the living.' (p. 10) The method of estimating a wealth distribution from estate duty returns employs a concept known as the 'mortality multiplier' and is simply described.

Estate duty returns are classified by the age and sex of the deceased persons. Persons of any age and sex group who die are regarded as a random sample of the population in that age/sex group. For example, if ten men from a population group of 1,000 die and their estates in total are valued at £10,000, the wealth of that group in the population is assumed to be £1 million. The mortality rate in the group is $10/1,000 = 0.01$; the value of the estates of the deceased is multiplied by $\frac{1}{0.01} = 100$. Hence the term 'mortality multiplier'; it is defined as the reciprocal of the mortality rate. The mortality rates themselves are calculated from Census of Population data (or intercensal estimates) and the numbers of estate duty returns.

This procedure is simple to operate if the tax authorities publish sufficient data. In Britain, and since mid-1974 in Northern Ireland, the Inland Revenue does so, but this is not the case in the Republic of Ireland. However, the estate duty method is far from being a satisfactory way of estimating the distribution of wealth, as its practitioners frequently emphasise, but this is usually forgotten in public discussion. The limitations of the method have been discussed in detail by Polanyi and Wood (1974) and Lyons (1974); a shorter account appears in Atkinson (1972), Chapter 1. They can be listed under two broad headings: on the one hand, limitations arising from the assumptions of the mortality multiplier and the nature of the data in estate duty returns, and, on the other hand, those arising from omissions from the returns. The following arise under the first heading.

(*a*) There are clear objections to treating the deceased in every age/sex group as a random sample of the population in that group. Some age/sex cells may have very few entries, thus increasing the risk that those who die may be unrepresentative of the group as a whole. In Britain in 1970–71 two men aged 25–34 died with property valued at more than £200,000; as Polanyi and Wood state, by the mortality multiplier calculation they could have raised by 10 per cent the number of people recorded as having wealth of that amount. Considerable variation in year-to-year estimates of wealth could arise in such circumstances, although operating within a longer time period than a year would reduce the likelihood and magnitude of such distortions.

(*b*) Estates valued below a certain amount are not liable for estate duty, and data for such estates are inadequate or non-existent. In the Republic of Ireland this amount was £5,000 in the year 1966 for which comparisons are made below. Thus adequate data exist only for the upper part of the wealth distribution, total wealth is likely to be understated, and the share of the largest wealth holders is therefore overstated. However, the credibility of the returns for the largest estates is affected by the incentives to avoid or evade estate duties. Avoidance, which is legal, may take many forms such as the transfer of property to relatives before death or switching into assets on which estate duty reliefs exist. Evasion, of course, is also accomplished in various ways. To the extent that these practices exist, the wealth of the largest wealth holders and their share of the total is understated.

(*c*) The valuation of assets causes a number of difficulties. It may be legal to undervalue some assets for estate duty purposes. For example, in the Republic of Ireland agricultural land is valued at below its market value, as are certain government and other securities. Undervaluation may occur for other reasons, such as the difficulty or inappropriateness of making a market valuation. Atkinson (1972) argues that the market value of company shares understates their true value and that, since they loom large in the portfolios of the rich, this leads to an understatement of the share of wealth. For further discussion of these and other valuation problems the reader is referred to the works already cited.

The second set of limitations of the estate duty method arises from assets which are omitted from the returns. Some assets disappear at death, e.g. pension and annuity rights. During life, of course, such assets constitute part of the individual's wealth. Polanyi and Wood argue that not only should pension rights be included when wealth distributions are calculated, but also claims to social security benefits such as unemployment and sickness benefit, family allowances, etc., as well as benefits such as subsidised education, health services and housing. Council houses, which in the Republic form almost a quarter, and in Britain one-third, of the non-farm housing stock, are not included in wealth estimated from estate duty returns, since at death the capitalised value of the difference between subsidised and market rent is not estimated. The importance of these omissions is that they are distributed either in favour of the less well off, or at least more equally than other wealth, so that the degree of inequality in the overall wealth distribution may be increased by the omissions. Their magnitude could be sizeable in view of the growth of expenditure in the Republic of Ireland and the U K on such human wealth-creating activities as education and medical care.

The limitations of the estate duty method, then, are considerable, and this should induce a critical response to wealth distributions so derived. Examples of these for the Republic of Ireland, Northern Ireland and Britain are now considered; for Britain, attempts have been made to remedy some of the shortcomings, and these also are presented.

The volume of work on the distribution of wealth in the Republic of Ireland has been small; most of it has been done by Patrick M. Lyons. His most recent work on the subject (1974), which includes references to his earlier papers, contains a detailed account of the calculations he made from unpublished estate duty returns for the year 1966, which were then grossed up by the mortality multipliers. His results, together with his estimates for Northern Ireland based on published data and estimates for Britain adopted from the official Inland Revenue estimates, appear in Table 5.12. The data for the Republic of Ireland suggest that 62 per cent of the adult population, i.e. those over twenty years of age owned no wealth at all in 1966. The equivalent figure for Northern Ireland was 59·65 per cent and for Britain 50·26 per cent. Wealth, of course, is a net concept, i.e. assets less liabilities. A further 32·64 per cent in the Republic of Ireland owned wealth valued at up to £5,000 and accounted for 35·6 per cent of total wealth, according to these estimates. This means that almost 65 per cent of total wealth is estimated to be owned by the top 5 per cent of wealth holders (the top 1 per cent holding 33 per cent) in the Republic in 1966. In Northern Ireland 35·4 per cent of the population were estimated to own wealth valued at up to £5,000 and accounted for 52·5 per cent of total wealth, a much higher proportion than in the Republic. The top 5 per cent owned 47·5 per cent and the top 1 per cent owned 23·6 per cent of total wealth in Northern Ireland. In Britain 40·7 per cent of the population were estimated to have wealth of up to £5,000 and accounted for 32 per cent of total wealth; the top 5 per cent owned 52 per cent, and the top 1 per cent owned 29 per cent of the total.

These estimates suggest that the degree of inequality of the distribution of personal wealth is greater in the Republic of Ireland than in Northern Ireland or Britain; concentration appears to be least in Northern Ireland. It is difficult to say how correct this ranking is, given the data shortcomings. However, it is of interest to compare these results with some obtained for

Table 5.12: Distribution of Adult Population and Personal Wealth in Northern Ireland, the Republic and Great Britain, 1966

Wealth (£)	Northern Ireland		Republic of Ireland		Great Britain	
	% of population	% of wealth	% of population	% of wealth	% of population	% of wealth
0 Up to 5,000	59·65	0·00	62·02	0·00	50·26	0·00
	35·42	52·51	32·64	35·61	40·65	31·77
5,001 — 10,000	2·85	12·66	2·72	13·97	5·40	17·71
10,001 — 20,000	1·55	16·13	1·57	16·01	2·19	14·58
20,001 — 50,000	0·28	6·28	0·82	18·28	1·10	15·36
50,001 — 100,000	0·21	8·95	0·18	8·85	0·27	8·72
100,000+	0·04	3·47	0·05	7·28	0·12	11·85
	100·00	100·00	100·00	100·00	100·00	100·00

Source: Lyons (1974), Table 3.

the United States and Canada. The U S estimates of the upper part of the wealth distribution were obtained by applying the estate duty method, while those for Canada employed data obtained in household *wealth* surveys which were incorporated in the Canadian household *budget* surveys in 1956. Since then, four surveys have been conducted. The main problem with such surveys has been the understatement of wealth, but they avoid many of the difficulties associated with the estate method. As Podoluk (1974) remarks, 'Even in the U S, which discontinued the funding of surveys some years ago, the possibility of conducting new surveys is being discussed. Imperfect as they are, surveys are still the only data available which are a comprehensive source of information on the wealth structure of the population.' (p. 216). The results for the U S A and Canada, together with comparable results from Table 5.12, appear in Table 5.13. By this comparison, the degree of inequality in the distribution of the Republic of Ireland remains the greatest. Even allowing for data limitations, it is clear that wealth is more equally distributed in the U S A and Canada than in Britain or the Republic of Ireland, with the position of Northern Ireland less clear. The Canadian result is of interest due to the method of computation, which also showed that the bottom 50 per cent of households owned 3·2 per cent and the bottom 60 per cent owned 8·4 per cent of total wealth.

Table 5.13: International Comparison of Shares of Major Wealth Holders in Total Personal Wealth (in Percentages)

Country	Year	Top 10%	Top 4%	Top 1%
U S A	1954	n.a.	n.a.	24
U S A	1969	n.a.	37	n.a.
Canada	1970	54	n.a.	n.a.
Great Britain	1966	70	52	29
Northern Ireland	1966	55	43	24
Republic of Ireland	1966	69	58	33

Note: Wealth group for U S A 1954 refers to the top *x* per cent of the total population; for U S A 1969, Britain and Ireland (North and Republic) it refers to the *adult* population (aged 20 or more); for Canada it refers to the top *x* per cent of households.

Sources: Atkinson (1972), p. 19; Smith (1974); Podoluk (1974); Table 5.11 above.

Atkinson (1972) and Polanyi and Wood (1974) have made estimates of the effects on the distribution of wealth in Britain of remedying some of the deficiencies of the estate duty method outlined above. Atkinson included a valuation for state pensions and an adjustment for the omission of small estates of £750 per man and £250 per woman. The result of these adjustments is summarised in Table 5.14; it clearly lowers the degree of concentration of personal wealth. Polanyi and Wood argue that further revisions on the lines already suggested would reduce the share of personal wealth of the top 10 per cent to about 40 per cent. Atkinson, however, places strong emphasis on the contrary tendency to understate the wealth of the rich due to underestimation of the value of company shares.[4]

Table 5.14: Adjusted Distribution of Personal Wealth, Great Britain,
1963–67: Share of Wealth (in Percentages)

% of population over 25 years	Unadjusted	Adjusted for omission of small estates	Further adjusted for state pensions
Top 1	32	29	22
Top 5	58	54	41
Top 10	73	67	52

Source: Atkinson (1972), p. 14.

The relationship between the distribution of income and wealth in the Republic of Ireland and Northern Ireland is illustrated in Figure 5.4. The Lorenz curves for income intersected and were very similar, so that only the curve for the Republic is reproduced in the figure. The degree of inequality revealed by the Lorenz curve for wealth is far greater than that for income, and furthermore, the Lorenz curve of the Northern Ireland wealth distribution lies strictly above the Lorenz curve of the Republic's wealth distribution. It is to be expected that the distribution of wealth should be more unequal than the distribution of income, and this is invariably found to be the case.

It is clear that the quality of existing data on the distribution of personal wealth is very variable and that conclusions about the degree of inequality may be decisively affected by the decision as to which items should be included in the definition of wealth. While adjustments to the wealth distributions of the Republic and Northern Ireland of the type incorporated in Table 5.14 would be of great interest, it is hard to avoid the conclusion that the household wealth inquiry approach, as operated in Canada, is more likely to produce data on whose merits there would be some agreement than modifications applied to the unsatisfactory estate duty method.

4 The recent report of the Royal Commission on Wealth and Incomes – the 1975 Diamond Report (No. 1, Cmnd 6171) confirms that adjusting for state and occupational pension rights has a significant effect on the shape of the wealth distribution. One calculation indicated that by 1974 the shares of personal wealth owned by the top 1 per cent and 10 per cent were 13 per cent and 39 per cent respectively (see *Sunday Times*, 3 Aug. 1975, p. 39).

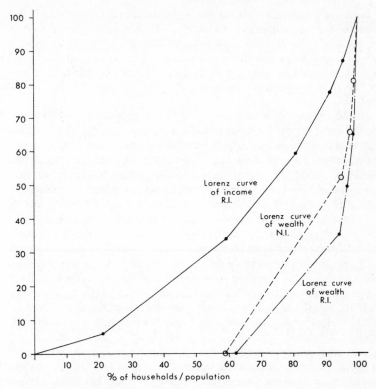

Figure 5.4: *Lorenz Curves of the Distribution of Personal Wealth, Northern Ireland and the Republic, 1966*

Source: Tables 5.7 and 5.12.

5 THE FUNCTIONAL DISTRIBUTION OF INCOME

The theory of the functional distribution of income, or theory of distributive shares, attempts to explain the distribution of national income among factors of production. Thus it is concerned with share of labour, rent, interest and profit in total income. In sharp distinction to the personal distribution of income, the functional distribution has been the subject of much theorising and controversy, associated with such eminent economists as Ricardo, Marx, Kaldor, Joan Robinson, Samuelson and Solow among others. Pen (1971) and Bronfenbrenner (1971) provide introductions to this literature; interested readers will wish to pursue the references they provide.

There are implications for the functional distribution of income in the models of the two economies in Chapter 1. Their structure is such that output, the level of employment and the price level can be solved for independently of wages. Thus, as noted in the introduction to this chapter, the 'adding-up' problem is not formally resolved. However, Spencer and Harrison discuss this issue and suggest mechanisms by which the problem may be resolved (see p. 34).

The distribution of income among factors of production has been investigated in detail for the Republic of Ireland by Hughes (1972). Income, appropriately defined, is divided into three categories: (*a*) remuneration of employees, which consists of all wages, salaries, pensions, etc. in cash and kind, arising from employment within the Republic, valued before the payment of tax and including employers' and employees' contributions to social insurance, (*b*) income from independent traders, which is defined as income in cash and kind accruing to individuals as sole proprietors, partners and independent professional persons in the agricultural and non-agricultural sectors of the economy, and (*c*) income from property, which consists of trading profits of private and public companies and certain corporate bodies operating within the Republic, after payment of indirect taxes and after the deduction of depreciation allowances for income tax purposes. It includes net rents, actual and imputed, arising from the ownership of dwellings as well as interest arising from the activities of the financial sector within the Republic. Hughes discusses the issue of the choice of the aggregate income concept appropriate to the analysis of income shares, e.g. whether to use net domestic income or national income (see Hughes (1972), pp. 10–16). The difference between them is that the latter includes net factor payments from abroad. However, his main conclusions about the behaviour of income shares are not much affected by the choice; net domestic income is employed here.

No such choice problem arises in the case of Northern Ireland, where functional distribution can be analysed only for personal income. This concept is roughly national income plus current transfers from public authorities, i.e. family allowances, national insurance benefits, etc., less undistributed profits. The Northern Ireland data allow the exclusion of transfers, and this has been done. However, the data are published for *financial years* (April to March) and are presented that way in Table 5.15(a). The first two categories of income in the Northern Ireland data are very similar to those in Table 5.15(b), but the category 'rent, dividends and interest' excludes items which appear in 'income and property'; undistributed profit has already been mentioned.

While care is necessary in comparing these tables due to data differences, some conclusions can be drawn from them. In the Republic of Ireland, as Hughes emphasises, there has been a steady growth in the proportion of income received by employees and a corresponding decline in the share of independent traders. The latter category is dominated by the agricultural sector, so that this change reflects the decline in the relative importance of agriculture and the growth of the industrial sector. This trend is common to most countries, as Pen (1971) points out. At the turn of the century the share of labour in total income in the U S A and U K was only just over a half, compared with about 70 per cent now, while in Africa the labour share in some countries is as low as 20 per cent. (For further details and discussion of the issues raised by these findings see Pen (1971), Chapter 5.) Hughes has shown that within the industrial sector itself, the share of employees fell between 1953 and 1968 (see Hughes (1972), Section 6). Hence the increase in the share of employees is due to the increased weight attached to the industrial sector. The reasons for the fall in the wage and salary share are not investigated by Hughes. Since the price of labour has risen sharply relative to the price of capital over the period 1953–68, the fall in the labour share is consistent with an elasticity of substitution between labour and non-labour inputs in excess of unity (see Geary, Walsh and Copeland (1975)). This is consistent with the discussion of the change in the industrial structure of the Republic in Chapter 2.

Table 5.15(a): Functional Distribution of Personal Income in Northern Ireland, selected years 1960–73 (in Percentages)

Year	Income from employment	Income from self-employment	Rent dividends and interest
1960–61	70·1	17·5	12·4
1965–66	71·8	15·2	13·1
1970–71	73·8	15·1	11·0
1972–73	74·9	15·4	9·7

Source: *Digest of Statistics,* No. 43 (Mar. 1975), H M S O, Belfast.

Table 5.15(b): Functional Distribution of Net Domestic Income in the Republic of Ireland, selected years 1960–73 (in Percentages)

Year	Remuneration of employees	Independent traders	Income from property
1960	56·4	29·5	14·1
1965	61·2	25·7	13·1
1970	65·4	21·5	13·1
1973	64·4	23·4	12·2

Sources: Hughes (1972), Table 2, and *National Income and Expenditure 1973,* Stationery Office, Dublin, various issues.

In Northern Ireland the share of income from employment has risen since 1960, though by much less than in the Republic. The agricultural sector in the Northern Ireland economy, as is pointed out in Chapter 2, is less important than in the Republic (its share in Gross Domestic Product in 1973 being roughly half that of the Republic's agricultural sector), so that its decline since 1960 has had a smaller impact on the share of the different income categories. These findings suggest that the growth in the share of employee remuneration in the Republic of Ireland will slow down as the agricultural sector's relative decline slows down. In Britain, where agriculture's share in GDP in 1970 was only 2·98 per cent, the share of income from employment in domestic income was 68·0 per cent, as compared with 67·7 per cent in 1961, when the share of agriculture in GDP was 3·8. Interestingly, in 1973 the share of independent traders in the Republic rose, reflecting the growth of agricultural incomes in 1972 and 1973; there was also a small rise in the share of income from self-employment in Northern Ireland in 1972–73. Whether the effects of developments in world agriculture and membership of the EEC will cause the share of this category to stabilise remains to be seen, but is unlikely.

Table 5.16: Share of Income from Property in Domestic Income in the Republic of Ireland, Disaggregated, 1960–73

| Year | Income from property | | | |
	Trading profits of companies	Rent	Other	Total
1960	10·2	3·5	0·4	14·1
1961	10·1	3·3	0·4	13·8
1962	9·9	3·2	0·4	13·5
1963	10·5	3·1	0·5	14·0
1964	9·1	2·8	0·5	12·3
1965	9·8	2·7	0·6	13·1
1966	9·0	2·9	0·7	12·6
1967	9·7	2·8	0·8	13·3
1968	10·2	2·7	0·8	13·7
1969	10·7	2·6	0·7	14·0
1970	9·8	2·6	0·7	13·1
1971	9·5	2·3	0·6	12·4
1972	9·1	2·2	0·7	12·0
1973	9·3	2·1	0·8	12·2

Source: As Table 5.5.

The main component of income from property is the trading profit of companies: it provided 10·2 per cent of the 14·1 per cent share in 1960 and

9·3 per cent of the 12·2 per cent share in 1973. Unlike the other categories, whose shares have either risen or declined steadily, the share of income from capital has fluctuated, almost entirely because of fluctuations in the share of profit. This can be seen in Table 5.16, which divides income from property into profits, rent of dwellings plus rent element in land annuities, and other income. A similar disaggregation for the Northern Ireland data is not possible, but it is noteworthy that the category 'rent dividends and interest' fluctuates more than the other two, which are trend-dominated. It is also worth noting that there has been no noticeable tendency in the Republic of Ireland for the share of profits in domestic income to fall in the post-war period, and the same appears to be true in Northern Ireland.

6 CONCLUSIONS

This chapter has ranged over a wide variety of topics, and the need for further research was evident at most points. Discussion of the behaviour of prices and wages in the two economies revolved around the hypotheses of the Spencer-Harrison model. Alternative price and wage equations were suggested, and the role of domestic factors in the price and wage determination process was assessed. Examination of price and wage data showed that the price level in the Republic had risen by more than that in the U K but that there was a strong similarity in the rates of inflation in the two countries. The increase in the ratio of industrial earnings in the Republic to those in both Northern Ireland and the U K was sizeable, but not big enough to prevent an increase in the difference between the levels of earnings. Minimum wage rates of agricultural workers in the Republic, however, did converge to the higher levels which obtained in Northern Ireland.

The analysis of personal expenditure was facilitated by an abundance of data for both the Republic and Northern Ireland; the expenditure patterns differed in ways which were readily explainable. Estimates of expenditure elasticities were presented for Northern Ireland to compare with those previously obtained for the Republic and proved, overall, to be similar. Savings data were available only for the Republic, however, and evidence on the behaviour of the ratio of personal savings to personal disposable income was examined.

The evidence relating to the distribution of income in the Republic of Ireland is, at the time of writing, lamentably scarce — in fact, inexcusably so. The evidence that is available showed that the distribution was similar to that in Northern Ireland. Evidence on the distribution of wealth in the Republic is even scarcer; in Northern Ireland the published data are now of the same type as those for Britain. The work on the distribution of wealth in the Republic of Ireland shows a high level of concentration of wealth — in fact, a level higher than that found in Britain and Northern Ireland using the same methods. The limitations of the method of calculation are severe, however; it appears to overestimate significantly the degree of inequality in the distribution of wealth. Determining the functional distribution of income presented nothing like the same difficulties for the Republic of Ireland, and the consequences of the relative decline of agriculture were evident. In Northern Ireland the pattern was influenced by the already smaller share of agriculture in total employment.

REFERENCES

Atkinson, A. B. (1970): 'On the Measurements of Inequality', *Journal of Economic Theory*, Vol. 2.

Atkinson, A. B. (1972): *Unequal Shares*, Allen Lane, London.

Atkinson, A. B., ed. (1973): *Wealth, Income and Inequality*, Penguin Modern Economics Readings, Harmondsworth.

Bronfenbrenner, M. (1971): *Income Distribution Theory*, Aldine, London.

Brown, A. and Deaton, A. P. (1972): 'Models of Consumer Behaviour: A Survey', *Economic Journal*, Vol. 82, No. 328 (Dec.).

Dernburg, T. F. and McDougall, D. M. (1960): *Macroeconomics*, 4th ed., McGraw-Hill, New York 1970.

Eckstein, O., ed. (1972): *The Econometrics of Price Determination – Conference*, Board of Governors of Federal Reserve System, Washington.

Geary, P. T. (1974): 'The Causes of Inflation', *Journal of the Statistical and Social Inquiry Society of Ireland* (1974–75).

Geary, P. T. (1975a): 'Expenditure and Price Elasticities for Northern Ireland 1967 and 1972'. (Mimeograph, Department of Economics, University College, Dublin.)

Geary, P. T. (1975b): 'The Northern Ireland Phillips Curve: A Note'. (Mimeograph, Department of Economics, University College, Dublin.)

Geary, P. T. and Jones, R. M. (1975): 'The Appropriate Measure of Unemployment in an Irish Phillips Curve', *Economic and Social Review*, Vol. 7, No. 1 (Oct.).

Geary, P. T., Walsh, B. M. and Copeland, J. (1975): 'The Cost of Capital to Irish Industry', *Economic and Social Review*, Vol. 6, No. 3 (Apr.).

Hughes, J. G. (1972): *The Functional Distribution of Income in Ireland 1938–70* (E S R I Paper No. 65), Dublin.

Johnson, M. B. (1971): *Household Behaviour*, Penguin Books, Harmondsworth.

Kennedy, K. A. and Dowling, B. M. (1970): 'The Determinants of Personal Savings in Ireland', *Economic and Social Review*, Vol. 2, No. 1 (Oct.).

Lipsey, R. G. and Parkin, M. (1970): 'Incomes Policy: A Reappraisal', *Economica*, Vol. 37, No. 146 (May).

Lyons, P. M. (1974): 'The Size Distribution of Personal Wealth in the Republic of Ireland', *Review of Income and Wealth*, Ser. 20, No. 2 (Jun.).

McDowell, J. M. (1975): 'The Control of Inflation in a Small Open Economy', *Studies* (Spring).

Pareto, V. (1897): *Cours d'Economie Politique*, Rouge, Lausanne.

Parks, R. W. and Barten, A. P. (1973): 'A Cross Country Comparison of the Effects of Prices, Income and Population Composition on Consumption Patterns', *Economic Journal,* Vol. 83, No. 33 (Sep.).

Pen, J. (1971): *Income Distribution,* Pelican ed., Penguin Books, Harmondsworth 1974.

Podoluk, J. R. (1974): 'Measurement of the Distribution of Wealth in Canada', *Review of Income and Wealth,* Ser. 20, No. 2 (Jun.).

Polyani, G. and Wood, J. B. (1974): *How Much Inequality?* (Institute of Economic Affairs Research Monograph No. 31).

Prais, S. J. and Houthakker, H. (1955): *The Analysis of Family Budgets,* 2nd impression, Cambridge University Press, 1971.

Pratschke, J. L. (1969): *Income and Expenditure Relations in Ireland 1965—66* (ESRI Paper No. 50), Dublin.

Roberti, P. (1974): 'Income Distribution: A Time-Series and Cross Section Study', *Economic Journal,* Vol. 84, No. 335 (Sep.).

Sen, A. K. (1973): *On Economic Inequality,* Oxford University Press.

Smith, J. D. (1974): 'The Concentration of Personal Wealth in America 1969', *Review of Income and Wealth,* Ser. 20, No. 2 (Jun.).

Stiglitz, J. E. (1969): 'Distribution of Income and Wealth among Individuals', *Econometrica,* Vol. 37, No. 3 (Jul.).

CHAPTER 6

Public Finance and Fiscal Policy*

J. A. BRISTOW

1   INTRODUCTION

Nowadays no area of economic life can escape the influence of government. Economic relationships between private individuals or organisations are constrained by physical planning legislation, laws limiting monopoly, laws governing conditions of employment, laws relating to foreign trade, to mention but a few. Governments also seek to influence the structure of economic activity by means of differential taxes, subsidies, etc. Again, governments directly supply goods and services 'consumed' by everyone to a greater or lesser extent. Finally, governments, through fiscal and monetary policy, incomes policies and so on, attempt to manipulate the overall level of economic activity. Because of this all-pervading influence, no chapter in this book can avoid making at least some reference to the operations of government.

However, in other chapters, government is not the primary subject for discussion: government is of interest to the other authors only to the extent that the authorities influence the activity under review. This chapter is different in that the concern is with the operations of government as a distinctive economic agent of interest in its own right.

This chapter begins with an outline of the structure of the public sector in Ireland, and continues with a comparative review of the tax systems of the two parts of the island. There then follows a section dealing with public expenditure; this is brief since many of the major items of expenditure are discussed elsewhere in the book. After a short descriptive section on public debt, the chapter ends with a discussion of the use in Ireland of fiscal policy as an instrument for manipulating the level of aggregate demand.

2   THE PUBLIC SECTOR IN IRELAND

The institutions of the Irish public sector can be divided into two groups:

Editors' Note: The reader should be aware that taxation changes referred to in Sections 3.4–3.6 have now (1976) become law.

first, the organs of direct government – central and local authorities – and secondly, semi-autonomous bodies which include what would usually be called public enterprises. In this section fiscal relationships within the former group are briefly set out and there is then a short discussion of the latter group. The remainder of the chapter concentrates attention on the activities of the first group as an entity; because of limitations of space no further reference is made to the second.

In the Republic there is central government and a system of local government based on the counties and the main towns. The responsibilities of local authorities cover such matters as housing, water supply, subsidiary roads, environmental services, and some aspects of public education and health programmes. However, the autonomy of these authorities is strictly limited in two senses: they have to operate within the constraints of national policies, and they have very little financial independence.

The current revenue of local authorities consists of the yield of local property taxes (known in Britain and Ireland as rates), trading income and grants from central government. The proportion accounted for by central government grants has risen steadily in recent years, reaching 50·0 per cent in 1972–73, and that represented by rates revenue has steadily declined, being 31·4 per cent in 1972–73. This dependence upon central government as a source of funds is as great on the capital side, although it has declined slightly in the immediate past with an expansion of loans other than from the exchequer. In 1972–73 75·3 per cent of revenue on capital account came from the central government – 19·9 per cent as grants and 55·4 per cent as loans.

In Northern Ireland the structure and functions of local authorities were very similar to those in the Republic, but there has recently been a very radical reorganisation. In 1972 local authorities were consolidated and deprived of all their major functions in the fields of housing, education, health and social services, these now being a central responsibility. Local responsibility is now limited to fairly minor environmental services. The fiscal aspect of this reorganisation abolished the old system of rates. There is now a single rate (property tax) for the province – and so rates will henceforth be a component of *central* revenue – plus district rates to contribute towards the cost of the remaining local functions.

Even before these changes, local government in the North was rapidly losing any financial independence. In 1972–73 rates accounted for a bare 16·7 per cent of local current revenue, whereas grants from government represented 73·4 per cent. The central government was the sole source of capital funds, in the form of grants or loans.

This declining financial independence of the local authorities in both parts of Ireland indicates that they are becoming little more than a system for implementing the policies of central government, and the recent changes in the North simply reflect this process. A number of reasons can be

or this. First, both areas have very small populations, and so
ernmental efficiency nor political forces provide much in the
way of pressure for local autonomy. Secondly, there has been increasing
pressure for countrywide uniformity in the standard of the kind of services
traditionally provided by the local authorities. Thirdly, the only local tax —
rates — has little automatic flexibility of yield, and so the kind of buoyancy
provided to the yield of central taxes by inflation and real income growth
does not exist. Fourthly, there is widespread dissatisfaction with the equity
of the rates, thus providing a political constraint on the local authorities in
increasing revenue from local sources. All these factors have led to a tendency to move functions from local to central government and to increase
the proportion of local services financed by means of transfers from the
central authority.

2.1 Northern Ireland and the United Kingdom Government

Throughout this chapter central government in Northern Ireland means the
administration in Belfast. However, that administration is itself subordinate
to the government of the United Kingdom in London.

At the time of writing, the future of the form of government for Northern Ireland is in the melting-pot and already significant changes have been
made in the fiscal relationship built up over a period of fifty years. Until
1973 the two main features of this relationship were as follows. First, the
major taxes on income and expenditure were called reserved taxes and
levied from London, but the Belfast government had certain taxing powers
of its own, e.g. death duties and motor vehicle duties. The tax revenue of
the Northern government therefore consisted of a sum transferred from
London representing the yield of the first group of taxes net of a small contribution to national services (this sum was called the residuary share of
reserved taxes) and the yield of its own taxes (transferred taxes). Secondly,
transfers were received from London to ensure that Northern Ireland could
enjoy no less a standard of social and other public services than was provided in Britain.

The Northern Ireland Constitution Act (1973) considerably simplified
all this. In effect, practically all taxes are now reserved taxes and Northern
Ireland receives a share of the taxes collected in the UK as a whole. In certain cases this share is the amount actually collected in the province, but in
the case of the major taxes it is calculated by reference either to the ratio of
the relevant tax bases in the two regions of the UK or to the ratio of the
populations. The second innovation was a movement towards replacing the
series of specific grants which had grown up over the years with a general
grant-in-aid designed to allow the North to achieve and maintain parity of
public services with the rest of the UK.

The financial subordination of Belfast is shown by the fact that in 1972—73
(before the new system was in operation) 47.4 per cent of current revenue

came from taxes controlled from London (a proportion which would have been 65 per cent under the new definitions), and 26·6 per cent was accounted for by transfers from the UK government. In the same year the whole of revenue on capital account took the form of borrowing from the government of the United Kingdom.

2.2 Public Enterprises

In Ireland there are semi-autonomous bodies which have a special relationship with government. They are either statutory (or public) corporations set up by special legislation or companies with a majority governmental shareholding. They perform three types of function: they operate public utilities, they engage in other forms of trading activity, or they implement certain aspects of policy where it is particularly valuable to have more flexibility than can be permitted or achieved in a normal government department. The last group includes, in the Republic, the agencies responsible for the disbursement of industrial development assistance, tourist and export promotion, and various other areas of micro-economic or social policy. Their sole source of finance is state grants.

Of more economic interest are those bodies with trading functions, known as public enterprises or nationalised industries. In Northern Ireland they have generally been restricted to the fields of electricity and gas supply and public transport, although the recent expansion of state participation in the Belfast shipyards has brought that company into this sector. In the Republic such enterprises have been similarly involved in public transport (land, sea and air) and in energy supply (electricity and solid fuel, but not gas), but have also played significant roles in other manufacturing and commercial areas.

Direct state participation has been an important feature of economic development in the Irish Republic, but there is no space here to go into this in any depth (see Bristow (1968) and C E E P (1973)) for a more extended discussion). As regards public utilities, the rationale for public involvement is well known. In electricity supply, nationalised in 1927, massive unexploited economies of scale required consolidation on the supply side. The state provided this, and the monopoly thus created needed close public regulation. In transport, state involvement originated in a need to preserve a railway system which could not be profitable, a desire to ensure the availability of merchant shipping in wartime, and the typical desire of a new state to have its own airline.

It is in other areas, however, that the Republic has had more in common with developing countries than with, say, Britain or, indeed, Northern Ireland. Thus two finance houses were established, in 1927 and 1933 (the Agricultural Credit Corporation and the Industrial Credit Company) to remedy deficiencies resulting from the underdevelopment of the domestic capital market by providing credit for agriculture and industry respectively.

Above all, a series of manufacturing enterprises were set up to produce import substitutes. Incorporated at intervals from the 1930s to the 1960s, their products range over peat (Ireland is the second largest producer of peat fuel in the world), industrial alcohol and glucose, steel, fertilisers, sugar and other processed foods.

The connection of these bodies with government is multi-dimensional. Government nominees occupy all or some of the seats on their boards of directors. The exchequer provides capital finance by purchasing shares or, more usually, granting loans. This is of diminishing importance since an increasing proportion of public enterprise investment is financed internally or from non-exchequer sources. More significantly from the economic point of view, the government determines the environment in which public enterprises trade. Thus hardly a single enterprise has not benefited from government influence on the market in which it buys or sells (Bristow (1968)). Also governments, by methods of varying degrees of subtlety, intervene in the investment and operating decisions of these enterprises.

It should be quite clear from this that these enterprises are regarded by governments as primarily instruments of public policy rather than as essentially commercial activities which for historical reasons find themselves in the public sector.

Finally, an idea of the magnitude of the public enterprise sector can be conveyed by a few figures. There are two problems here. First, there is no firm boundary to this sector. Secondly, no aggregate information is published for the sector on a regular basis. However, a compilation by the European Centre for Public Enterprises (C E E P (1973)) for 1970–71 reveals the following information (some non-trading activities are included, but their influence on the figures is negligible). In that year public enterprises accounted for 8 per cent of G D P, 6 per cent of total employment, 37 per cent of public sector employment, 15 per cent of total gross investment, and 46 per cent of public gross investment.

This brief review has concentrated almost entirely upon the Republic. This is because that country has departed so much from the British tradition in this area. It has used semi-autonomous bodies to perform functions allocated to government departments in Britain and has established publicly owned enterprises in activities extending far beyond the public utility area. Northern Ireland is much more like Britain in these respects.

3   TAXATION

The two tax systems under review share a common parentage in the United Kingdom system applying to the whole of Ireland prior to 1921. Since that time the fiscal structures of the two parts of Ireland have diverged considerably: the Republic has gone its own way, especially in the field of consumption taxes, and the U K (and therefore Northern Ireland) has made changes, notably in relation to income taxes, as yet only partially emulated by the Republic. Very recently some convergence has been taking place in three respects. First, the two countries now have value-added tax. This represents a move by the U K in the direction of the Republic, since for the former a broadly based retail sales tax was an entirely new venture whereas in the latter such a tax (though not V A T) was already an established part of the system. Secondly, the Republic is currently moving in the direction of the U K in relation to the taxation of capital gains and of agricultural incomes. Thirdly, a number of changes are at present taking place or are being proposed in the two countries which would make their tax systems more alike. Examples are the amalgamation of personal income tax and surtax, the taxation of gifts, annual wealth taxation, and the form of corporate income tax. In relation to both V A T and corporate income tax, practice in the E E C has been of primary importance in producing the recent changes in both countries.

Despite this convergent process, however, differences in tax structure remain, and it is the primary purpose of this section to explore these differences.

3.1 The Level of Taxation

In both parts of Ireland taxation has been increasing over the past decade as a proportion of Gross Domestic Product. In 1972–73, total tax revenue (including social insurance contributions and local rates) was £697·6 million (35·5 per cent of G D P) in the Republic and £404·61 million (36·4 per cent of G D P) in Northern Ireland. Ten years earlier the proportions were 25·8 per cent and 34·4 per cent respectively. In the North the proportion has declined somewhat recently – in 1969–70 it reached almost 43 per cent – but the general trend is quite clear.

When the distribution of income does not vary much, such a trend would be the expected result of the application of a generally progressive system, in times of inflation and real growth, to a base denominated in money terms. In other words, such a trend is built into the system. It provides opportunities for a similar expansion in the ratio of public expenditure to GDP, and social pressures to expand this latter ratio ensure that governments do little to mitigate the tax trend by downward adjustments in statutory tax rates. This interrelationship between tax and expenditure trends is discussed below.

Throughout the past decade taxes have represented a higher proportion of G D P in Northern Ireland than in the Republic, although the gap is now almost closed. This would appear to be partly the result of the higher *per capita* income in the North, i.e. since the systems are at least slightly progressive overall, the application of common statutory rates throughout the island would produce a somewhat higher overall effective rate in the North.

Of at least equal, or possibly greater, significance is the fact that differences in the structure of taxes between the two areas would almost certainly produce a higher ratio of tax revenue to income in Northern Ireland, even if *per capita* incomes were equal. These differences will be discussed in more detail shortly; suffice it to say at this stage that of great importance would appear to be the fact that the statutory base of personal and corporate income tax is narrower in the Republic than in the North.

3.2 The Structure of Tax Revenue

Table 6.1 indicates the relative importance of different types of taxes as sources of revenue. In that table direct taxes cover personal and corporate income taxes, capital gains tax, and death duties (the only form of wealth taxation operating in Ireland at the time of writing, though innovations are imminent – see below). Rates refer to local authority property taxes, social insurance contributions cover both employers' and employees' payments, and indirect taxes refer to all other taxes, i.e. customs duties, excises, V A T, motor vehicle duties, stamp duties, etc.

The outstanding feature of Table 6.1 is that throughout the decade the Republic has collected a much lower proportion of its revenue from direct taxes and a much higher proportion from indirect taxes than has been the case in Northern Ireland. One reason for this is, of course, that *per capita* incomes are lower in the Republic, but contributory differences in the tax systems (which will be taken up shortly) include the facts that the law defines the base of income tax more narrowly in the Republic and that, although the Republic did not have a wholesale-stage sales tax analogous to the purchase tax in Northern Ireland until 1966, it had since 1963 a remunerative retail-stage sales tax which had no equivalent in the North.

Also of note in Table 6.1 is the much greater significance of social insurance contributions in the North. The discussion of social security in the Appendix to Chapter 3 indicates reasons for this.

The difference in the structure of public revenue is narrowing over time as a result of two factors: a narrowing of the difference in income per head and, more generally, in the economic structures of the two areas; and, as already mentioned, a marked tendency for the tax laws of the Republic of Ireland and the United Kingdom to converge in recent years. It is now appropriate to look more closely at those laws.

3.3 Personal Income Tax

This tax operates in a very similar way in the two areas, even to the extent that major structural changes instituted in the U K (and therefore in Northern Ireland) in 1973 were followed in the Republic a year later. Until these changes were made there were two personal income taxes in both North and South. Income tax was levied at a flat rate (the 'standard' rate) on all income after the deduction of exemptions and allowances. On income above a certain level a further tax, surtax, was imposed with graduated marginal rates.

Table 6.1: Percentage Composition of Total Taxes, Northern Ireland and the Republic, 1962–63 and 1972–73

Year	Northern Ireland					Republic			
	Direct taxes	Indirect taxes	Soc. ins. contribs	Rates	SET	Direct taxes	Indirect taxes	Soc. ins. contribs	Rates
1962–63	34·1	43·5	13·7	8·7		25·7	54·2	6·5	13·6
	(36·0)	(40·6)	(15·9)	(7·6)					
1972–73	35·2	39·7	15·6	7·4	2·2	29·8	50·8	9·0	10·4

Note: The figures in parentheses are the percentages when selective employment tax is excluded

Sources: N I: *Digest of Statistics*, H M S O, Belfast, various issues; R I: *National Income and Expenditure*, Stationery Office, Dublin, various issues.

The changes just mentioned did two things. First, in the Republic they abolished, and in the North they changed the form of, a system which discriminated in favour of wages and salaries against other forms of income.

Secondly, the two-tier system of income tax and surtax was dismantled and replaced by a single tax with graduated rates (simply called income tax) which is applied to income net of allowances.

The main exemptions are of a similar order North and South, but the structure of marginal rate progression differs markedly (the following discussion relates to the tax year 1974–75). The South has a somewhat lower maximum marginal rate – 80 per cent compared with 83 per cent (or 98 per cent on non-labour income) but reaches that maximum at a much lower income. In the Republic there are only six steps to the maximum rate, and that rate is applied to taxable income over £8,350. In Northern Ireland the maximum rate is not charged until taxable income reaches £20,000, and it takes ten steps to reach the top.

If one combines the allowances and the marginal rates, one has the effective, or average, rate. For a single person (with an exemption of £625 in the North and £500 in the South) all of whose income is earned, the effective rate is lower in the North for incomes up to approximately £1,000, lower in the South for the range £1,000–£5,000, and then lower in the North until one reaches approximately £83,000.

One might speculate on possible economic effects of these differences – e.g. on work or savings incentives in the South relative to the North – but such speculation would not be fruitful. Research elsewhere has not found significant tax effects in this area, and no relevant work has been done in Ireland. Furthermore, even if such effects did exist, the income tax systems of the two parts of the island are on such definitely convergent paths that the rather marked differences just noted may well be transitory.

Similarly, one cannot tell whether the Republic or Northern Ireland has the income tax with the greater redistributive impact. Unless the pre-tax distributions of income are the same, a mere comparison of tax schedules cannot reveal which of two economies has the tax system with the greater redistributive effect. However, no information is available on the distribution of pre- or post-tax incomes in either part of Ireland.

The notion of a redistributive effect of taxation is closely related to the ethical concept of vertical equity, i.e. if it is to be fair, how should a system discriminate between individuals having different taxable capacities? Even more fundamental, however, is the concern for *horizontal* equity. Deriving from more general notions of the need for equality before the law is the view that a tax should treat equally individuals in equivalent positions. Operationally, this is the question of the definition of the tax base, and this is the next item to be considered.

A major problem in the Republic and the UK is that in neither country are the income taxes based on any general definition of income, which is perhaps not surprising since only comparatively recently has the economist's definition of income (the maximum level of consumption which can be undertaken without dissaving) been at all widely accepted as a reasonable starting-point for a personal income tax. The income tax codes in both the Republic and the U K simply list sources of taxable income, and so any income (in the economist's sense) not on the list is not taxed. The three major anomalies produced by this method concern agricultural incomes, the income from owner-occupation of dwellings, and 'casual' capital gains.

In Northern Ireland, farmers' incomes are treated for tax purposes as the profits of a trade, but in the Republic they have been traditionally untaxed or treated peculiarly leniently. This discrimination in favour of farmers was impossible to justify in terms of equity, and attempts to justify it on other grounds were unconvincing. A government commission recommended its removal fifteen years ago, but to no avail. However, as the Republic becomes increasingly urbanised, more and more people have no direct economic, social or emotional connection with agriculture. This has made reform more feasible politically. More positively, as tax allowances have failed to keep pace with inflation, real effective rates have risen, and pressures have been generated to make farmers, many of whom have above-average incomes, subject to tax. The result of this has been a change in the law in 1974. The owners of large farms are now to be subject to income tax, and it can be only a matter of time before all farmers are so treated.

An important change in the code in the Republic in 1969, and the equivalent step in Northern Ireland in 1963, also had the effect of exempting from tax the imputed income of the owner-occupiers of dwellings. If one accepts the economist's definition of income as the relevant index of taxable capacity, this exemption represents a clear contravention of the principle of horizontal equity. In effect, it means that the income tax in both parts of Ireland discriminates, not only according to the level of income, but also according to the form of income: income in the form of the services of an owner-occupied house is untaxed, whereas the same value of income from, say, securities is taxed.

3.4 Capital Gains Taxation
The present situation in the Republic is similar to that in Britain and Northern Ireland before 1962. Capital gains arising in the normal course of one's business are taxable as the profits of a trade, but gains arising otherwise (so-called 'casual' gains) are not. Since that date the law in the U K has gone through a number of changes. The current situation is broadly that such gains are subject not to income tax but to a separate flat-rate tax called capital gains tax of 30 per cent. The government of the Irish Republic is proposing to introduce an almost exactly equivalent system, with gains being taxed at a flat rate of 26 per cent, this being the lowest positive marginal rate of income tax.

The most basic question is whether capital gains should be taxed differently from other income. Perhaps the greatest problem is that of what is called 'bunched gains'. There can be little doubt that an economic definition of income requires gains to be taxed as they accrue, but this is administratively difficult and it is usual for tax systems to restrict their attention to realised gains, i.e. gains on assets sold or otherwise disposed of. However, if gains are subject to a progressive levy, such as the typical income tax, a gain on an asset held for longer than a tax period would attract more tax on a realisation than on an accrual basis.

There is no way of completely solving this problem, but a number of partial solutions exist. For example, one could use an averaging procedure or have a sliding scale whereby the proportion of the gain taxable is inversely related to the length of the holding period. The crudest solution is to charge *all* gains to a proportional tax, i.e. the method currently operated in the UK and proposed for the Republic.

This is a classic example of the conflict between equity and administrative simplicity. For instance, separate treatment of capital gains at a flat rate is simple but hardly equitable: averaging is more equitable but also more complex. How one weighs equity against simplicity is a matter of personal judgment, but it is not obvious why the compromise chosen in the UK and that proposed for the Republic (all gains taxed proportionally, other incomes progressively) should command support. There seems to be no case for charging gains on assets held for less than a year to other than the ordinary income tax, and there is no obvious reason why the income tax – on a sliding scale to take account of the length of the holding period – could not be applied to longer-term gains.

Attention has been concentrated on the fundamental question of the equity of the distinctive treatment of capital gains because this distinction has been, and remains, a significant feature of the systems of income tax in both the Republic and the UK. Space does not permit a consideration of the large number of other economic and legal issues surrounding this controversial tax (an excellent discussion can be found in the Final Report of Royal Commission (1955), Chapters 1 and 4, and the Memorandum of Dissent to that report, Chapters 1 and 3), but two points deserve mention.

First, since a capital gain is part of the income from non-human capital, to tax such gains differently from other income may have allocative consequences: in particular, to treat them more favourably may form an inducement to saving. The strength of such an effect is unknown. Certainly there is no evidence that the reduction of the discrimination in favour of capital gains in Britain in 1962 and again in 1965 had any effect on savings. Secondly, capital gains taxes are typically not very remunerative, and therefore little of the difference in the ratios of direct to total taxes in the two parts of Ireland may be explained by their absence in the Republic but their presence in Northern Ireland. But even this is not certain, since the inclusion of capital gains in the tax base may improve the revenue efficiency of the income tax system as a whole by removing an incentive to arrange to receive income in the form of capital gains.

3.5 Corporate Income Taxes

Like personal income tax, taxes on profits have diverged in their structures North and South, but are now converging. In the past fifteen years the system in Northern Ireland has gone through three phases in both its legal form and its economic objectives. From 1958 to 1965 corporate profits were charged to two taxes, income tax and profits tax (both at a flat rate), with the income tax component (but not the profits tax) being credited to the shareholder as a tax on any dividend received. The main administrative feature of that system was the link between corporate and personal income tax, the same tax (income tax) being levied on both companies and individuals. The main economic feature was that, by crediting the shareholder with the income tax, the system did not discriminate between retained and distributed profits.

A radical reform was instituted in 1965. Profits tax was abolished, and since then income tax has not been levied on companies. A new proportional tax (corporation tax) was created: During the period 1965–72 the main feature economically was that the shareholder paid income tax (and surtax if appropriate) on his dividend and received no credit for the corporation tax paid by the company. As a result, taking company and shareholders together, more tax was payable on dividends than on retained profits. This was a deliberate act of policy by the government, designed to raise the corporate savings ratio with the object of stimulating fixed investment.

There are strong arguments against imposing heavier taxes on dividends than on retentions. Some of these arguments were persuasively presented by a Royal Commission in the 1950s, when recommending the abolition of the administratively different but economically similar system operating until 1958, and need not be repeated here. The greatest fear was that such a policy would, by restricting dividend distribution, reduce the flow of funds passing through the capital market. This, in turn, would increase the possibility of a misallocation of capital resources and would strengthen monopolistic tendencies.

The discrimination against dividends in the operation of the corporation tax without shareholder credits produced a reincarnation of these arguments in the late 1960s and led to a further reform in 1972. Since then the so-called imputation system has been in effect, which is designed to remove much of the discrimination. Of course, if share prices are positively correlated with retentions rather than with dividends, and if, as at present, capital gains are taxed more favourably than other income (including dividends), there may still be a tax advantage attaching to the retention of profit. However, that is the result of the special treatment of capital gains and not of the system of corporate taxation as such.

In effect, though not in form, the imputation system represents a return to the system operating in the United Kingdom between 1958 and 1965. The shareholder is credited with enough of the corporation tax paid by the company to ensure that he pays no further tax on his dividend unless his own marginal rate is higher than the lowest marginal rate of personal income tax.

In the Republic the form of company taxation is at present almost exactly as it was in the UK (and therefore Northern Ireland) in the period 1958–65. There is a two-tier structure, with the old link with personal taxation and with no discrimination against distributed profits. There is income tax at 35 per cent and corporation profits tax (CPT) at $7\frac{1}{2}$ per cent on the first £2,500 and 23 per cent on the remainder of profit. The nominal rates are not simply additive since CPT is deductible before income tax is charged: the effective combined marginal rates are therefore approximately 40 per cent and 50 per cent. It will be seen that, unlike the system in the UK, corporate taxes in the Republic are very slightly progressive as a result of the two rates of CPT.

The government of the Republic has recently indicated its intention of changing the administrative form of these taxes to make the system identical to that now operating in Britain and Northern Ireland (see *Company Taxation in Ireland* (1972) and *Proposals for Corporation Tax* (1974). It is proposed to break the link with personal taxation but to maintain the equality of treatment between distributed and retained profits by introducing an imputation-type corporation tax to take effect in 1975.

So much for the main features of these systems as applied to a given level of taxable profit. It now remains to look at the definition of the base — specifically, the structure and level of allowances and exemptions. The main economic interest here lies in the way allowances etc. have been used as an instrument to stimulate investment.

Since depreciation is a cost of using capital, taxable profit has in all countries been defined net of an allowance for depreciation. The most significant economic point about these annual allowances in Ireland and Britain is that they are on the historic-cost principle. This principle has great administrative attractions since it enables the allowance to be derived from a known value. It is also consistent with the rest of the tax system, which takes no account of changes in the purchasing power of money. However, the justification for depreciation allowances is that the flow of funds needed to keep capital intact is not properly regarded as part of income. Therefore, if replacement cost exceeds historic cost, to give an allowance equal to the amount of historic cost means that the tax bears on something which is not properly described as profit.

An allowance for depreciation is required by the economic definition of

income, but refinements of such allowances have been used in both parts of
Ireland, as in many countries, as a stimulus to fixed investment. In broad
terms, the refinements fall into two categories: an acceleration of the
normal allowance, and an addition to that allowance.

Accelerated depreciation means that, for tax purposes, an asset is written
down more quickly than would happen under the normal allowance. This
changes the time profile of the net income stream from an asset and is beneficial to a firm for two reasons. First, it raises company liquidity at the time
the asset is being purchased, thus easing the problems of financing the investment. Secondly, at any given positive discount rate, the acceleration of an
income stream (keeping the undiscounted total constant) will raise the present value of that stream. Thus if companies make investment decisions by
reference to the present value of the expected post-tax profit-stream from
an asset (i.e. they use a discounted-cash-flow technique), accelerated rather
than normal depreciation allowances should encourage fixed investment.

In Ireland accelerated depreciation itself comes in two versions. In one
(the system of initial allowances) the rate of acceleration is determined
by the tax authorities; in the other (free depreciation) the company can
write off an asset as fast as it likes for tax purposes.

It will be noted that, since the normal allowance applies to the remaining,
depreciated value of an asset, the initial allowance does not add to the total
allowances over the whole lifetime – it merely gives more in the first year
at the expense of the later years – and total lifetime allowances sum to the
original historic cost. However, there used to be in Northern Ireland, and
still is in the Republic, an additional allowance, called the investment
allowance. Such an allowance is added to the other first-year allowances
but does not affect allowances in the remaining years. As a result, total
write-off exceeds historic cost, and so this device is a straightforward subsidy to investment.

There is no evidence for Ireland, but experience elsewhere suggests that
these refinements to the system of depreciation allowances do influence
the volume of fixed investment. However, it must be recognised that these
allowances will have the desired effect only if businessmen make their investment decisions in a way which takes account of *post*-tax expected profit (allowances do not influence pre-tax profit). This is why capital grants
are thought to be a more potent stimulus to investment: such grants do
increase the pre-tax return on investment by reducing its cost. Capital grants
are a major instrument of development policy North and South and are discussed in more detail in Chapter 2.

As has been seen, the system of corporate taxes and allowances is very
similar in both areas. There is, however, one respect in which the two
systems differ significantly. This is the exemption given to export profits
in the Republic, an exemption which has no counterpart in Northern
Ireland.

In the mid-1950s the whole philosophy of industrialisation changed in the Republic. From being based on import-substitution and the discouragement of foreign capital it became orientated towards exports and the attraction of capital inflows. Part of the policy package introduced as a result of this change in strategy was that profits on exports of manufactured goods (or on the increase of such sales above the level at a base date) were partially relieved of tax for a limited period.

The effect of this exemption on the revenue from corporate taxes is far from negligible. The information needed to measure this effect on an annual basis is not publicly available. However, it has been estimated that in 1970–71 the tax revenue forgone as a result of these reliefs amounted to £21·8 million. This represents some 15 per cent of the total revenue actually derived from direct taxes in that year.

The economic effects are difficult to disentangle, even at the theoretical level. Depending on the way companies shift corporate taxes, these reliefs could reduce export prices relative to domestic prices or could raise the profitability of exporting compared with production for the home market. One could get a different answer in the long run as compared with the short run (e.g. if the short-run effect were to raise profits, this could attract capital to the activity in question and the result could be to have firms based in the Republic competing with each other in the same export markets, the result being a reduction in prices). However, it is probable that, in the minds of the policy makers anyway, the effect on profitability is paramount and that this is seen as a device for attracting to the Republic foreign capital and entrepreneurship which brings export markets with it. Thus it is of interest that over 80 per cent of the relief given in the Republic in 1970–71 went to subsidiaries of foreign firms. The role of this type of tax relief is discussed in Chapter 2.

3.6 Wealth Taxes

At present, wealth taxes in Ireland are restricted to death duties. In both Northern Ireland and the Republic the systems have changed little since the introduction of the progressive estate duty for the whole of the United Kingdom in 1894, and so there is little difference between them. The law is extraordinarily complicated, and dramatic changes are imminent. Therefore the exposition here will be restricted to the barest outline necessary to give the flavour of how this tax works. After exemptions and reliefs, the tax is levied on the estate of the deceased, which is counted as including gifts made in the last years of his lifetime. Estate duty is progressive. In the Republic tax starts at a lower level of estate, but rises in smaller steps, and the rate levels off at both a lower rate and a lower estate than in the North. Thus, ignoring exemptions, tax starts when an estate reaches £10,000 in the South, whereas no estate below £15,000 is taxed in the North. However, the Northern rate immediately jumps to 25 per cent, a rate not levied in the South until an estate reaches £40,000. Indeed, for any estate valued at more than £15,000, the rate is higher in Northern Ireland than in the Republic.

The most important economic objective of wealth taxes is the redistribution of wealth. Dissatisfaction with the performance of estate duty in this matter, as well as unease at the generally unsophisticated tax treatment of wealth in these islands, has led to major proposals for reform in both the Irish Republic and the United Kingdom.

Before proceeding to a review of these proposals, it is necessary to stress one feature of the present estate duty. Estate duty is not an inheritance tax. It is a liability on the estate of a deceased, and the size of the liability depends on the total dutiable size of that estate. There is therefore no tax inducement for someone to divide his estate among a number of beneficiaries. An inheritance tax, if it were progressive, would provide such an incentive, since the effective rate on each inheritance would be determined by the size of that inheritance and not by the size of the estate from which it was derived. An inheritance tax forms part of the proposals for reform mentioned above.

For the Republic, these proposals are contained in a recent White Paper, *Capital Taxation* (1974). Apart from the introduction of a capital gains tax, which has been referred to already, the White Paper proposes the introduction of a capital acquisitions tax and an annual wealth tax, and the abolition of death duties.

Briefly, the proposed *acquisitions tax* would be a combination of an inheritance and a gifts tax. The tax would be progressive, the rate depending on the size of the gift or inheritance after allowances, which in turn would depend upon the degree of consanguinity between the benefactor and the beneficiary.

Such a tax is clearly superior to estate duty. First, the inclusion of all gifts eliminates a major reason why the existing tax has been called a voluntary one. Secondly, it contains a very substantial incentive to distribute one's wealth among several recipients, an incentive which estate duty does not provide. As a result, an acquisitions tax could be a powerful engine for the redistribution of wealth.

Two main criticisms can be levelled at this proposal as it stands at the time of writing. First, the exemption limit for transfers to a spouse or children is inordinately high. It stands at £150,000, which means, for example, that a man may give or bequeath to his wife and four children a total of £750,000 without their attracting any tax. This sort of thing will severely limit the redistributive properties of this tax.

Secondly, it is proposed not to make the tax cumulative except with respect to transfers between a given benefactor and a given beneficiary. Thus a person who receives a total of £x from several benefactors can pay less tax than another person who receives less than £x but from a single benefactor. This again weakens the tax as a redistributive device, particularly, given the high exemption levels, with respect to transfers between parents and children. Without doubt, full accumulation would be a desirable amendment to these proposals.

The proposed *annual wealth tax* would be made progressive by having an exemption limit and a single positive effective rate. (This is an amendment subsequent to the White Paper, which indicated a staircase of three positive rates.)

A major criticism is that an annual wealth tax, if it is to be at all comprehensive in its coverage, is extremely cumbersome to administer. This is less of a problem in countries where a high proportion of personal wealth is held in the form of assets which are easy to value because of the existence of a well-developed market (quoted securities and urban real estate would be examples). In the Republic, however, probably a much higher proportion of personal wealth than is normal in Europe or North America is held in such assets as rural land and interests in private companies. The valuation problem here could be very severe.

It is also of interest that for the purposes of both the wealth tax and the acquisitions tax, it is proposed to introduce the kind of discrimination in favour of farmers already noted with respect to income tax. For both taxes, land valued at less than £200,000 would be taxed on only half its value.

Broadly equivalent proposals for the reform of wealth taxation have been made for the U K (see *Wealth Tax* (1974) and *Capital Transfer Tax* (1974)). It is worth noting that one of the criticisms voiced above in relation to the Republic's acquisitions tax would not apply to the U K *capital transfer tax* in that the exemption levels proposed are much lower than in the Republic's case. However, the U K government proposes to make its transfer tax cumulative only with respect to a given benefactor, and so there is no incentive for a person to give or bequeath his wealth to several persons rather than to one, an incentive which does exist in the Republic's proposal to accumulate with respect to any given pair of benefactor/beneficiary.

3.7   Indirect Taxes

Until quite recently the structure of indirect taxation differed significantly between the Irish Republic and Northern Ireland. There is now, however, no major difference.

Indirect taxes used in Ireland can be divided into three groups: single-stage sales taxes; value-added tax; and customs or excise duties on particular commodities. In the early 1960s the Republic had no taxes of the first type, whereas Northern Ireland had the purchase tax, a multiple-rate wholesale tax. Purchase tax, which was eventually abolished on the introduction of V A T in 1973, was restricted to a fairly narrow range of consumer goods, in particular consumer durables. Services, and what were regarded as the more necessary consumer goods such as food, children's clothes and housing, and commodities on which major excises were levied such as liquor, tobacco and hydrocarbon oils, were not covered by this tax.

In 1963 the Republic introduced a tax which had no equivalent in the United Kingdom — a broad-based retail sales tax known as turnover tax. This was levied at a single rate on, in principle, all retail transactions, be they concerned with visible goods or services.

Then in 1966 the Republic adopted, in addition to the retail tax just mentioned, a multiple-rate wholesale tax almost identical in form to the purchase tax in the UK.

In their last full year of operation (1971—72) wholesale and turnover tax accounted for 26 per cent of total indirect tax revenue in the Republic. The proportion accounted for by turnover tax alone, which had no counterpart in the North, was 16 per cent.

Both parts of Ireland now have value-added tax, a non-cumulative, multi-stage sales tax. Introduced as a result of accession to the E E C, this was seen in the Republic as a straight swap for the wholesale and turnover taxes, even to the extent of setting the rates of V A T equal to the combined rates of the two taxes it replaced. In Britain and Northern Ireland V A T was only partially seen as a replacement for an existing tax, viz purchase tax. As a result, the V A T rate structure is somewhat simpler in the North than in the South.

That leaves the traditional customs and excise duties and such items as stamp and motor vehicle duties. The main point of interest is that there has been, over the past decade, a significant change in the source of indirect tax revenue, certainly in the Republic and very probably in Northern Ireland also. The development of general sales taxes in the South, and of V A T in both areas, has already been mentioned, but perhaps the clearest way of indicating the change is to note the greatly reduced importance of the 'big three' customs and excise duties — those on liquor, tobacco and hydrocarbon oils. In 1972—73 these accounted for 56 per cent of total indirect tax revenue in the Republic, whereas ten years earlier they accounted for 81 per cent. A similar trend cannot be demonstrated for Northern Ireland because in recent years no breakdown is publicly available of the revenue from individual indirect taxes. However, as a result of the introduction of V A T, it almost certainly exists there, although if one takes the ten-year period, it will be less dramatic than in the Republic because in 1962—63 the North had the purchase tax, which had no equivalent in the South.

On both allocative and distributional grounds, these changes are to be welcomed. Taxes on individual commodities distort relative prices whereas general sales taxes do so less, and there must be a strong presumption that, unless a tax system is designed to change particular price ratios in the interests of improved resource allocation, the less distortion the better.

Of course, the sales taxes and now the V A T used in both parts of Ireland were multiple-rate and so had some distorting effect. However, this can probably be justified on distributional grounds.

Since the traditional taxes, with the exception of that on hydrocarbon oils, were concentrated on goods with a low income elasticity of demand, the broadening of the base should have egalitarian consequences. The changes in indirect taxation over the period have almost certainly increased the degree of progression of the tax system as a whole, North and South.

4   PUBLIC EXPENDITURE[1]

In the economic or national income accounting sense, public expenditure is less homogeneous than taxation. All taxes are transfer payments from the private sector to the government; public expenditure is different in that some of it consists of transfer payments, though not all. Governments trade in markets, particularly as buyers. Governments buy labour and goods and services; they also make loans (as opposed to grants). Therefore, although a government is unique in its taxing powers, a good deal of its expenditure takes a form which in principle is no different in national accounting terms from what goes on in the private sector.

A result of this heterogeneity of public expenditures is that care has to be used in the interpretation of any aggregate. There are, however, good reasons for taking note of changes in the ratio of total government expenditure to national income. First, although governments buy in a market, they buy primarily in order to produce services which are not sold in a market. Further, transfer payments do not involve a market at all. Therefore a rise in the ratio just referred to indicates that an increasing proportion of total economic transactions is taking place wholly or partially outside the market mechanism. Such a phenomenon is worthy of consideration. Secondly, the almost universal secular increase in that ratio is an interesting fact about societies at large and has been the subject of research.

4.1   Current Expenditure
In both the Republic and Northern Ireland there has been a substantial and continuous increase in government current expenditure as a proportion of G D P, with the rate of increase being somewhat higher in the South than in the North. In 1972–73 the Republic's expenditure of £770·70 million represented 39·2 per cent of G D P and the North's expenditure of £504·59 million represented 46·1 per cent of G D P. The equivalent percentages ten years earlier were 29·4 and 38·2 respectively.

1 The figures for Northern Ireland in this section cover, with one exception, only public expenditure involving a budgetary authority in the North, and exclude certain direct expenditures of the U K government, such as on the armed forces. The one exception is agricultural subsidies, which are paid from London but which are included.

The tendency for public expenditure to rise more quickly than national income was noticed many years ago, and became known as Wagner's Law. However, plausible explanations for this phenomenon had to wait until comparatively recently. Perhaps the best known work is that of Peacock and Wiseman (1961) in relation to the U K. They noticed that the ratio did not rise steadily over a long period of time, but moved upwards in a series of steps, or displacements.

The most significant displacement effects were associated with wars, and the following hypothesis was presented. Government expenditure is, at any point in time, limited by the amount of taxation which society is prepared to tolerate. In wartime, tax tolerance increases, but does not, after the war, return to its pre-war level. People just get used to higher taxes. Thus the ratio of government expenditure to national income can be maintained at its wartime, rather than its pre-war, level. This gives the step-like progression revealed over a long period.

Hence there is a constraint upon public expenditure provided by the public's degree of tolerance of any given level of taxes — a revenue constraint. This was put forward as an explanation for the U K experience. A parallel study for the Irish Republic revealed the same pattern of periodic displacements, but the authors suggested that the tax tolerance hypothesis was less plausible for the Republic (O'Donoghue and Tait (1968)). The timing of displacements was influenced by events in Britain, and debt was more important than taxation in financing those displacements.

In recent years the situation appears to be different. The past decade reveals no modern displacements, nor does it show either a constancy in the relevant ratio or a slightly declining trend which would be expected if the pattern indicated by the earlier experience were continuing. There is instead a secular upward movement. Can this be explained by reference to a hypothesis based on tax tolerance?

If the tolerance in question is supposed to relate to effective rates, the experience of recent years must be regarded as inconsistent with the hypothesis. However, such an inconsistency does not arise if the hypothesis is taken to refer to statutory, or nominal, rates. The application of a generally progressive tax system to a base primarily defined in money terms has, during a period characterised by both real growth and continuous inflation, produced an increase in the overall effective rate. Changes in nominal rates — and indeed the introduction of new taxes — have been much less significant than this underlying feature in explaining the secular increase in the ratio in question.

This is reinforced, in the Republic anyway, by what appears to be part of the fiscal philosophy of its governments in recent years. There can be little doubt that a prime intention has been to achieve a balance in the current account of central government, although this principle has been breached in the very recent past. It is true that the inflationary pressures endemic in the Republic's economy since the early 1960s have made the avoidance of budget deficits desirable from the point of view of aggregate demand management, but what is of most interest here is that governments have avoided surpluses just as much as they have avoided deficits. There has, in other words, been a tendency for governments to spend on current account the total proceeds of the tax system. As a result, the ratio of current public expenditure to national income has simply risen in line with the equivalent tax ratio.

Table 6.2 shows that there has been a marked convergence over the past decade in the economic structure of public current expenditure in the two areas. None the less, certain obvious differences remain. First, social services expenditure, which dominates the transfers component, has been higher — per head of population and as a proportion of GDP — in Northern Ireland than in the Republic (see Chapter 3). This is, in a sense, a fiscal abnormality which biases the whole structure of public expenditure and arises from the massive support received from the United Kingdom government specifically for social welfare services. In other words, if Northern Ireland were fiscally independent as the Republic is, transfers would probably not be so significant.

Secondly, the difference in the proportion represented by debt interest is very striking. Capital expenditure and borrowing are dealt with below, but at this stage it should be said that the differences shown in Table 6.2 seem to be adequately explained by the fact that the proportion of public capital expenditure financed by borrowing has traditionally been much higher in the Republic than in Northern Ireland.

The economic structure of expenditure is, of course, related to the functional structure, and this is shown in Table 6.3 for 1970–71 (at the time of writing this was the latest year for which such a table could be constructed). The individual columns in that table show noticeable differences between the North and South. The differences in the functional composition of subsidies arise primarily from two factors. First, there was very little current (as opposed to capital) support for industry in the Republic, whereas in the North such assistance accounted for a quarter of all subsidies. Of particular importance here is the Regional Employment Premium — a payroll subsidy for manufacturing industry in the development areas of the United Kingdom — which has no equivalent in the Republic. Secondly, the high relative incidence in the South of subsidies to transport and communications arises almost wholly from a large subsidy to cover the deficit of Córas Iompair Éireann, the state transport company.

The functional composition of transfers is very similar in the two areas (there is a slight difference in education which will be referred to shortly), but there are marked differences with respect to goods and services expenditure: in particular, the proportion of government consumption represented by educational expenditure is much lower in the Republic and that accounted for by 'other' expenditure is much higher.

Table 6.2: Percentage Economic Composition of Public Current Expenditure, Northern Ireland and the Republic, 1962–63 and 1972–73

Year	Northern Ireland				Republic			
	Subsidies	Transfers	Goods and services	Debt interest	Subsidies	Transfers	Goods and services	Debt interest
1962–63	18·2	33·2	44.1	4·5	14·2	23·8	50·9	11·1
1972–73	11·4	39·3	43·6	5·7	12·6	27·4	49·0	11·1

Sources: As Table 6.1.

Table 6.3: Percentage Functional Composition of Public Current Expenditure (excluding Debt Interest), Northern Ireland and the Republic, 1970–71

	Northern Ireland				Republic			
	Subsidies	Transfers	Goods and services	Total	Subsidies	Transfers	Goods and services	Total
Housing	10·1		0·1	1·8			0·3	3·0
Education		13·1	25·8	16·5	17·0	17·1	17·9	14·7
Health and Social Services		81·8	43·6	49·8		81·0	26·7	39·1
Agriculture	63·9	0·1	3·0	12·8	68·5	0·1	8·1	15·6
Industry	25·0	1·6	2·1	6·0	2·5		1·7	1·3
Transport and Communications	0·8		5·5	2·6	10·4		9·6	6·7
Other	0·2	3·4	20·0	10·3	1·5	1·8	35·8	19·5
	100·0	100·0	100·0	100·0	100·0	100·0	100·0	100·0

Sources: As Table 6.1.

It will be noted that the proportion of total current expenditure (excluding debt interest) accounted for by education is very similar in the two parts of Ireland. The difference occurs in the division between transfers and expenditure on goods and services. This is because of the differences in the way this sector is organised. In the South almost all educational establishments are, according to normal national accounting conventions, counted as being in the private sector. Much of government finance for education therefore takes the form of grants to those institutions. This is not the case in the North, where substantial parts of the educational sector are publicly owned and therefore where direct public financing of goods and services expenditure is more normal.

The large difference under the 'other' heading seems to stem from two sources. First, as already explained, the Northern Ireland figures exclude expenditure on the armed forces. The figures for the Republic include this. Secondly, and more generally, the Republic is an independent state, whereas Northern Ireland is not. As a result, the South is involved in certain expenses of government (e.g. a diplomatic service) which do not have to be borne in the North.

4.2 Capital Expenditure

In 1972–73 public capital expenditure in the Republic was £170·30 million, or 7·6 per cent of GDP, and in Northern Ireland £197·52 million, or 18·1 per cent of GDP. The relevant ratios for 1962–63 were 7·4 per cent and 11·0 per cent respectively, indicating quite different trends in the two areas.

Table 6.4 provides clues as to the reasons for this difference (since the economic structure of capital expenditure can change dramatically from year to year, that table shows the whole decade to permit the observation of the underlying trends). In neither part of the island has physical capital formation by the central or local authorities (as opposed to public corporations, which are excluded from the figures) been a source of relative growth of the public capital budget, in the sense that the ratio of this item to GDP has changed little over the period in question. The major changes have come in the other items – capital transfers and net loans (which equal loans less repayments).

In recent years capital grants to industry have represented approximately half of total capital transfers, and this item has shown very substantial growth in the Republic (for example, it increased four-fold in the second half of the 1960s). These grants are an even more significant component of capital transfers in Northern Ireland, but in that region they have shown very little growth. Similarly, capital grants for education, which account for around one-eighth of transfers in both areas, have grown much faster in the South than in the North. The effect of these trends is that the very definite upward movement seen in the Republic in the proportion of total

Table 6.4: Percentage Economic Composition of Public Capital Expenditure, Northern Ireland and the Republic, 1962–73

	Northern Ireland			Republic		
Year	GPCF[a]	Capital transfers	Net loans	GPCF[a]	Capital transfers	Net loans
1962–63	72·9	25·5	1·5	52·6	17·1	30·3
1963–64	71·9	21·4	6·7	55·3	20·1	24·6
1964–65	65·3	21·0	13·7	55·1	19·2	25·8
1965–66	65·7	20·6	13·7	58·4	18·9	22·6
1966–67	65·2	19·1	15·7	59·9	23·5	16·6
1967–68	61·6	23·1	15·3	59·6	27·2	13·2
1968–69	56·7	27·7	15·6	56·4	27·9	15·7
1969–70	50·8	31·4	17·8	49·0	26·0	25·0
1970–71	50·7	28·9	20·3	56·8	30·6	12·6
1971–72	46·3	26·7	27·0	54·0	33·7	12·4
1972–73	39·1	25·2	35·7	58·2	27·1	14·7

[a]Gross Physical Capital Formation, equals gross fixed capital formation plus stock changes.

Sources: As Table 6.1.

public capital expenditure accounted for by capital transfers has not similarly manifested itself in the North.

Net loans represented an increasing proportion of total capital expenditure in Northern Ireland but a strongly declining proportion in the Republic. Of course, by the arithmetic of proportions this has already been partially explained, but there appears to be at least one other factor worth mentioning. In the North in the recent past very nearly the whole of these loans have gone to public corporations, and this item has shown massive growth. The situation in the South has been quite different. Since the mid-1950s the tradition in the United Kingdom as a whole has been that central government has been the sole source of long-term finance for nationalised industries, apart from any internal funds those industries may possess. In the South the government has, of course, been involved in the provision of such finance, but in a much less exclusive manner.

 ## 5   PUBLIC BORROWING

The management of public debt is normally treated as an aspect of monetary policy and so will not be dealt with here. However, simply to complete the picture of public finance, it is appropriate to present a brief descriptive survey of the course of public borrowing in recent years.

In 1972–73 the net borrowing requirement of central and local authorities combined was £128·30 million in the Republic, or 6·5 per cent of G D P, and £84·26 million in Northern Ireland, or 7·7 per cent of G D P. These figures are of gross borrowing less repayments. Of course, only transactions with other sectors are included: including intrasectoral borrowing, e.g. by local authorities from central government, implies double-counting.

Two points are of interest. First, although net borrowing as a proportion of G D P fluctuates quite substantially from year to year, definite patterns emerge. There seems to be a fairly constant trend in that ratio in the Republic, but a strongly rising trend in Northern Ireland over the past ten years. The very much lower ratio of borrowing to G D P in the North in the early 1960s (1−2 per cent compared with 5−6 per cent in the South) must at least help to explain what was shown earlier, i.e. the lower proportion of public current expenditure accounted for by debt interest in the North. Indeed, there seems to have been a definite change in policy by Northern Ireland since the mid-1960s, with annual borrowing, especially from the United Kingdom government, rising dramatically. This seems to be associated with the substantial increase, relative to GDP, of public capital expenditure in the North − a phenomenon not manifest in the Republic. Because of the severe limitations on the taxing powers of the Northern Ireland government, such an increase in public expenditure could only have been debt-financed.

Secondly, there are very different situations in the two areas as regards the proportion of public capital expenditure financed from borrowing. Not only has this proportion, throughout the past decade, been much lower in the North than the South, but the trends are moving in opposite directions. Until the mid-1960s this ratio was fairly constant at 75−80 per cent in the Republic, but since then it has not been higher than 70 per cent, and in 1966−67 it went as low as 55 per cent. In Northern Ireland, however, the ratio was only around 10 per cent at the beginning of the decade, but in the last seven years of the period under review it was between 30 and 40 per cent.

The explanation for these differences in the trends partially lies in the starting-point, where the ratio was remarkably low in the North and remarkably high in the South. But it is also rooted in the differences in the political and monetary situations of the two parts of Ireland. Over 90 per cent of the borrowing of the Northern Ireland administration is from the government of the United Kingdom, and clearly, as an act of regional development policy, the U K government has been prepared to provide the loan finance for the massive increases in public investment already observed. Furthermore, the Northern administration does not feel that it has any responsibility in relation to the balance of payments of the area, or for the rate of inflation. In the South, however, the situation is somewhat different. When the Dublin government borrows abroad, it does so in international markets and its borrowing is limited by the conditions imposed by those markets. Furthermore, it is a sovereign government for whom domestic inflation and payments deficits are relevant policy considerations. As a result, it is subject to constraints not felt by the administration in Belfast.

6 FISCAL POLICY

So far in this chapter, although aggregates of taxation, public expenditure and borrowing have been referred to and related to other aggregates such as Gross Domestic Product, the main framework of reference has been micro-economic, i.e. concerned with the way public authorities obtain and use scarce resources and with the way fiscal operations such as taxes may influence the allocation of resources in the private sector. In this section attention is switched to macro-economic issues — the effects of budgetary actions on variables such as the level of national income, the level of unemployment, the rate of inflation, and the balance of payments.

The context will be essentially short-run — that is, the effects of fiscal policy on such things as the long-run rate of growth of productive potential will be ignored. In other words, one is thinking here of an economy with a given volume of resources (such as labour and capital) and a given state of technical knowledge and organisation, attention being focused on the extent to which those given resources are used. Thus, for example, net investment would be considered as a component of aggregate demand rather than as something which adds to productive capacity. This is essentially the world of the model set out in Chapter 1.

However, the treatment of the level of productive capacity as given can be justified, not only on the grounds of being a simplification but also for the following reason. An economy's capacity to produce is, above all, determined by things like the size and quality of the labour force and the size and quality of the stock of capital. These things are not susceptible to short-run influences and, to the extent to which they are sensitive to fiscal measures at all, will be affected only in the longer run by, for instance, the nature of the social services, educational policy, the structure of personal and corporate income taxes, and so on. The discussion here, however, will be more concerned with variables which are more likely to respond quickly to the kind of year-to-year changes made in annual budgets. These variables fall into the realm of aggregate demand, which is certainly more policy-elastic than aggregate supply.

The relationships between aggregate demand and the instruments of fiscal policy are brought out clearly in the model in Chapter 1. The fiscal instruments are G_1 (public current expenditure on goods and services), t_1 (the marginal tax rate), G_2 (domestic transfers), and B (borrowing), although by the assumptions of Chapter 1, only three of these can be determined exogenously (see pp. 21—2).

Why should governments be concerned with short-run movements in aggregate demand or its components? The relevant policy objectives here

are, primarily, full employment (i.e. to ensure that the given level of productive capacity is used to the full so as to avoid unemployment created
by demand deficiency); price stability (i.e. to ensure that the degree of unused capacity is not so low that excessive inflationary pressures are generated); and balance of payments equilibrium (i.e. to ensure that domestic
demand is not so high in relation to domestic capacity that excessive imports are sucked in, either directly or as a result of domestic inflation).

The problem is that the first of these objectives will, because it requires
a low margin of unused capacity, conflict with the other two, which require a higher margin. Governments therefore have to compromise: to
decide on a target margin of spare capacity designed to produce acceptable
unemployment and acceptable inflation.

An obvious difficulty is that an economy tends to experience cyclical
fluctuations in output and employment. Difficulties arise in trying to
counteract these cyclical movements in such a way that they are stabilised
rather than exacerbated. In relation to fiscal policy, perhaps the greatest
limitation of the general model in Chapter 1 is that it is static and so cannot
take account of the lags which may generate the cycles referred to and
which make 'fine tuning' so difficult. If significant lags exist, even the
direction of desired fiscal intervention cannot be determined solely by
reference to the *current* state of excess or deficient demand.

It is true that this whole question is less important in Ireland than in
many other places. A high proportion of Ireland's unemployment is probably structural and not sensitive to changes in aggregate demand. Also a
high proportion of Ireland's inflation is imported and thus independent
of domestic demand conditions. This again would require a development
of the model if it were to be analysed at any level of rigour. The insertion
of a balance of payments constraint with, perhaps, some disaggregation of
the labour market, would serve to provide an explanation of why, for instance, full employment cannot be achieved in Ireland simply by increasing
the budget deficit to a large enough size. However, no country wants un-
necessarily high unemployment or inflation, and so even an Irish government rightly takes an interest in the level of aggregate demand and attempts
to influence that level through its budgetary and other policies.

Before examining the course of fiscal policy in Ireland in recent years,
two more introductory points need to be made. First, the budget is only
one instrument available to governments who wish to influence aggregate
demand: there is also, for instance, monetary policy, which is discussed
in Chapter 7. Secondly, administrations in Northern Ireland have little part
to play in all this since their fiscal autonomy is so limited. The discussion
here will therefore concentrate entirely upon the Irish Republic.

6.1 Fiscal Policy in the Republic

It would be most satisfactory if one could somehow encapsulate the experience of fiscal stabilisation policy over the past decade or so and pass an overall judgment on its success or otherwise in minimising fluctuations in the relevant variables. This, however, would be a major research project in its own right and will not be attempted here. This section's ambition will be limited to fairly general qualitative conclusions as to the relationship between budgetary policy and economic conditions in recent years, referring at times to particular instances to substantiate or illustrate a point.

To give a simple picture of the Republic's business cycle for the years 1960–73, Table 6.5 shows the annual growth in real Gross Domestic Product at factor cost.

Table 6.5: Annual Percentage Growth of G D P in the Republic of Ireland, 1960–73 (Factor Cost, Constant Prices)

Year	%
1960	5·0
1961	4·1
1962	3·6
1963	3·0
1964	5·5
1965	1·3
1966	1·5
1967	5·0
1968	6·9
1969	4·2
1970	2·3
1971	5·0
1972	4·4
1973	7·0[a]

[a]Estimate.

Source: *National Income and Expenditure,* Stationery Office, Dublin, various issues.

If productive capacity were growing at a constant rate, and if the government's preferences regarding the weighting of unemployment against inflation remained unchanged, perfect stabilisation policy would have existed when output grew at a constant annual rate. This has clearly not happened, but one must not overestimate the magnitude of the fluctuations: the trend rate of growth is constant and the variations around that trend quite small. Over the period the mean annual rate of growth was 4·2 per cent and the standard deviation 1·7 per cent.

The experience of the 1960s has been reviewed by Ryan (1972), and it is worth summarising his conclusions on that period before looking at the more recent past, since there seems to have been a significant change in the attitude of the Dublin government towards the role of fiscal policy in relation to demand management.

The most remarkable feature of the 1960s was the dominance of the desire to maintain balance in the current budget. In no year during that decade did the government plan anything other than balance on current account, with the exception of 1968—69 when a supplementary budget turned a planned balance into a planned deficit. Fortunately, built-in flexibility (see below) meant that the current budget went into deficit in recession years, despite the intentions of the policy makers. This occurred in, for instance, 1962—63 and 1965—66 which Table 6.5 shows to be low years in the business cycle.

Of course, balance in the current budget does not necessarily imply fiscal neutrality in the macro-economic sense. As is well known from the balanced budget theorem, an increase in the size of the current budget, even though balance is maintained, will exert upward pressure on aggregate demand. Furthermore, public current expenditure and public current revenue are each aggregates of heterogeneous items whose effects on overall economic activity vary markedly. Just as an example, suppose a desired relationship between the two sides of the current budget is produced alternatively by an increase in social welfare benefits or by a reduction in rates of tax on corporate profits. Clearly, one would expect the former to have a significant and immediate effect on consumption whereas the latter will not. Thus it is not enough to look merely at the size of, and relationship between, the two sides of the account. The structure of budgetary changes is also important. Of course, a model of the degree of aggregation as in Chapter 1 cannot readily demonstrate this point, but it should be intuitively quite clear.

None the less, this determination to maintain current balance was obviously a severe limitation on the stabilising capacity of fiscal policy. It seems that, in framing budgets, more attention was given to longer-term objectives of economic development, improvements in social services, etc. Deficits were eschewed because it was feared that to use borrowing to finance current expenditure would reduce the volume of funds available to both public and private sectors for fixed capital formation, and surpluses were avoided since revenue availability was seen as an opportunity to do such things as improve the quality of publicly provided services, increase social welfare provisions, etc.

But this attitude to the current account does not mean that the government made no attempt to use the budget to influence short-run movements in aggregate demand. It was the capital budget which was seen as the main instrument for this purpose, although publicly expressed governmental views are ambiguous on this, and here again demand management very much took second place. Public capital expenditure was seen as a major instrument of growth policy, and the government was predisposed to keep this item as large as possible, the substantial annual variations in both planned and actual growth in public investment being explained more by borrowing problems than by any intention to use the capital budget as a stabilisation tool.

This is really a matter of monetary policy, which is the subject of another chapter, but it is necessary to record here two points. First, real or imagined monetary constraints (e.g. the fear that excessive government borrowing would inhibit private capital formation) were of major importance in producing fluctuations in the rate of growth of public capital expenditure. Furthermore, in some years such fluctuations were contrary to what would have been required if governments had been more interested in stabilising the rate of growth of domestic income. This can be illustrated by reference to what happened in the mid-1960s.

In 1963—64 and 1964—65 the public capital programme in money terms grew at an annual rate in excess of 20 per cent. This was a major contribution to a surge in aggregate demand which accelerated inflation and produced serious balance of payments problems compounded by a falling-off in capital inflows. The severe cut-back in public investment which followed (money expenditure on this item rose by less than 3 per cent in 1965—66 and actually fell in 1966—67) must have contributed to the dramatic reduction in the rate of growth of output shown clearly in Table 6.5.

Secondly, the apparent priority accorded to maintaining a high level of public capital expenditure has certainly added to the difficulty of using what little power monetary policy may have as an instrument to restrain aggregate demand in a small open economy. Briefly in the middle of the last decade, and more consistently in recent years, the public sector in the Republic has not allowed itself to be subject to the credit constraints imposed by the Central Bank on the private sector. In particular, when monetary constraints would have made it difficult to finance the proposed public investment from domestic resources, there has been resort — by both the government and the nationalised industries — to foreign borrowing. This inconsistency between fiscal and monetary policies also casts doubt on the intentions of the government in the stabilisation field.

The general impression which emerges from the 1960s is of a government which gave short-term counter-cyclical policy a much lower priority than longer-term matters. The insistence upon balancing the current budget and on maintaining, regardless of its immediate effects on aggregate demand, as high a level of public capital spending as financial constraints would allow, certainly does not suggest that the Irish Republic had a government which felt it important that fiscal policy should be used to maintain a target relationship between aggregate demand and supply.

In the last few years, however, things have changed quite dramatically in this respect: above all, governments have departed from the practice of the balanced budget by allowing planned deficits on current account. In fact, the budgets of 1972, 1973 and 1974 were highly expansionary in two ways: in each year substantial real increases in the public capital programme were budgeted for, and the current budget was, for all three years, run at a deficit.

At the time of the 1972 budget the forecasters were predicting a below-capacity growth rate and an improvement in the balance of payments. The latter was significant because concern over international payments had inhibited any departure from a balanced budget in 1970 and 1971, when the trend of output suggested the need for stimulus. This expected improvement in the balance of payments encouraged the government to budget for a current deficit of £35 million, or nearly 6 per cent of total revenue.

In fact, because of a combination of accelerating inflation and the built-in flexibility of the tax system, the actual deficit for 1972–73 turned out to be only £5½ million. Here was a case where the automatic flexibility of a tax system based on money values inhibited real recovery at a time of inflation.

The budget of 1973 was prepared by a new government which had at the election committed itself to various reforms. The implementation of some of these reforms (e.g. improvements in social welfare benefits) and a general preference for growth over price stability led to a very expansionary budget, with an increase of 23 per cent in the public capital programme and a current deficit of £39 million, or 5 per cent of revenue. This budget, combined with other expansionary forces, produced an extremely high rate of growth of output in 1973. But again, inflation and automatic revenue buoyancy conspired to produce a deficit barely one-quarter the size of what was planned. This was perhaps fortunate, given that, as it was, real output rose by 7 per cent, unemployment fell, inflation accelerated and the balance of payments deteriorated, and may have been an example of desirable built-in stabilisation.

If other things had behaved normally, the scene would have been set in 1974 for a neutral or mildly deflationary budget. However, in 1973 the situation became quite abnormal due to the extraordinary increase in oil and other commodity prices. The deflationary impact of this was recognised in the spring of 1974 – although, as it turns out, it was seriously underestimated. So another expansionary budget was delivered, with an increase of 20 per cent in the capital budget and a planned current deficit of £67 million, or over 7 per cent of total revenue. At the time of writing, the outcome for 1974 is unknown, but it looks as if the budget has done little more than offset the depressing effects of the international situation.

6.2 Built-in Stability in the Republic

The emphasis so far has been on discretionary fiscal policy where the government varies the level of public revenue and expenditure by legislative or administrative action. However, since tax yields and, to a much lesser extent, expenditure are linked to variables outside public control, these fiscal magnitudes will to a degree vary independently of governmental action on tax rates and so forth. Thus, for example, the yield of personal income tax will rise as personal income rises, even though statutory rates and allowances remain unchanged; similarly, expenditure on unemployment benefits will vary with the level of unemployment, even though the rates of benefit and the rules defining eligibility may not change. This phenomenon is called built-in, or automatic, flexibility.

However, what is of interest here is not this flexibility as such, but its effect on the stability of an economy. If tax yields rise as income rises, taxes constitute a leakage from the multiplier process just as, for example, savings and imports, being functions of income, are leakages. The reduction in the value of income and output multipliers resulting from the incorporation of built-in flexibility gives a more stable system. This stabilising effect is known as built-in, or automatic, stability.

The Republic of Ireland has a fiscal system of this kind, and the model in Chapter 1 contains a simplified version of it. That model clearly shows how built-in stabilisers work, since if the tax system had no built-in flexibility (i.e. tax revenue were fixed), $Q \cdot Y_D$ would be constant and the parameter t_1 would disappear. The disappearance of this parameter would increase the values of the multipliers.

A point of clarification is needed, however. Although the Republic definitely has a fiscal system with automatic stabilisation properties, the full effects may have been mitigated (especially in recent inflationary times when the massive growth of money income, combined with a progressive income tax, has led to a severe tendency for real resources to be transferred automatically to the government) by a tendency for governments to use revenue buoyancy as an opportunity to expand current public expenditure.

To evaluate the effectiveness of built-in stabilisers, one proceeds in two stages: one first estimates the degree of built-in flexibility (i.e. the sensitivity of a tax's yield to changes in its base) and then inserts these estimates into a macro-economic model to evaluate the effect on income.

It has been estimated that, with the rates and allowances ruling in 1967–68, personal income taxation had an overall marginal rate of approximately 10 per cent, i.e. that, *ceteris paribus*, a rise of £1 in aggregate personal income produced an increase in tax yield of 10p (see Lennan (1972)). One would guess that the overall marginal rate has increased since the late 1960s because exemption levels have not risen in proportion to average money incomes and so, nowadays, a higher proportion of any increment in aggregate personal income would be liable for tax. This tendency for the built-in flexibility of yield to increase will be strengthened as capital gains and agricultural profits are included in the tax base.

The same author estimated that the combined overall marginal rates of the two corporate taxes with respect to undistributed profits was 30 per cent at the rates ruling in 1967–68.

These figures, of course, relate changes in yield of a tax to changes in the base of that tax. However, what is more important for the stability of the system is the yield-flexibility of taxes with respect to national income. The work under review here suggests that the total tax system of the Republic has a marginal rate with respect to Gross National Product of approximately 28 per cent.

When these estimates were inserted into a macro-economic model, Lennan estimated that the existence of built-in flexibility reduced by about 8 per cent the fluctuations in G N P: in other words, if tax revenue had not responded automatically in the way described, movements in G N P would have been around $8\frac{1}{2}$ per cent larger than they actually were. In relative terms, the system was estimated to be significantly more effective in stabilising consumption than in stabilising income: on average, about 23 per cent of movements in consumption were thought to have been prevented by the existence of this built-in stability.

Of course, too much credibility must not be attached to the precise results obtained in an exercise of this kind. Because of data and other difficulties, certain simplifications have to be made, and the results can be quite sensitive to changes in the specification of the model. Furthermore, they apply only to the system at a point in time (in this case, 1967–68). As already suggested, the automatic flexibility of the Republic's income tax has almost certainly increased in recent years, and so the built-in stabilisation properties of the overall system have presumably also increased. However, *ceteris paribus,* the higher the marginal propensity to import, the lower the stabilisation index used in studies of this kind. As a result of the extreme openness of the Republic's economy, therefore, one would not expect this index to reach the kind of levels suggested, for instance, for the United Kingdom. However, such an open economy is, again *ceteris paribus,* inherently more stable, since a high marginal propensity to import reduces the domestic multiplier effects of an exogenous shock and thus a lower value for built-in stabilisation would not necessarily be a cause for concern.

REFERENCES

Bristow, J. A. (1968): 'Public Enterprise' in J. A. Bristow and A. A. Tait, ed., *Economic Policy in Ireland,* Institute of Public Administration, Dublin.

Capital Taxation (1974) (Prl 3688), Stationery Office, Dublin.

Capital Transfer Tax (1974) (Cmnd 5705), H M S O, London.

Company Taxation in Ireland (1972), (Prl 2628), Stationery Office, Dublin.

C E E P (1973): *The Evolution of the Public Enterprises in the Community of Nine,* C E E P editions, Brussels.

Lennan, L. K. (1972): 'The Built-in Flexibility of Irish Taxes and their Contribution to Economic Stability'. (Unpublished M. Litt. dissertation, Trinity College, Dublin.)

O'Donoghue, M. and Tait, A. A. (1968): 'The Growth of Public Revenue and Expenditure in Ireland' in J. A. Bristow and A. A. Tait, ed., *Economic Policy in Ireland,* Institute of Public Administration, Dublin.

Peacock, A. T. and Wiseman, J. (1961): *The Growth of Public Expenditure in the United Kingdom,* Oxford University Press.

Proposals for Corporation Tax (1974) (Prl 3713), Stationery Office, Dublin.

Royal Commission on the Taxation of Profits and Income (1955): *Final Report* (Cmd 9474), HMSO, London.

Ryan, L. (1972): 'Fiscal Policy and Demand Management in Ireland 1960–70' in A. A. Tait and J. A. Bristow, ed., *Ireland: Some Problems of a Developing Economy,* Gill and Macmillan, Dublin.

Wealth Tax (1974) (Cmnd 5704), HMSO, London.

CHAPTER 7

The Banking System

N. J. GIBSON

1 INTRODUCTION

It will be recalled that the models presented in Chapter 1 included equations for the demand and supply of money and that these were referred to as the monetary sector. The two equations for the Republic were written as follows: $\frac{M^D}{P} = 1(Y, R^N)$ and $M^S = M^D$. The demand for money equation suggests that if income rises, other things being equal, the real quantity of money demanded increases and vice versa for a rise in the rate of interest.

In the model it is assumed that income (Y) is an endogenous variable, and thus any change in the model which impinges on Y will, given that the rate of interest (R^N) is exogenous, change the quantity of money demanded. In this respect the model is highly interdependent in the sense that any changes anywhere in the model which affect Y will affect the quantity of money demanded.

The position as regards the rate of interest (R^N) is somewhat different since this variable is assumed to be exogenous and hence is not influenced by changes anywhere in the model. However, if R^N changes because of influences outside the model, it will, as already indicated, necessarily affect directly the quantity of money demanded. But it will also, through its effects on the variables of the model generally, affect Y and thus in addition indirectly affect the quantity of money demanded.

As the model stands it says that the money supply is endogenous and therefore not directly under the control of the authorities. This is not to say, however, that they cannot influence the monetary situation indirectly. For instance, according to the model an increase in, say, government expenditure (G_2) or the rate of taxation (t_1) may be expected to affect income and other variables and thus to affect the monetary sector. Nevertheless, the model, as it exists, implies no role for monetary policy as ordinarily understood, in that the monetary authorities have no direct control over the money supply or the rate of interest.

To use a model which permits no role for monetary policy as commonly defined, as a background to a chapter dealing with the banking system, may seem rather puzzling. The fundamental reasons for doing so are the fixed exchange rate with sterling, the ease with which funds can move between the Republic and Britain, and the smallness economically of the former relatively to the latter. These factors make it difficult, if not impossible, for interest rates in Ireland to differ much from those in Britain. However, they can and do differ to some extent, and thus the model must be interpreted, at least for the moment, as abstracting from this kind of complication. Indeed, this chapter may be looked upon as in part an elaboration and modification of the monetary sector of the model, as well as an exploration of its relationship with other sectors.

The next section considers the banking structure of both the Republic and Northern Ireland, concentrating on the development of the Central Bank and the various kinds of commercial bank. There then follows a discussion of the relationship between money and economic activity which is basic to an understanding of monetary and credit policy. This is followed by an examination of certain features of the monetary sectors, including the setting of interest rates, the behaviour of selected monetary and credit aggregates and the demand for money in the Republic (there is unfortunately no information about the stock of money in Northern Ireland). Next comes a discussion of monetary and credit policy in the Republic. Particular attention is given to the credit advice of the Central Bank, the inflow of foreign funds, the introduction of variable liquid asset ratios, the banks' interest rates, and other policy matters, including government financing, official and semi-state foreign borrowing, and the parity link with sterling. A short section deals with credit policy in Northern Ireland, and finally some conclusions are presented.

2   THE BANKING STRUCTURE

The major banking institutions within Ireland comprise the Central Bank of Ireland; a number of different kinds of commercial banks, each of which is more fully described below; the Post Office Savings Bank and Trustee Savings Banks in the Republic, and the National Savings Bank and Trustee Savings Banks in Northern Ireland. In addition, though not normally described as banks, brief mention is made of hire purchase finance companies and building societies.

2.1 The Central Bank of Ireland
The Central Bank, which is publicly owned and whose activities are, of course, confined to the Republic, formally came into existence in 1943 under the Central Bank Act (1942) some twenty years after the establishment of the state. The Central Bank evolved from what was called the

Currency Commission which had been established under the Currency Act (1927). The major responsibility of the Currency Commission was to keep the Saorstát (Irish Free State) pound at absolute parity with the pound sterling. This was accomplished by the Commission accumulating sterling assets and being always ready to exchange in London, and later in Dublin, without charge or fee, the Saorstát pound for the pound sterling. This responsibility is still carried out, only now for the Irish pound, by the Central Bank. However, under the Central Bank Act (1971) the par value of the currency may now be changed by government order after consultation with the Central Bank. Before this development a change in the par value of the currency would have required an act of the Oireachtas (the National Parliament).

The Central Bank Act (1942) gives the Central Bank 'the general function and duty of taking (within the limit of the powers for the time being vested in it by law) such steps as the Board may from time to time deem appropriate and advisable towards safeguarding the integrity of the currency and ensuring that, in what pertains to the control of credit, the constant and predominant aim shall be the welfare of the people as a whole' (No. 22 of 1942, s.6, ss.1). This statement, which is adopted from the Constitution, is perhaps necessarily vague and difficult to interpret (Constitution of Ireland, Article 45, s.2, ss.(iv)). The 'integrity of the currency' might refer to the stability of the internal or external purchasing power of the Irish pound or both, and if so, the Central Bank's responsibility in this matter is clearly qualified by the first part of the statement. If 'the integrity of the currency' refers to both the internal and external purchasing power of the Irish pound, then it may be doubted that both aims can be achieved simultaneously. This point can perhaps best be appreciated by considering it in terms of the model presented in Chapter 1. The model suggests – and this was reinforced by the arguments of Chapter 5 – that the price level in the Republic (and indeed also in Northern Ireland) is greatly influenced by prices in Britain, granted the fixity of the exchange rate between the two currencies. Alternatively, an attempt to stabilise the price level in the Republic would require variation in the exchange rate, and this is not and has never been the sole prerogative of the Central Bank.

As regards the 'control of credit' in the interests of 'the welfare of the people as a whole', this too raises many difficult questions. The concept of 'national welfare' is a notoriously difficult one. However, if it is interpreted in terms of maintaining full-employment levels of income more or less continuously, which would imply an absence of involuntary emigration, then clearly it is an aim which has hardly ever been achieved. But it would be unrealistic to saddle the Central Bank alone – and it was presumably not the intention of the Central Bank Act to do so – with this kind of responsibility. It would be unrealistic because if the model of Chapter 1 is at all plausible, it suggests that the determination of output and employment, and their full-employment levels, is essentially outside the control of the Central Bank. Thus, however extensive the Central Bank's powers to control money and credit (these are discussed more fully below), it is doubtful, in the circumstances of the economy and the maintenance of the parity link with sterling, if they could have been employed in ways which would ensure full-employment levels of income and employment.

The Central Bank Act (1942) gave the Bank the powers traditionally associated with central banking, including the power to engage in open market operations and act as a lender of last resort. For many years these powers lay dormant. It was not until 1955 that the Central Bank first exercised its powers as a lender of last resort, when it rediscounted for some of the banks both Dublin government exchequer bills and commercial bills of exchange. One of the basic reasons for the long period of inactivity of the Central Bank was that the banks, with large holdings of net external assets — accumulated mostly during the Second World War — had no need of its services and in the management of their assets relied on the facilities of the London money and capital markets. However, a succession of deficits in the balance of payments in the post-war period seriously depleted the net sterling assets of the banks, and in 1955 they turned to the Central Bank for help on a small scale.

In 1958 the banks began to keep clearing balances with the Central Bank for inter-bank settlements, whereas previously these had been carried out through their London agents. Some ten years later the major banks were encouraged to transfer their 'net' external assets to the Central Bank in exchange for interest-bearing deposits and certificates of deposit of varying maturity and yield. By early 1970 the transfer was complete, with the banks retaining only working balances in London. The transfer, together with the movement of some government-held external assets to the Central Bank, gave it control over the country's official external monetary reserves. This had the effect of greatly increasing the resources of the Central Bank and fundamentally changed its relationship with the major banks. For the first time they became dependent on the Central Bank as an important source of liquidity.

Meanwhile in 1969 the Central Bank had taken a number of steps to encourage the development in Dublin of a money market for short-term deposits and a market for short-dated government securities. As regards short-term deposits, the Central Bank accepts them on call and at various periods of notice. It is prepared to make a market in short-dated government securities by buying and selling in sufficiently large amounts to facilitate the banks and other institutions. It also took over from the government at about this time the issue of exchequer bills, which takes place monthly to the banks and the public.

In 1970 the Central Bank started a foreign exchange market to meet the requirements of the banks, which previously had relied almost entirely on the facilities of the London market. The Bank sets daily exchange rates for currencies other than sterling, which, as already mentioned, is held at par with the Irish pound. Because of the parity link the non-sterling rates of exchange are kept 'equal to or within the margins prevailing between sterling and . . . other currencies' (Whitaker (1972b), p. 116).

The next major stage of development of the Central Bank followed the coming into force of the Central Bank Act (1971). This enhanced the powers of the Central Bank in three main ways: it became responsible for the licensing of banks, a task hitherto the preserve of government and over which little control had been exercised; it acquired the power to impose liquid asset ratios on the banks, with different ratios for different kinds of bank; and it made provision for the transfer of the exchequer account in the Bank of Ireland to the Central Bank. The last-mentioned development took place on 1 January 1972, and liquid asset ratios were introduced in the autumn of 1972. Thus the last five years or so have seen a great extension of the powers of the Central Bank in relation to the banking and financial system. The use that the Central Bank has made of these powers and their significance for economic activity in the Republic is examined below (see pp. 246–60).

2.2 The Commercial Banks

There are five main types of bank operating in Ireland: the traditional and long-established deposit banks with their extensive system of branches which, with the exception of the Belfast Banking Company which carried on business only in Northern Ireland, became known, as far as the Republic is concerned, as 'Associated Banks' under the Central Bank Act (1942); the merchant banks; the North American banks; the industrial banks; and a category known as 'other banks'. Each type is discussed briefly below.

There were nine distinct deposit banks operating in Ireland up to the 1960s. All but two of them carried on business in both the Republic and Northern Ireland. During the 1960s, however, there was a series of bank amalgamations, which in all cases did not legally come fully into effect until early 1972. The Hibernian Bank, which had been acquired by the Bank of Ireland in 1958, was amalgamated with the Irish interests of the National Bank to form the Bank of Ireland Group which has some 280 branches in the Republic, over 30 in Northern Ireland, and 8 in Britain. The Munster and Leinster Bank, the Provincial Bank of Ireland and the Royal Bank of Ireland became the Allied Irish Banks, with over 260 branches in the Republic, some 40 in Northern Ireland, and 15 in Britain. The three remaining banks, each of which had its head office in Belfast, were the Northern Bank, the Belfast Banking Company and the Ulster Bank. In 1970 the first two became the Northern Bank, which is owned by the Midland Bank, a London clearing bank. The Northern Bank has some 40 branches in the Republic and over 120 in Northern Ireland. The Ulster Bank is also owned by a London clearing bank, the National Westminster Bank, and has over

60 branches in the Republic and about 70 in Northern Ireland. Thus both the Republic and Northern Ireland share a common system of deposit banks, and hence each is likely to be affected by the monetary and credit policies pursued in the other area.

The merchant banks, of which there are seven altogether, confine their activities to Dublin and Belfast. Each operates in Dublin, and three have offices in Belfast. They offer a highly specialised type of banking and financial service, tending to accept only large deposits, generally not less than £50,000, and to gear their lending specifically to the requirements of their customers. 'Their other activities range from advice on methods of financing, on mergers and takeovers to the management of portfolios on behalf of large investors.' (Whitaker (1972a), p. 68) The liabilities of the merchant banks within Ireland are generally less than their assets there, and so they tend to be net external borrowers.

The next group of banks are known in the Republic as North American banks. There are five of them, one being a joint undertaking with the Bank of Ireland. Three of the five have branches in Belfast. Like the merchant banks, they tend to cater for the larger customer, offer a full range of banking services and in so doing are strong competitors of the traditional deposit banks. Again like the merchant banks, their liabilities within Ireland are generally less than their assets, and so they too tend to be net external borrowers.

Both the merchant banks and the North American banks have been active participants in the inter-bank money market that has developed in recent years in Dublin. Indeed, its development is partly a consequence of their arrival and their particular methods of operation in that they, like the industrial and other banks still to be discussed, often first seek out lending business and then find the funds to finance it.

'Deposits in the inter-bank market are repayable at call, two and seven days' notice, and for fixed periods ranging from seven days to twelve months. Most activity is centred in the call to one month range. The normal amount dealt in is £250,000 and each bank has limits on the amounts it will lend to each of the other banks. As in the case of its British counterpart, all lending in the Dublin Inter-Bank Market is unsecured.' (*ibid.*, p. 72)

The fourth category of banks, called industrial banks in the Republic, concentrate their business on instalment credit. To begin with they mainly provided hire purchase loans in connection with consumer durables. More recently they have extended their activities into such areas as industrial loans, the finance of foreign trade and company finance. There are about eleven of these banks operating in the Republic. Like the merchant and North American banks, their domestic assets generally exceed their domestic liabilities, and so they tend to be net external borrowers.

The final group of banks, of which there are currently sixteen, is known as 'other banks' in the Republic and, in effect, covers those excluded from the previous categories. The group includes foreign banks such as Algemene Bank Nederland (Ireland) Ltd, and Banque Nationale de Paris (Ireland) Ltd — sometimes described as continental banks — as well as domestic banks. Like each of the previous groups of banks, with the exception of the Associated Banks, they tend to be net external borrowers.

2.3   Post Office and Trustee Savings Banks
The Post Office and Trustee Savings Banks in the Republic and Northern Ireland both date from the nineteenth century. The Post Offices have, as is well known, an extensive system of branches throughout the whole island. The same is true of the Trustee Savings Banks, though they are much less extensive in their coverage. Both sets of institutions are, as regards their deposit business, essentially a means of channelling small funds from a large number of owners to the respective governments in Dublin and London. To that extent both sets of institutions are a significant source of finance for government expenditure.

2.4   Hire Purchase Finance Companies and Building Societies
There are about 40 hire purchase finance companies operating in the Republic and an unknown but probably smaller number in Northern Ireland. Each of the four Associated Banks has a finance house subsidiary in Northern Ireland and, in addition, there is a small number of companies which are members of the Finance Houses' Association. Some finance companies carry on business in both parts of Ireland. Most of the companies are small, and they are mainly concerned with the financing of consumer durables.

Building societies are highly developed in both the Republic and Northern Ireland, with about 26 operating in the former. Their major business is, of course, the granting of mortgages against the security of house property. The interest rates they pay on their share and deposit liabilities offer strong competition to other financial institutions interested in smaller deposits.

3   MONEY AND ECONOMIC ACTIVITY
The relationship between money and economic activity is highly controversial but is clearly of crucial importance to the discussion of monetary and credit policy. In this section an attempt is made to discuss briefly some of the issues concerning money and economic activity as they may relate to the banking system in Ireland and in the light of the model of Chapter 1.

It will be recalled that the model allows no role for monetary policy as ordinarily understood since the money supply is assumed to be endogenous and hence outside the direct control of the authorities, while the interest rate is also outside their control and, in effect, determined by conditions in Britain (see pp. 254—6 and also Chapter 1, pp. 22—4). However, it has already been made clear that this formulation is highly simplified, and it is instructive to develop the matter further.

It is broadly agreed amongst monetary economists, despite areas of controversy, that what are called substitution and wealth effects are important to an understanding of the linkages between money and economic activity. In addition, some economists, generally with Keynesian leanings, emphasise the role of credit availability in the process and to that extent stress the significance of imperfection in money and credit markets — the provision of credit on criteria other than or in addition to prices.

Substitution effects refer to changes in relative prices and relative interest rates induced by a monetary change. Wealth effects generally refer to changes in wealth brought about by a monetary change. It should perhaps be stressed that, while substitution and wealth effects are formally distinguishable and analogous to the substitution and income effects of ordinary price theory, in practice a change induced by monetary factors will bring about both substitution and wealth effects.

The substitution effect may be loosely described as follows. Suppose a central bank, in an economy where interest rates are not exogenous, purchases government securities in the open market. This will tend to raise the price of government securities and so lower their interest rates and at the same time increase the cash reserves of the banks. The banks may be expected to acquire additional assets and in so doing expand the money supply. In general, the prices of financial assets will rise relatively to existing real assets and encourage at the margin a substitution of real assets for financial assets. But this will tend to raise the price of existing real assets relatively to the cost of producing them and hence stimulate an expansion of expenditure on production. As economic activity rises the demand for money balances may be expected to expand and possibly prices will tend to increase. These consequences will eventually dampen or eliminate the effects of the monetary expansion, though the actual time taken and the lags involved in the process may be highly variable.

To incorporate the foregoing into the models of Chapter 1 would require their substantial modification and give rise to considerable difficulties. For instance, it would be necessary to introduce a price level for existing real assets which could differ from the general level of prices of currently produced goods and then postulate some dynamic adjustment process which would bring the system to equilibrium. This issue is not pursued further here.

To discuss the wealth effect requires a definition of the term wealth. Emphasis is usually placed on domestic non-human wealth which may be defined as follows:

$$\frac{W_{nh}}{P} = \frac{D}{P} + \frac{\gamma S}{R^N P} + K$$

where W_{nh} is non-human wealth, P is the general price level, D is outside money, S is the number of government securities outstanding such that the nominal yield on each is one unit, R^N is the nominal interest rate, K is the real value of the stock of capital, and γ is a fraction generally assumed to lie between 0 and 1. By definition, outside money is money that is deemed to be a net asset of the non-government sector of the economy. It is to be distinguished from inside money, which is money backed by private sector securities and is generally considered not to give rise to a net asset as regards that sector. This last point is, however, controversial, as indeed is the value to be attributed to γ and hence the proportion of the value of government securities which should be included in net wealth. The usual argument is that if holders of government securities fully anticipate the discounted present value of tax liabilities needed to service the debt, then the net wealth effect will be zero or, at the other extreme, if they fail to anticipate them, it will be unity. However, it has been argued that in conditions of risk and government transaction costs in relation to debt management, the net wealth effect could be negative (Barro (1974)).

Putting these complications aside, however, it is clear that if an increase in the money supply raises D, the amount of outside money, then net wealth is increased. This is also commonly called the real balance effect. If at the same time interest rates decline and γ is positive, net wealth will be further increased. Finally if, along the lines suggested in the discussion of the substitution effect, the real value of the stock of capital rises, this too will give rise to a net wealth effect. These last two effects are sometimes known as the Keynes windfall effect.

The question still remains how a change in net wealth affects economic activity. The usual argument is that wealth is relevant to consumption expenditure, though there is no reason in principle why it should not also influence investment expenditure, and hence a change in net wealth will lead to changes in expenditure.

The credit availability effect emphasises the importance lenders attach to credit standards in relation to their lending policy. The usual inference is that credit standards become more stringent in periods of monetary restraint and the opposite in periods of monetary ease. The more stringent standards 'may take the form of stiffer requirements for the safety of proposed projects, for the net worth of the borrower, for the competence of management, for the quality of collateral etc.' (Lindbeck (1959)). This may happen without any change in explicit interest rates and so may be interpreted as a shift to the left of the demand curve for 'eligible' credit.

As far as the ability to undertake expenditure is concerned, credit availability may be an important factor, especially if there are few, if any, alternative sources of credit available to borrowers. This may be of particular importance in Ireland because of the dominance of the banks in the financial system, though perhaps this point should not be overstressed in economies as open as those in Ireland.

In discussing money and economic activity in the Republic the Central Bank has placed most emphasis on the credit availability effect, though some attention has also been given to the substitution effect, with apparently little or none to the wealth effect. This point is returned to in the section below on 'Monetary and Credit Policy in the Republic'.

As regards the models of Chapter 1, the foregoing discussion in one sense implies an important modification of them but in another does not fundamentally alter their operation. The important modification is that the introduction of substitution, wealth and credit availability effects relaxes the assumption of one-way causality from the expenditure sector to the monetary sector and allows the latter to affect the former. However, this does not affect what is fundamental to the model, i.e. the endogeneity of the money supply. The latter, however, does not necessarily imply that the domestic credit of the banking system is endogenous, though in the model of Chapter 1 it is so if the money supply is defined to be equal to domestic credit plus foreign exchange reserves since the latter is endogenously determined through equation (1.39) (see p. 26). In contrast, Hoare (1973) assumes that domestic credit is exogenous, but the validity of this assumption is open to doubt (see pp. 250–4).

4   FEATURES OF THE MONETARY SECTOR

4.1   Interest Rates

One of the basic assumptions of the models of Chapter 1 is that the nominal rate of interest (R^N) is determined outside the model and in effect is a consequence of the ease with which funds can move between Ireland and Britain. Any attempt, in the circumstances of a fixed exchange rate and freedom of movement of capital, to maintain indefinitely interest rates in Ireland substantially different from those in Britain would be doomed to fail. Indeed, the Governor of the Central Bank has written 'that interest rates in Ireland cannot for any extended period of time be significantly different from those prevailing in Britain' (Whitaker (1973), p. 73). It comes therefore as no surprise to find that in practice movements in interest rates, especially in relation to highly mobile funds, closely parallel each other in the two islands. This may be seen in Figure 7.1.

It will be seen that the Central Bank's rediscount rate is generally slightly higher than the minimum lending rate of the Bank of England and that both move in a similar way, though the former has on occasion been below the latter. The relationship between the inter-bank three months' money rate and the corresponding rate in London tends to be more regular, with the former almost invariably above the latter. The third figure shows the yields to redemption on government securities with eight years to maturity in Dublin and ten years to maturity in London. These were the closest comparisons that could be made on the basis of the data readily available. It

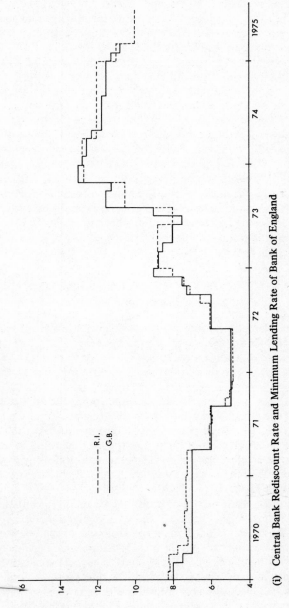

(i) Central Bank Rediscount Rate and Minimum Lending Rate of Bank of England

Figure 7.1: *Selected Interest Rates: Republic of Ireland and Great Britain, 1970–75*

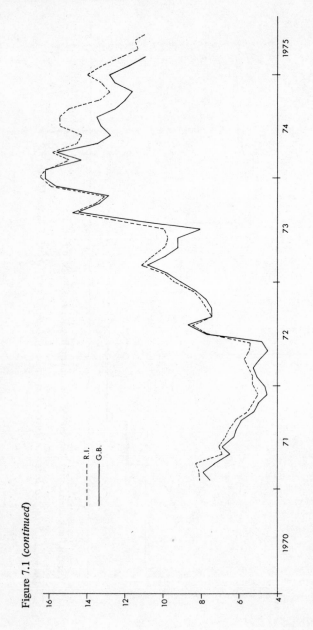

Figure 7.1 *(continued)*

(ii) **Inter-bank Three Months' Money Rates**

Figure 7.1 (*continued*)

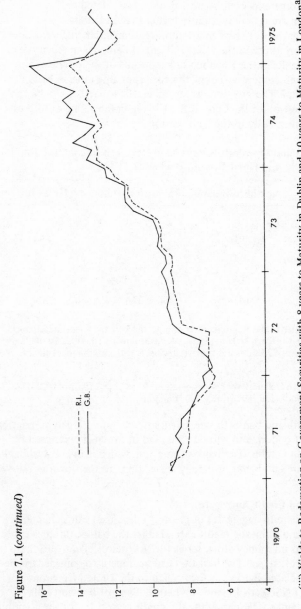

R.I. - - - -
G.B. ———

(iii) Yields to Redemption on Government Securities with 8 years to Maturity in Dublin and 10 years to Maturity in London[a]

[a]For the Republic from March 1970 to December 1971 the security is $7\frac{1}{2}$ per cent exchequer stock 1975 and thereafter representative yields.

Sources: *CBQB* and *BEQB*, various issues.

will be noticed that the movements in rates parallel each other very closely
but, as is perhaps to be expected because of the longer-dated securities,
the rates in London are generally slightly higher than in Dublin.

Notwithstanding the difficulty in attempting to maintain different rates
in the Republic from those in the UK, the Central Bank has in recent years
'encouraged' the banks in the Republic to keep some of their deposit and
lending rates at levels somewhat below the corresponding rates in Britain
and Northern Ireland. The position in December 1974 may be seen in Table
7.1. The whole question of the Central Bank's role in the fixing of interest
rates is discussed more fully in the next section.

Table 7.1: Deposit and Overdraft Rates (%) in Northern Ireland, the Republic
and Great Britain, December 1974

	Northern Ireland	Republic	Great Britain
Deposit Rates:			
Under £5,000	$9\frac{1}{2}$	8	$9\frac{1}{2}$
£5,000 to £25,000	$10\frac{1}{2}$	9	$9\frac{1}{2}$
Over £25,000	$10\frac{1}{2}$	$10\frac{1}{2}$	n.a.
Overdrafts	14	$11\frac{3}{4}$–14	13–18

Note: The interest rates in the Republic refer only to those of the Associated Banks.
The deposit rates for Northern Ireland refer to deposits under £10,000, £10,000 and
under £25,000 and over £25,000, and the overdraft rate is the minimum ordinary
rate.

Sources: N I: Northern Ireland Bankers' Association; R I: *C B Q B* (Spring 1975);
G B: *Financial Statistics* (Jan. 1975), H M S O, London.

The Northern Ireland banks fix their own interest rates, largely in relation
to those ruling in London, and without the kind of oversight exercised by
the Central Bank in Dublin. The Bank of England, which is the central bank
for the Northern Ireland banks, generally leaves them to their own initiative
in this matter.

4.2   Monetary and Credit Aggregates

The monetary and credit aggregates of greatest relevance to this chapter are
the money stock and domestic credit extended by the banks. But as already
mentioned, there is no money stock series for Northern Ireland, and there
is also no bank credit series. The best that can be done is to consider the deposits of the 'Associated Banks', as they relate to the United Kingdom as a
whole and not just Northern Ireland — what the Bank of England calls the
Northern Ireland banks. The monetary and credit aggregates for the Republic
are considered first.

The Central Bank publishes three monetary aggregates, M_1, M_2 and M_3. M_1 refers to the amount of currency outstanding plus the Associated Banks' current accounts; M_2 includes M_1 and the deposit accounts of the Associated Banks; and M_3 includes M_2 plus the non-Associated Banks' current and deposit accounts less all inter-bank balances. Thus M_1, M_2 and M_3 are progressively broader definitions of the money supply. Data on M_1 and M_3 are shown in Table 7.2. M_2 has not been included as it is of less interest than the other two series.

Table 7.2: Monetary Aggregates (£m) and Velocities, Republic of Ireland, 1966—74

Year	M_1	V_{M_1}	M_3	V_{M_3}
1966	315·7 ·	3·37	647·2	1·64
1967	329·7	3·51	709·6	1·63
1968	356·4	3·70	815·6	1·62
1969	376·5	3·99	918·3	1·64
1970[a]	B D	B D	B D	B D
1971	400·5	4·72	1,120·6	1·69
1972	451·3	4·95	1,234·6	1·81
1973	505·6	5·29	1,513·3	1·77
1974	521·0	5·56	1,832·9	1·58

[a]The behaviour of 'money' and credit during the bank dispute period, when the Associated Banks were closed for some seven months, is of considerable interest since the economy, despite the closure, continued to operate at a 'high' level of activity. Space limitations prevent any discussion of the matter other than to say that one of the factors that greatly ameliorated the economic consequences of the closure was the widespread willingness of firms and individuals to draw and accept cheques on the banks which were closed. How much longer this could have continued is another matter. For further discussion see Central Bank of Ireland (1971).

Note: M_1 and M_3 are *averages* for the calendar year. V_{M_1} and V_{M_3} are velocity of circulation for M_1 and M_3 in relation to G N P. B D refers to the bank dispute in 1970 when no statistical returns were available.

Source: *C B Q B* (Winter 1974) and its Statistical Supplement.

Over the period 1966 to 1974 M_1 has grown at a compound rate of growth of 6·5 per cent per year, while the corresponding rate for M_3 was more than twice as rapid at 13·9 per cent. These average rates of growth hide, of course, considerable variation in the year-to-year rates of growth. These varied for M_1 from a low rate of 3·0 per cent during 1974 to a high rate of 12·7 per cent during 1972. For M_3 the corresponding low and high rates were 9·6 per cent and 22·6 per cent and occurred during 1967 and 1973 respectively.

What, if any, interpretation can be put on the behaviour of M_1 and M_3? The inclination of the monetarist would be to attempt to interpret them within a quantity-theory framework — in other words, by making use of the relationship $M = kPY$. The reciprocal of k, namely velocity, for both M_1 and M_3 are shown in Table 7.2, where PY is taken to be Gross National Product at market prices.

It is clear that neither velocity series gives support to the notion of a constant velocity of circulation of money. On the contrary, the V_{M_1} series has a strong upward trend and the V_{M_3} series, which showed little variation in the first four years of the period, rose in the next few years to a peak in 1972 and subsequently declined to a level below that at the beginning of the period.

However, monetarists do not assume constancy of velocity and accept that it is not independent of interest rates and other variables. But in taking this step they are moving, at least to some degree, in the direction of a liquidity preference explanation of money holdings.

In so far as the velocity of circulation of M_1 has risen substantially it suggests an attempt on the part of money holders, over a period when on the average nominal interest rates and prices have been rising at historically rapid rates, to economise on their holdings of what presumably are largely balances held for transaction purposes. In contrast, the behaviour of V_{M_3} shows little indication of a trend, though it exhibits some signs of cyclical influences but on the average has shown relatively slight variation. Another way of putting this is that over the eight years 1966–74 M_3 and GNP have grown at much the same annual rates, in fact, at 13·9 per cent and 13·3 per cent respectively. This suggests at the least a fairly systematic association between GNP and the money stock, whatever may be the direction and strength of the causal links. The model of Chapter 1 requires, of course, that they run from PY to M and not the other way round. However, the discussion of the previous section indicates that the matter may be more complex.

Some data on domestic credit in the Republic may be seen in Table 7.3. The table distinguishes between domestic credit extended by the Associated Banks and the non-Associated Banks and between that extended to government and to non-government borrowers. The rate of growth of domestic credit extended by the two groups of banks has been markedly different. Domestic credit of the Associated Banks has grown over the eight years 1966 to 1974 at 15·1 per cent per year while that of the non-Associated Banks has grown at 32·0 per cent; in 1966 the domestic credit extended by the non-Associated Banks was 13·6 per cent of the total; by 1974 it was 32·2 per cent.

Borrowing by government from the banks has increased more rapidly than non-government borrowing. In 1966 the former was 20·4 per cent of total domestic credit and in 1974 some 25 per cent. The tendency of

Table 7.3: Domestic Credit, Republic of Ireland, December 1966–74 (£m)

Year	Associated Banks	Non-Associated Banks	All Licensed Banks Government	All Licensed Banks Non-Government	Total
1966	407·8	64·2	92·2	379·8	472·0
1967	440·5	78·4	103·7	415·2	518·9
1968	543·1	92·5	137·9	497·6	635·5
1969	614·7	170·0	182·3	602·4	784·7
1970	BD	BD	BD	BD	BD
1971	718·2	273·2	259·1	732·3	991·4
1972	911·3	316·7	292·6	978·7	1,271·3
1973	1,096·1	315·6	371·6	1,202·7	1,574·3
1974	1,256·0	595·7	462·3	1,389·4	1,851·7

Source: As Table 7.2.

government to increase its share of domestic credit provided by the banks has been a matter of concern to the Central Bank. This point is taken up again in the discussion of monetary and credit policy.

As already mentioned, there are no money stock figures for Northern Ireland. It is not known, for instance, what amount of Bank of England notes are in circulation, and there are no figures for deposits in Northern Ireland of all the banks operating there. There is only information on the Northern Ireland banks' activities in the United Kingdom as a whole. However, for what it is worth, it may be useful to consider briefly the Northern Ireland banks' notes outstanding, together with what are called their United Kingdom residents' deposits, even though the latter include some deposits held in Britain.

These figures may be seen in Table 7.4. The table also has columns showing total deposits and their division between sterling and other currencies. Total deposits include, in addition to United Kingdom residents' deposits, deposits of United Kingdom banks and deposits of overseas residents. It is clear from the table that the banks are heavily involved in inter-bank transactions and in the holding of foreign currency deposits. Granted the mobility of international funds, the fact that the same banks operate in the Republic, Northern Ireland, Britain, and indeed elsewhere, helps to emphasise the highly integrated nature of international money markets — a point which has already been stressed in the discussion earlier on interest rates.

Table 7.4: Northern Ireland Banks' Deposits and Notes in the United Kingdom, 1972–74 (£m)

| Year | U K residents' deposits | Deposits | | | Notes outstanding |
		Total	Sterling	Other currencies	
1972	274	414	378	36	26
1973	342	601	524	77	28
1974	416	877	742	135	29

Note: All figures are annual averages.

Source: *B E Q B*, various issues.

Data on the banks' deposits, as shown in Table 7.4, are only available for the three complete years 1972–74. The compound rate of growth of United Kingdom residents' deposits has been 23·3 per cent — a rate slightly faster than the 21·7 per cent of M_3 in the Republic over the same period — and probably somewhat faster than the rate of growth of G D P at current prices, though to compare the two may not be very meaningful. Total deposits, on the other hand have shown a much faster rate of growth at 45·6 per cent, which highlights the scale of the banks' activities in the handling of United

Kingdom banks' and overseas residents' deposits, but these are not directly relevant to the Northern Ireland economy.

The notes outstanding are something of a curiosity and are a survival from the Bankers (Ireland) Act (1845) (8 & 9 Vic. c. 37), as amended by subsequent legislation and, in particular, the Bankers (Northern Ireland) Act (1928) (18 & 19 Geo. V, c. 15). Under the 1928 act the six banks, which previously had issues under the 1845 act, were allocated a fiduciary note issue of £1,624,000, and any issue in excess of this figure had to be covered by Bank of England notes and coin.[1] This is the position up to the present, except that the National Bank is excluded from the figures.

One of the curious features of the banks' note issue is its size. It is, for instance, well known that a large volume of Bank of England notes circulate in Northern Ireland alongside those of the banks. It thus seems that the banks do not find it in their interests to try to substitute entirely their own notes for those of the Bank of England. The main reason seems to be that it would not be profitable for them to do so, since they would have to incur the costs involved in producing their own notes and also hold additional Bank of England notes as cover for their own issues. Broadly speaking, though it is obviously more complicated than this, it seems to pay the banks to issue their own notes up to the amount that is roughly in keeping with their desired holdings of Bank of England notes and coin for their general banking purposes. Such holdings are usually in excess of their fiduciary issues.

4.3 The Demand for Money

In the monetary sector a key relationship which is fundamental to making monetary policy possible is the demand for money. This relationship has already been referred to a number of times in this chapter.

The demand for money equation may be written as

$$\frac{M^D}{P} = 1 \, (Y, R^N, \pi)$$

for both the Republic and Northern Ireland, where Y refers to gross national disposable income. The equation is the same as in Chapter 1 except that a price expectations variable, which is discussed below, has been included.

The earlier discussion of the monetary sector presupposes that the demand for money is stable. In the particular context of the model, this implies, granted Y, R^N, π and P are determined outside this equation, that there is a systematic and, in principle, predictable relationship between these variables and the quantity of money demanded (M^D).

---

1 The six banks were the Bank of Ireland, Provincial Bank of Ireland, National Bank, Belfast Banking Company, Ulster Bank and Northern Banking Company.

The formulation or specification of the money demand equation reflects the influence of much recent work in monetary economics and especially that which stems from the pioneering work of Friedman (1956). The equation states that the demand for real money balances $\left(\dfrac{M^D}{P}\right)$ is dependent on an income or output variable, nominal rate of interest and a price expectations variable.

It is common enough in both theoretical and empirical work to find real income and nominal interest rate variables in a demand for money equation, and so little time need be spent discussing them. This is not to say that the matter of how they are defined and measured is straightforward. There are both theoretical and empirical difficulties involved in determining what are the appropriate income and interest rate variables for inclusion in demand for money relationships: for instance, whether the income variable should refer to permanent income and, if so, how it should be defined and measured; similarly, whether the appropriate interest rate (or rates) should be a short rate or long rate and/or an expected rate. However, space prevents these matters being pursued further here. But the expected price variable π is perhaps less familiar and requires some discussion, especially concerning its relationship to the nominal rate of interest (R^N).

It is common practice in discussing the demand for money to argue that a measure of the opportunity cost of holding real money balances in comparison with holding bonds or fixed interest securities is their nominal rate of interest, where the latter is assumed to allow for expected changes in the general level of prices. In other words,

$$R^N = R + \pi$$

Analytically, however, there is no reason to suppose that holding bonds is the only alternative to holding money balances. In general, it is clearly possible to hold equities or physical assets or both. Thus it seems that there is an argument for including in the demand for money relationship the respective rates of return on equities and physical assets. This is, of course, what Friedman does in his famous 1956 article (*ibid.*).

However, even if it is held that there is no direct substitution between money and physical assets, it may still be argued that a price expectations variable should be included in the equation in so far as there may be substitution between such assets and bonds or if for some reason nominal interest rates do not take full account of expected price changes. For reasons such as these, and in a period like the present (1975) of rapid price change, a price expectations variable π is included in the demand for money equation. However, it was not felt necessary to include a variable reflecting the rate of return on equities, partly because in both the Republic and Northern Ireland there is a very narrowly based equity market.

There is unfortunately relatively little empirical work on the demand for money in the Republic and apparently none for Northern Ireland. Furthermore, the work known to this writer and undertaken for the Republic was severely handicapped by lack of suitable data and by statistical and other difficulties (Pratschke and O'Connell (1973) and Hill (1969)). It cannot therefore be considered as definitive but nevertheless is of considerable interest. Some of the results of one of these studies is presented in Table 7.5.

Table 7.5: Empirical Results on the Demand for Money in the Republic of Ireland, 1946–68

Dependent variable	Income	Interest rate	Lagged money	R	D W
(1) $\frac{M_1}{P}$	0·384 (24·95)	− 3·460 (0·984)		0·972	1·38
(2) $\frac{M_2}{P}$	0·524 (10·81)	−39·99 (3·61)		0·854	0·97
(3) log $\frac{M_1}{P}$	0·985 (22·48)	− 0·086 (0·96)		0·966	1·44
(4) log $\frac{M_2}{P}$	0·657 (10·56)	− 0·518 (4·09)		0·848	1·05
(5) $\frac{M_1}{P}$	0·317 (12·66)	− 5·188 (2·71)	0·282 (4·17)	0·992	
(6) $\frac{M_2}{P}$	0·384 (4·10)	−26·79 (2·26)	0·445 (2·30)	0·893	

Note: M_1 is currency outstanding plus current accounts of the Associated Banks, while M_2 is M_1 plus deposit accounts of the Associated Banks; income is real national income in equations (1) and (2); in (3) and (4) it is in logarithmic form, and in (5) and (6) a measure of permanent income is used, defined as a three-year weighted moving average of real income; the interest rate is a computed yield to maturity on $3\frac{1}{2}$ per cent exchequer bonds 1970 for the years 1946–62 and on 6 per cent exchequer stock 1980–85 for the years 1962–68; log r is used in equations (3) and (4); P is the consumer price index; R is the multiple correlation coefficient and D W the Durbin-Watson statistic.

Source: Hill (1969).

In so far as the results may be taken at their face value they suggest that there is a stable demand for real money balances in the Republic and that real income, either current real income or permanent income, is an impor-

tant determinant of that demand. The importance of interest rates is somewhat more problematic since the coefficients are not significant in every
case, though the signs are as suggested by the theory. The lagged dependent
variable is of some note, as it indicates that the adjustment of actual to
desired real money balances may not be complete within the period of one
year and that the adjustment is more rapid for M_1 than for M_2.

However, too much should not be made of these results for the reasons
already mentioned, and it is well to remember that perhaps one of the best
tests of such relationships is how they forecast outside the sample period.
Unfortunately, this is not a straightforward matter, as there are problems
of finding comparable data. Furthermore, the rapid development of the
non-Associated Banks and other structural changes since the late 1960s
would make any attempts at forecasting with these equations extremely
hazardous. They should be treated as illustrative rather than as conveying
well-founded empirical evidence on the demand for money in the Republic.

5　MONETARY AND CREDIT POLICY IN THE REPUBLIC

It has been indicated on a number of occasions that, strictly interpreted, the
models in Chapter 1 allow no role for monetary policy. Yet it is well known
that the Central Bank in the Republic has for many years given advice to the
banks and the government about monetary and credit policy and more recently has attempted to implement its policies through the introduction of
reserve ratios and by other means. In this section the policies recommended
and pursued by the Central Bank since the early 1960s are examined from
both a theoretical and empirical viewpoint. Most attention is given to the
period since the late 1960s.

5.1　Credit Advice
Up until 1965, while the Central Bank expressed repeatedly in its reports
concern about balance of payments deficits, the growth of government expenditure and rising prices, it seems to have offered little or no public advice
on monetary and credit policy to the banks, nor does it seem to have
attempted, however limited the scope for such action might have been, to
implement a monetary and credit policy. This inactivity, as already mentioned above (p. 228), had much to do with the fact that the banks had
relatively large holdings of sterling assets and could mostly operate without
having to rely on the services of the Central Bank, except in relation to the
issue of notes. The Central Bank has recently described its subsequent
approach to credit policy as follows:

> In 1965 the Central Bank issued to the Associated Banks what was to be
> the first of a series of letters of advice on credit policy. These letters set
> guidelines for the expansion of domestic credit by the Associated Banks.

They related generally to a full year, but were subject to review from time to time in the light of economic developments and of changes in outstanding bank credit and resources. Until April 1969 the credit advice of the Central Bank was directed exclusively towards the Associated Banks but in that year the Bank also issued its advice to the non-Associated Banks. (*CBR* (1975), p. 85)

In its early letters on credit policy the Central Bank 'indicated a minimum "Central Bank Ratio" which the Associated Banks should observe in regulating their lending within the country' (*CBR* (1968–69), p. 41). The minimum ratio was defined in terms of the ratio of their net external assets plus their net balances with the Central Bank to their domestic liabilities on current and deposit accounts. In the early 1960s this ratio had averaged about 30 per cent of current and deposit accounts but by 1965 was around 21 per cent.

The Central Bank seems to have considered the ratio as being useful from two main points of view. First, the ratio was some indication of the liquidity of the banks in the sense of their 'ability to meet their short-term demand liabilities' (*ibid.*). Secondly, in so far as the ratio was defined in terms of net external assets and net balances with the Central Bank, the remaining assets of the banks had to be domestic assets and so a change in the ratio necessarily reflected an opposite change in the proportion of their resources devoted to domestic lending.

It is clear, however, that since the Central Bank had throughout the 1960s no effective control over the assets comprising the 'Central Bank Ratio', it cannot have been very meaningful as an indicator of monetary and credit conditions. It·is, for instance, possible that the ratio could remain constant and yet permit either increases or decreases in the money supply or domestic credit. Furthermore, with the complexities involved in forecasting exports and imports and especially capital flows, the task of deciding upon an appropriate Central Bank Ratio was extremely difficult.

It scarcely comes as a surprise therefore that the Central Bank tried to find a further policy instrument and from early 1966 employed, in conjunction with the ratio, 'a quantitative indication of the desirable amount of bank lending' (*ibid.*, p. 41). 'It estimated the amount of credit expansion by the banking system which was required if the money supply were to be of the desired size and then conveyed to the Associated Banks its advice on the total amount of lending, by way of bills, loans, advances and investments, which would be economically appropriate in the period concerned.' (*ibid.*, p. 43)

Unhappily from the Central Bank's point of view, the credit advice it gave and the actual outcome were frequently very different, as may be seen from Table 7.6. From 1972 somewhat less emphasis was placed by the Central Bank (which is not to say it dispensed with them) on precise quantitative guidelines for credit expansion for the banks. This development coincided with a move on the part of the Central Bank towards a system of liquidity ratios which it was anticipated would 'enable the Central Bank to exercise more flexible control over the growth in bank lending' (*CBR* (1971–72), p. 31). The liquidity ratios are discussed below.

Table 7.6: Credit Policy Advice to Associated Banks, 1967–72 (£m)

Year ended	Actual bank credit	Advised expansion
March 1967	40·5	43·0
March 1968	68·2	40·4
April 1969	109·4	64·0
April 1970	82·0	75·0 to 80·0
April 1971	130·0	75·0
April 1972	64·0	78·0

Note: The table includes Chase and Bank of Ireland (International) up to January 1969, and the advised credit expansion figure of £64·0 m for 1968–9 was somewhat relaxed from November 1968.

Source: *CBR*, various issues.

5.2   Non-Associated Banks and Inflow of Foreign Funds

The credit advice considered above refers only to the Associated Banks. However, from the late 1960s the Central Bank began to give increasing attention to the activities of the non-Associated Banks. 'This is a reflection of the fact that, as the scale of operations of the non-Associated Banks has grown, it has become more difficult to distinguish between them and the Associated Banks as regards the monetary effects of increases in their domestic liabilities.' (*CBR* (1970–71), p. 40) The feature of the non-Associated Banks' activities which attracted most attention from the Central Bank at this time was the inflow of foreign funds. The following typifies the approach of the Central Bank to this matter. 'It is desired that the inflow of external capital through the non-Associated Banks in 1970–71 should be allocated as follows' (*CBQB* (Spring 1970), p. 15):

North American Banks	£15 m
Merchant Banks	£ 5 m
Industrial Banks	nil
Other Non-Associated Licensed Banks	nil

The Central Bank also stipulated that the lending of the North American banks and merchant banks should be for 'industrial development purposes only' and that there should be 'no growth in non-productive lending (including lending for consumer purposes)' (*ibid.*).

It is of interest that the outcome was somewhat different with an inflow of £26 million, of which 'about £11 million relates to the Industrial Banks, almost £10 million to the North American Banks, while the remainder came through the Merchant Banks and other non-Associated Banks' (*CBR* (1970–71), p. 44).

The behaviour of the industrial banks was a source of concern to the Central Bank. It stated that 'From February 1971 onwards these banks did not adhere to the limit placed on inflows. Furthermore, some of this inflow was used to finance new instalment credit of a non-productive nature, although no increase in the level of such lending was desired.' (*ibid.*, p. 44)

The Governor of the Central Bank had previously explained the Bank's preoccupation with inflows of funds from abroad in the following terms:

Inflows of money from abroad (and these cover direct external borrowing by the government and state bodies as well as inflows through non-Associated Banks) boost the domestic money supply in exactly the same way as credit creation and, where they are excessive, can have equally harmful results. They increase the pressure of demand with the result that either immediately or ultimately the foreign money flows out of the country to pay for the extra imports which it was intended to finance or which its arrival helped to generate. Even after this has happened, of course, the debt to the foreigners who lent us the money in the first place remains and must be repaid. When foreign money arrives here it does, naturally, cause a temporary rise in our external reserves until the imports which it generates are paid for. When the non-Associated Banks come to pay back their foreign depositors, the repayment will cause a fall in our external reserves. This is a net fall, because the temporary rise will in all probability have been dissipated on imports. Therefore we end up with reserves which are lower than they were before the inflow of capital occurred. The lesson to be learned is that if a substantial proportion of the inflow is being spent on consumption goods, there is obviously a good case for curtailing it. We cannot afford to have an externally financed consumption boom which sends our imports soaring but must ultimately be paid for by a running-down of our external monetary reserves. Long-term capital inflows are welcome if they are used for investment designed to increase our productive capacity, particularly export capacity. Inflows, whether long- or short-term, are not welcome if they merely boost an already high level of consumption. (Whitaker (1970), pp. 75–6)

It is informative to consider the Governor's statement in the light of the model of Chapter 1 and of the discussion on money and economic activity. The Governor clearly sees strong links between the monetary and balance

of payments sectors and the expenditure sector of the model. To that extent he seems to rule out the simplifications of the formal model of Chapter
1 — putting aside the various qualifications made in the text — and in this
context appears to see the links between the monetary and expenditure
sectors in terms of some credit availability variables — though possibly not
substitution and wealth effects — which may enter into either the consumption or investment equations or both. The emphasis on credit availability
seems to be highly plausible and is of obvious significance in relation to
monetary and credit policy, the behaviour of the balance of payments, and
as regards effects on the holdings of external reserves. However, a qualification needs to be made. So long as there is no fear — and this is an extremely
important qualification — that the exchange rate parity will be altered, then,
from a monetary point of view, the credit availability effects need not be
unduly disturbing, as the balance of payments position should adjust automatically. The latter remains true whether the inflow of funds finances
directly or indirectly consumption or investment goods. The Governor's
concern is fundamentally with the allocation of expenditure between consumption and investment and, strictly speaking, is not the direct concern of
monetary policy.

Furthermore, as regards the inflows of foreign funds referred to, the
model of Chapter 1 sees them outside the control of the Central Bank; this,
as will be seen, is not to say that within limits the Central Bank cannot take
measures to influence them. However, the exogeneity assumption certainly
suggests that target inflows of funds announced as desirable by the Central
Bank are unlikely to be realised, and indeed this has generally been true.
Incidentially, a similar point can be made as regards desirable rates of expansion of domestic bank credit. For, a plausible extention of the model
implies, and the discussion below (pp. 250–4) supports it, that not all forms
of domestic bank credit are under the control of the authorities and, as
already argued, if foreign exchange reserves are endogenously determined,
for example through equation (1.39), aggregate domestic bank credit must
be endogenous and is unlikely to be consistent with the credit advice
offered by the Central Bank.

5.3   Variable Liquid Asset Ratios
During 1972 the Central Bank began to implement its proposals for the introduction of variable liquid asset ratios. By early 1973 these seem to have
been more or less in full operation for the Associated Banks, the North
American and merchant banks, as the Central Bank announced some changes
in them in February of that year. The main reasons given by the Central
Bank for the introduction of the ratios was that they would 'give scope for
more competition by relating bank lending capacity to success in attracting
deposits and . . . promote greater efficiency in the allocation of funds among
borrowers' (*CBQB* (Spring 1973), p. 21). The Central Bank was, of course,

contrasting the operation of liquid asset ratios with the former emphasis it placed on quantitative guidelines on credit expansion as a policy instrument. Moreover, it saw the liquid asset ratios as a means of 'influencing the growth in the money supply rather than directly controlling bank lending' (*CBR* (1975), p. 86).

The Central Bank operates two liquid asset ratios: a primary liquidity ratio and a secondary liquidity ratio. The assets which are included in the primary ratio 'comprise the sum of banks' holdings of notes and coin and balances with the Central Bank (including statutory deposits) and reserve bonds issued by the Central Bank' (*CBR* (1974), Statistical Appendix, p. 20). '*Secondary liquid assets* comprise the sum of banks' holdings of government paper (including exchequer bills and rediscounts)' (*ibid.*).

The ratios are defined as a percentage of 'relevant resources', which 'comprise the sum of banks' current and deposit accounts and net external liabilities (adjusted for any exemptions that have been granted by the Central Bank), less balances with and lending to all other licensed banks within the state' (*ibid.*). In the case of the Associated Banks their current accounts are adjusted for uncleared cheques to obtain a net figure. The exemptions granted by the Central Bank include capital inflows for the purpose of financing major industrial development projects. Thus, broadly speaking, 'relevant resources' are made up of net domestic deposit liabilities to the non-bank public plus the banks' net external borrowing and less any exemptions granted by the Central Bank. The ratios in operation in June 1975 are shown in Table 7.7. It should be noted that the primary ratio is made up of what might be called Central Bank funds and the secondary ratio of Irish government paper — putting aside rediscounts. Taking the secondary ratio first, it may be looked upon as a way of guaranteeing a demand for government securities; to the extent that the banks have to hold more than they would otherwise do, it constitutes a tax on their activities and will necessarily have other distributional effects.

At first sight the Central Bank, as supplier of funds for the primary ratio and controller of its size, seems to be in a powerful position to determine

Table 7.7: Minimum Liquid Asset Ratios, June 1975

Banks	Primary Ratio (%)	Secondary Ratio (%)	Total (%)
Associated	13	30	43
North American	13	10	23
Merchant	13	10	23
Continental	13	10	23
Industrial	10	10	23
Other	10	10	20

Source: *CBR* (1975), Statistical Appendix, pp. 20–1.

the volume of bank deposits. However, the matter is much more complicated than this suggests. For one thing, the general public also holds Central Bank funds in the form of notes and coin, and, in principle, the banks might be able to influence to their advantage the volume of such funds held by the public. More important, perhaps, from the point of view of the Central Bank's powers of control, is the banks' ability to attract inflows of foreign funds and so augment their Central Bank funds in this way.

However, the Central Bank is alert to this possibility and from the bank-return date in January 1973 stipulated that of any net inflows after that date — other than those exempted — at least 50 per cent would have to be deposited with the Central Bank and would be excluded from assets counting towards the primary liquidity ratio and would 'not attract commercial rates of interest' (*CBR* (1975), p. 92). This ratio relating to net inflows is variously called 'the special ratio' (*CBR* (1972–3), p. 17) and the 'incremental liquidity ratio' (*CBR* (1975), p. 92). The Central Bank has, of course, the power to vary the ratio and indeed may request the banks to bring about no net inflows, difficult though this may be to accomplish in practice.

There is one further way in which the banks might augment their Central Bank funds, and that is by borrowing from the Central Bank. However, this can only be done on the Central Bank's terms and generally takes the form of rediscounting exchequer bills for the Associated Banks, though it has authority to extend credit to other banks and financial institutions. The Central Bank has stated:

> Access to Central Bank credit is in all circumstances a privilege, and the Bank retains discretion to grant or refuse a request for rediscounting. . . . Licensed banks are strongly encouraged to regard the Bank as lender of last, rather than first, resort. The Bank discourages banks from using its rediscounting facility on a continuous basis or as a source for financing long-term lending. Appropriate rediscount rates discourage frequent calls on Central Bank credit and, thus, provide an incentive to the banks to manage their affairs without resorting to the Central Bank. (*CBR* (1975), p. 88)

It should be made clear that 'appropriate rediscount rates' may and have meant in practice penal rates well above the minimum rediscount rate, which 'is fixed by reference to the discount rate on the issue of exchequer bills and is not designed to influence that rate. The exchequer bill rate is, in turn, set by the Minister for Finance and tends to be influenced by short-term rates in Britain.' (*ibid.*, p. 87)

Notwithstanding the far-reaching powers of the Central Bank to influence the liquid asset holdings and control the size of the minimum liquid asset ratios of the banks, and hence apparently affect the volume of bank deposits, it may be doubted that the Central Bank can, as it were, determine exogenously the volume of bank deposits, and certainly not in the long run. The fundamental reason for this is the fixity of the exchange rate and, in particular, the parity link with sterling. Any successful attempt to maintain the volume of bank deposits, and more generally the money supply, at levels different from those determined endogenously by the economy would result in balance of payments surpluses or deficits which would ultimately result in a break in the parity link.

There are, of course, other factors at work which make it difficult or impossible for the Central Bank to control the money supply in the short run. One of these has already been mentioned: shifts in the note and coin holdings of the general public; and another is the holding by the banks of liquid assets in excess of their actual and anticipated requirements. A further factor is the behaviour of the government's balances with the Central Bank. These are subject to substantial seasonal fluctuations, and, for instance, a reduction in government balances with the Central Bank may greatly augment the primary liquidity funds of the banks. This indeed happened in the autumn of 1973 and in the view of the Central Bank contributed to 'the large increase in non-government lending over the period' (*CB QB* (Winter 1973), p. 22).

Expansion of bank credit in the early part of 1974 was also much more rapid than the Central Bank felt was desirable, and in June 1974 it announced increases in the primary ratio of the merchant banks and North American banks, to be operative from mid-August, from 10 per cent to 13 per cent, while leaving the primary and secondary ratios of the Associated Banks unchanged at 13 per cent and 30 per cent respectively. At the same time it extended the secondary liquidity ratio requirements to the industrial and other banks. They were requested to raise their holdings of Irish government paper to 5 per cent of their 'relevant resources' by mid-August and to 10 per cent by mid-November.

The Central Bank, however, was not satisfied to rely entirely on these measures and supplemented them by the reintroduction of quantitative guidelines on certain specific forms of credit. The Central Bank issued the following statement:

All banks are being requested to permit no net increase in lending over the months ahead . . . for personal and other non-productive purposes and there should be no lending whatsoever for speculative purposes. In particular, there should be no increase between the quarterly return dates in May and November next in the following categories of advances: . . . (Banks and hire purchase finance companies), . . . (Property companies), . . . (Other financial) and . . . (Personal). . . . If the level of lending outstanding in November next in the categories indicated exceeds the May figure, the bank concerned will be obliged to maintain on deposit with the Central Bank an amount equal to such excess, for as long as the latter continues to obtain. These deposits would not be included when calculating primary liquidity ratios, and would not attract commercial rates of interest. (*CBR* (1973–74), p. 15)

The subsequent behaviour of these lending categories suggests that the Central Bank's request was highly effective, at least in the short run. But clearly the Central Bank is either unable or unwilling to rely exclusively on its powers of control over the banks' liquid asset ratios as a means of implementing its monetary and credit policy. This point is reinforced, as explained below, by its role in determining the banks' interest rates.

5.4   The Banks' Interest Rates

The Central Bank now exercises strict control over changes in both deposit and lending rates of the Associated Banks. This is a relatively recent development of the last few years. The Central Bank has argued that it is obliged to do so under the Central Bank Act (1942) (*CBQB* (Spring 1973), p. 36). It has stated that its 'objective . . . has been to moderate fluctuations in interest rates here, so as to minimise the effects of external fluctuations – and particularly of increases in external rates – on the Irish economy' (*ibid.*, p. 37). And it continues: 'It has been possible for a margin to exist between interest rates here and in Britain, and in particular for rates here to be moderately lower than those prevailing elsewhere, without precipitating a major outflow of capital. This tendency towards a lower rate [*sic*] here has generally been appropriate in view of the developmental needs of the economy.' (*ibid.*)

Thus the thrust of Central Bank policy has been to try to maintain deposit and lending rates of the Associated Banks somewhat lower than in Britain. This, as might be expected, has clearly given rise from time to time to difficulties for the Associated Banks. For instance, in the early summer of 1972 interest rates rose rapidly in the United Kingdom and other European countries, while Associated Bank rates remained unchanged. However, the non-Associated Banks

> increased their deposit rates in response to movements in rates abroad. This had the effect of diverting deposits to the non-Associated Banks which would otherwise have been placed with the Associated Banks. . . . At the same time the demand for relatively cheap loanable funds from the Associated Banks resulted in a reduction of Associated Bank liquidity. In order to minimise these pressures which reduced their capacity to attract resources and which at the same time put a strain on their liquidity, the Associated Banks, after consultation with the Central Bank, increased their rates in September. (*CBQB* (Autumn 1972), p. 32)

The Central Bank, largely with a view to greater control over lending by the Associated Banks, had prevailed upon them to introduce from April 1972 a system of term lending. This was to replace, except for seasonal purposes, the overdraft system by which borrowers could at will call upon their unutilised borrowing facilities. Two new types of bank loan were introduced, term loans and loan accounts:

Term loans are granted for specific purposes and are repayable by negotiated amounts within fixed periods. . . . Loan accounts [arise] where the term of the borrowing exceeds seven years, or cannot be determined beforehand.

Under the term lending system there are three categories of borrowers (AAA, AA and A). Loans and advances in the AAA category relate to:

1. Government, Local Authorities and government-granted borrowers;
2. Large-scale limited companies satisfying certain profit criteria; and
3. Schools, charities, churches and hospitals.

The AA category relates to consumers in the *Primary (including Agriculture) and Construction, Manufacturing* and *Service* sectors. The A category relates to all other categories of borrowers, including personal borrowers. In April 1975 term lending incorporated the following interest rate structure: [Table 7.8]. (*CBR* (1975), p. 93)

Table 7.8: Associated Banks' Lending Rates, April 1975

Category	Term Loans				
	Overdrafts and Term Loans up to 1 year	Over 1 year and up to 3 years	Over 3 years and up to 5 years	Over 5 years and up to 7 years	Loan Accounts
AAA	10·75	11·25	11·75	12·25	12·75
AA	11·50	12·00	12·50	13·00	13·50
A	13·50	14·25	15·00	15·50	16·25

Source: *CBR* (1975), p. 94.

The non-Associated Banks would seem to be much more fortunate, from their point of view, in having rather more freedom to determine their interest rates without the direct involvement of the Central Bank. This is because their rates are particularly responsive to interest rates abroad and especially in the United Kingdom, because of the high mobility of funds between the different markets. As already indicated, this behaviour of the non-Associated Banks is not without its difficulties for the Associated Banks, and it certainly gives rise to the question whether or not it is appropriate for the Central Bank to pay such particular attention to the interest rates of the Associated Banks, either on grounds of credit control or the distributional effects involved. However, it is clearly evident from the foregoing, and is what the model of Chapter 1 assumes, that the capacity of the Central Bank to impose a structure of interest rates, in a regime of a fixed exchange rate with sterling and freedom of movement of capital, is severely limited.

5.5   Other Policy Issues

Three other policy matters remain to be considered: government financing, foreign borrowing, and the parity link with sterling. Each is now considered in turn.

The growth of the government sector, the difficulties it may pose for economic policy, and in particular the consequences of the government borrowing requirement and the way or ways in which it is financed, have been a source of concern to the Central Bank for a number of years. In its latest report it states:

> The rate of increase in public expenditure has swept ahead . . . of gross domestic expenditure in money terms. Public finance is absorbing a rising proportion of total national output: total public expenditure, current and capital, which represented 30 per cent of G N P in 1961–62, now represents at least 42 per cent of G N P. This drive to obtain extra resources for public purposes conflicts with private spending aspirations and sets up inflationary tensions. Prices and costs are raised by the need to increase indirect taxes and by the general effect on wage and salary demands of what people consider to be excessive government 'take'. . . . The private sector in general has shown itself unwilling to yield up the purchasing power which the government seek to obtain for public purposes through taxation and borrowing. (*CBR* (1975), pp. 10–11)

The Central Bank has also drawn repeated attention to the size and financing of the government borrowing requirement. The position for the last three years is shown in Table 7.9. In financing its borrowing requirement the government has found it impossible to do so by borrowing from the non-bank public and has had to turn to the banking system and abroad; the latter is discussed below.

In the view of two of the Central Bank's economists, 'Experience suggests that the private sector is extremely reluctant to permit a reduction in its expected share of additional [bank] lending. The tendency has been for the banking system to be under severe pressure to supply credit to the private sector, irrespective of the amount lent to the government. Thus additional government borrowing is reflected in an increase in aggregate demand, without any offsetting moderation in private expenditure.' (Doherty and O'Neill (1973), p. 120)

Table 7.9: Government Expenditure and the Borrowing Requirement,
Republic of Ireland, 1973–75 (£000)

	1973	1974	1975
Current Expenditure	767,103	956,719	1,251,700
Capital Expenditure	198,656	277,183	309,332
Total	965,759	1,233,902	1,561,032
Borrowing Requirement	207,491	334,940	431,609
Percentage of Total	(21·5)	(27·1)	(27·6)

Note: The 1975 figures are post-budget estimates, and all the figures exclude expenditure under the European Communities Act (1972). The 1975 figures have subsequently been substantially increased by the budget statement of 26 June 1975. The borrowing requirement is the difference between expenditure and revenue on both current and capital accounts.

Source: *CBR* (1975), p. 30.

The Central Bank's analysis of the effects of government expenditure seems to be supported in part by the model of Chapter 1. Clearly an increase in government expenditure will tend to expand income and have repercussions on the quantity of money demanded and on the volume of imports, hence affecting the balance of payments. However, running through the Central Bank's account is the notion that, in principle, government expenditure need not give rise to any further increases in the money supply or domestic credit to the private sector. This notion is not upheld by the model. Furthermore, if the model is modified to allow for wealth and credit availability effects in relation to private expenditure, then the income and other consequences are likely to be accentuated. Whether or not government expenditure is financed by borrowing from the banking or non-bank sector should have no lasting effects on the outcome as interpreted in terms of the model of Chapter 1. This interpretation necessarily assumes that the scale of the operation in no way threatens the fixed exchange rate. This is a very important assumption, and there is no guarantee that it would hold if the government were to borrow on a really large scale, especially from the banking system. Just how large a scale this would have to be is impossible to say on the basis of the model of Chapter 1, since it does not tell us in what circumstances expectations about the fixity of the exchange rate would be revised and what would be the behavioural consequences of such a revision. That they might be substantial and dramatic is clearly possible, but to attempt to explore them further would require a much more complicated model than that developed in Chapter 1.

The matter of foreign borrowing is closely related to the previous topic, as the government has been one of the major parties involved, together

with what the Central Bank calls state-sponsored bodies. The Central Bank
has shown concern about what may be called official foreign borrowing on
two main grounds. First, it increases the liquidity of the banking system
when the funds are spent domestically, and thereby makes credit policy
more difficult to implement. Secondly, it leads to an accumulation of foreign
debt which must be serviced and eventually repaid, perhaps in currencies
that will have appreciated in value in relation to the Irish pound. To the extent that the latter takes place — and it has done so already — it may make
foreign borrowing very expensive (see *CBR* (1973—74), p. 11).

The growth and distribution by currency of official foreign borrowing
is shown in Table 7.10. One of the striking things about Table 7.10 is the
rate of growth of the debt during the last nine months of 1974. It should,
however, be stressed that much of the borrowing is medium- to long-term.
Of the £310·7 million borrowed by government some £220 million has a
maturity date of more than five years, and of the £204 million borrowed
by state-sponsored bodies the corresponding figure is £134 million.

Table 7.10: Recent Growth and Distribution by Currency of Official Foreign
Borrowing by the Republic of Ireland (£m)

Currency	Government		State-sponsored bodies	
	31 Mar. 1974	31 Dec. 1974	31 Mar. 1974	31 Dec. 1974
Sterling	29·0	28·5	27	23
Dollars	48·5	128·9	70	102
Deutsche Marks	46·9	45·6	9	8
Swiss Francs	20·0	20·0	12	15
Dutch Guilders	15·5	23·8	1	1
Belgian Francs	0·0	10·2	28	28
European Units of Account	7·5	27·0	13	27
Kuwait Dinars	0·0	10·5	0	0
U A E Dirham	0·0	16·2	0	0
Total	167·4	310·7	160	204

Note: Some of the figures are estimates. It is reckoned that if exchange rate changes
are allowed for, the amount of £310·7 million for government foreign borrowing
would become £360 million.

Source: *CBR* (1975), Statistical Appendix, pp. 7—8.

It should be clear from the foregoing that the question of the parity
link with sterling, or more generally the exchange rate with sterling and
whether it should be fixed or variable, is closely related to such issues as

government financing and foreign borrowing. More fundamentally, the question of exchange rate policy is related to the basic policy goals of the society, as expressed through government, and its knowledge and understanding of its economic and other relationships with the rest of the world. Such knowledge is necessarily incomplete, as indeed is true of all policy areas, and to that extent the problem of determining the best or most appropriate policies is shrouded in difficulty and uncertainty. This seems to be especially true in the area of exchange rate policy.

Nevertheless, in the last couple of years there has been much public discussion about 'breaking the parity link with sterling'. The immediate background to this discussion seems to be the wish to protect the Republic from the rates of inflation experienced in the United Kingdom and the realisation that this is almost certainly impossible as long as the parity link is maintained and there is freedom of movement of goods and capital.

It is not always clear that all those who support the breaking of the parity link appreciate that the logic of their position, as regards protecting the Republic from United Kingdom rates of inflation, requires that they should advocate a floating exchange rate *vis-à-vis* sterling. The basic reason for this assertion is that to choose a fixed exchange rate different from the parity link — assuming that to be possible — would still be a means by which the inflation experience of the United Kingdom would be transmitted to the domestic economy. Alternatively, if domestic price behaviour is to be markedly different to that in the United Kingdom, then a necessary condition for achieving this is to let the exchange rate with sterling float, though, as argued below, this may be far from being a straightforward exercise. An apparent alternative to a floating Irish pound would be to permit periodic changes in the 'fixed' exchange rate with sterling. However, it seems doubtful whether this would be possible, as it might give rise to serious instability as foreign exchange positions were entered into in anticipation of changes in the exchange rate.

To let the Irish pound float freely against all other currencies would mean, if taken literally, that its exchange rate with each other currency would be determined by the forces of supply and demand. It seems likely that this would make for considerable instability in the exchange rates unless a highly sophisticated market emerged and operated in such a way as to stabilise or smooth fluctuations in the rates. This would require entry to the market of professional dealers, which seems an unlikely eventuality, at least in the short run, for a currency such as the Irish pound which is not widely used in international transactions.

For reasons such as these it is generally argued that if the link with sterling were broken, it would be necessary to fix the exchange rate of the Irish pound in terms of some other currency or group of currencies, such as those members of the EEC who have entered into arrangements, known as the 'snake', to keep their currencies within a certain fixed relationship to each other. To the extent that these currencies are experiencing a lower rate of domestic inflation than the United Kingdom and are appreciating in terms of the pound sterling, then in principle the Irish pound would be less subject to inflationary pressures emanating from the United Kingdom. However, the transitionary period to such a state of affairs might be very painful for the Irish Republic, as it would have to bring down its rate of inflation to that experienced in these other countries, and this could scarcely be accomplished without sustained unemployment and low or even negative rates of growth of output, possibly for a period of years.

It is thus hard not to feel that a good deal of the discussion, though by no means all, of 'breaking the link with sterling' has been somewhat facile. Furthermore, there has been little attempt to specify those domestic economic conditions which would be favourable to a break in the link with sterling. These would include full or over-full employment and a balance of payments surplus on current account. Neither of these conditions are at present (1975) to be found in the Republic, and it may well be a considerable period before they arise.

6   CREDIT POLICY IN NORTHERN IRELAND

The Bank of England appears to have taken little direct interest before the early 1970s in the credit policies pursued by the banks in Northern Ireland. However, with the introduction in 1971 of its new 'Competition and Credit Control' arrangements it announced that these applied in principle to all banks in the United Kingdom. But the Bank agreed that there were certain difficulties about implementing them in Northern Ireland because the branch banks there also operated in the Republic. Furthermore, the Bank accepted that in the future as in the past special consideration needed to be given to economic conditions in Northern Ireland before applying specific credit policies to it.

Nevertheless, after discussion with the Northern Ireland Bankers' Association, which concluded in the summer of 1972, the banks agreed 'to move gradually, from the end of June 1972, towards a $12\frac{1}{2}$ per cent minimum reserve ratio, observing it in full from the end of December 1972' (*BEQB* (Mar. 1973), p. 51). Those banks which are outside the Northern Ireland Bankers' Association also agreed to observe the $12\frac{1}{2}$ per cent ratio. The ratio, like the corresponding ones for all other United Kingdom banks, is defined as a percentage of eligible liabilities and in terms of reserve assets. Broadly speaking, eligible liabilities consist of 'sterling deposit liabilities, excluding deposits having an original maturity of over two years, plus any sterling resources obtained by switching foreign currencies into sterling' (*BEQB* (Mar. 1975), Additional notes to Table 9). Inter-bank transactions and sterling certificates of deposit are included on a net basis in the eligible liabilities of individual banks, and certain adjustments are made for transit items. Notes are not counted as eligible liabilities and a 'bank may exclude its net liability (if any) to its offices in the Republic of Ireland' (*BEQB* (Mar. 1973), p. 51).

Reserve assets in the Bank of England were defined as follows:

> Reserve assets comprise balances with the Bank of England (other than special and supplementary deposits), British government and Northern Ireland government treasury bills, company tax reserve certificates, money at call with the London money market, British government stocks and stocks of nationalised industries guaranteed by the government with one year or less to final maturity, local authority bills eligible for rediscount at the Bank of England, and (up to a maximum of 2 per cent of eligible liabilities) commercial bills eligible for rediscount at the Bank of England. (*BEQB* (Mar. 1975), Additional notes to Table 9)

In addition, each member bank of the Northern Ireland Bankers' Association was permitted up to June 1975 as part of the transitional arrangements to 'include among its reserve assets its holdings of certain liabilities of the Central Bank or government of the Republic of Ireland which have traditionally been regarded as liquid assets by the Northern Ireland banks. Any holdings so included must be in excess of those required by the Dublin authorities to satisfy ratios or quotas calculated in relation to deposits originating in the Republic, and should form only a modest proportion of the $12\frac{1}{2}$ per cent ratio.' (*BEQB* (Mar. 1974), p. 51)

The Bank also undertook to give consideration, 'if occasion arises, to the inclusion in reserve assets of special lending, e.g. under government guarantee, arising from the emergency in Northern Ireland or from the needs of reconstruction, if otherwise adherence to the $12\frac{1}{2}$ per cent ratio would severely impair the banks' ability to advance funds for essential purposes' (*ibid.*).

Mention was made above of special and supplementary deposits being excluded from reserve assets. There is little need to discuss these categories of deposits, which are broadly designed to restrict the credit and deposit expansion of banks, as the banks in Northern Ireland have been exempted, as regards their business there, from calls for these deposits. However, Northern Ireland banks which carry on business through offices in Britain are subject to calls for these deposits.

Thus, apart from the introduction of the reserve assets ratio, the banks in Northern Ireland have been essentially free from credit or monetary policy measures directed specifically at their activities. This fact, together with the model of Chapter 1, suggests that monetary and credit conditions are basically demand-determined, and to that extent Northern Ireland has not experienced direct monetary and credit restriction. This is not to say, however, that in some sense monetary and credit conditions in Northern Ireland are optimum. To do that would, among other things, require a discussion of policy objectives for Northern Ireland. And in so far as sustained full employment might be one of these objectives the persistent record of heavy unemployment clearly calls strongly in question any notion of optimum monetary and credit policies. However, this argument cannot be pursued further here, as it would raise wide-ranging and far-reaching questions about the nature of Northern Ireland's economic, financial and political relationships with the rest of the United Kingdom.

7 CONCLUSIONS

The banking system in Ireland is extensive and well developed, and this development has accelerated in the last ten years, especially in the Republic with the growth of the non-Associated Banks and the enlargement of the powers of the Central Bank.

Notwithstanding these developments, the dominant impression which emerges from the preceding discussion is the way in which the banking system of both the Republic and Northern Ireland is powerfully influenced by monetary conditions in Britain. It was argued repeatedly that this influence stemmed from the 'fixed exchange' relationship with sterling and the freedom of movement of funds between the two areas. This last point carries some important implications.

It implies, for instance, that as long as the fixed exchange rate and freedom of movement of funds is strictly adhered to, then attempts by the Central Bank to pursue monetary and credit policies (including interest rate policy) substantially different from those in Britain are bound to fail. Furthermore, such attempts are likely to create distortions between the different kinds of bank and suppliers of credit generally, to the detriment of some and the benefit of others, and probably an overall decrease in the efficiency of credit processes. It is not entirely clear that the Central Bank has been as aware as it might have been of these consequences. More basically, it seems to have frequently assumed that it has power to control domestic monetary and credit conditions in a way that is incompatible with a fixed exchange rate with sterling and freedom of movement of funds. By implication, fiscal policy seems in these circumstances to be a more potent instrument of economic policy than monetary and credit policy, though the openness of both economies also reduces the potency of fiscal policy.

Alternatively, if the government and the Central Bank wish to pursue monetary and credit policies geared specifically to such policy goals as full employment and price stability, then, unless the pursuit of these requires monetary and credit conditions identical or almost identical with those in Britain, which seems highly improbable, they must, as a minimum, be prepared to contemplate a variable exchange relationship with sterling. This would clearly be a major decision to make and would carry profound economic and political consequences, not least the establishment of (presumably) a variable exchange rate between the Republic and Northern Ireland.

Another useful way of looking at the relationship between the monetary and banking systems in Ireland and Britain is to consider them as in fact constituting a 'monetary union'. This is obvious enough as regards the banking system in Northern Ireland, which is not so much part of a union as part of the U K banking system and necessarily has a formal relationship with the U K monetary authorities, namely the treasury and the Bank of England. However, the relationship between the monetary authorities of the Republic and Britain would seem to be much less formal, despite the 'monetary union' and what that entails, especially for the former.

To put the matter differently, the Republic has a strong interest in the kinds of monetary and credit policies pursued by the U K authorities, yet, as far as is known, there is no machinery for systematic discussion and consultation between the two sets of authorities. However, this may well change as and when substantial progress is made towards a wider monetary union within the context of the European Economic Community. It would certainly be in the interests of the Republic to ensure, as a condition of moving towards such a monetary union, that proper institutional machinery was established for the discussion and co-ordination of monetary and credit policy.

Furthermore, it is widely appreciated that monetary union, in the sense of fixed exchange relationships and freedom of movement of capital, may contribute to very different rates of economic development in different parts of the union and that to try and deal satisfactorily with these may require an economic union, especially as regards regional and social policy. These also are noticeably absent as regards relationships between the Republic and the U K. Thus, despite its separate currency, the Republic has not found it desirable to pursue a really independent monetary and credit policy from the U K and apparently did not attempt or find it possible to achieve a co-ordination of such policies in the interests of both, quite apart from the greater problem of the co-ordination of economic policies generally. It may be hoped that the working of monetary union within the European Economic Community will be less one-sided in its effects.

REFERENCES

Barro, R. J. (1974): 'Are Government Bonds Net Wealth?', *Journal of Political Economy*, Vol. 82, No. 6·(Nov.–Dec.).

Central Bank of Ireland (1971): *Survey of Economic Effects of Bank Dispute 1970*, Dublin.

Doherty, J. H. and O'Neill, J. P. (1973): 'Recent Trends in Public Finance', *CBR* (1972–73).

Friedman, M. (1956): 'The Quantity Theory of Money – A Restatement' in *Studies in the Quantity Theory of Money*, ed. M. Friedman, University of Chicago Press.

Hill, T. (1969): 'The Demand for Money in the Republic of Ireland: An Econometric Analysis'. (Unpublished M. Sc. dissertation, New University of Ulster.)

Hoare, T. F. (1973): 'Money, Autonomous Expenditure and Aggregate Income', *C B R* (1972–73).

Lindbeck, A. (1959): *The 'New' Theory of Credit Control in the United States,* 2nd ed., Almqvist and Wiksell, Stockholm 1962.

Pratschke, J. L. and O'Connell, T. J. (1973): 'The Demand for Money in Ireland, 1948–69: A Preliminary Report'. (Mimeograph, Central Bank of Ireland.)

Whitaker, T. K. (1970): 'The Role of the Central Bank', *C B Q B* (Spring).

Whitaker, T. K. (1972a): 'Ireland and Foreign Money', *C B R* (1971–72).

Whitaker, T. K. (1972b): 'The Changing Face of Irish Banking', *CBQB* (Spring).

Whitaker, T. K. (1973): 'Monetary Integration: Reflections on Irish Experience', *C B Q B* (Winter).

Index